The Psychology of Illustration

Volume 1

The Psychology of Illustration

Volume 1

Basic Research

Edited by
Dale M. Willows
Harvey A. Houghton

With 52 Illustrations

Springer-Verlag
New York Berlin Heidelberg
London Paris Tokyo

Dale M. Willows
Ontario Institute for Studies in Education
Toronto, Ontario M5S 1V6
Canada

Harvey A. Houghton
Ontario Institute for Studies in Education
Toronto, Ontario M5S 1V6
Canada

Library of Congress Cataloging in Publication Data.
The Psychology of illustration.
  Includes bibliographies and index.
  Contents: v. 1. Basic research—v. 2.
Instructional issues.
  1. Visual learning. 2. Illustration of books—
Psychological aspects. 3. Textbooks—Illustrations.
4. Learning, Psychology of. I. Houghton, Harvey A.
II. Willows, Dale M.
LB1067.5.P78   1987   370.15′23   86-31477

© 1987 by Springer-Verlag New York Inc.
All rights reserved. This work may not be translated or copied in whole or in part without the written permission of the publisher (Springer-Verlag, 175 Fifth Avenue, New York, New York 10010, USA), except for brief excerpts in connection with reviews or scholarly analysis. Use in connection with any form of information storage and retrieval, electronic adaptation, computer software, or by similar or dissimilar methodology now known or hereafter developed is forbidden.
The use of general descriptive names, trade names, trademarks, etc. in this publication, even if the former are not especially identified, is not to be taken as a sign that such names, as understood by the Trade Marks and Merchandise Marks Act, may accordingly be used freely by anyone.

Typeset by Publishers Service, Bozeman, Montana.

9 8 7 6 5 4 3 2 1

ISBN-13: 978-1-4612-9110-7   e-ISBN-13: 978-1-4612-4674-9
DOI: 10.1007/978-1-4612-4674-9

Preface

From the earliest stages of elementary school to the advanced college level, various types of illustrations are included in educational materials in order to promote learning. These illustrative adjuncts are often profuse and, in many cases, they may be the most striking feature that distinguishes one set of learning materials from another. In addition, the perceived effectiveness of the illustrations clearly plays an important role in the marketing of many educational materials. Despite this pervasiveness and salience in education, there has never been a systematic effort to bring together the results of research on illustrations in order to provide some level of guidance to the developers of commercial learning materials. There is, however, a considerable research literature that is directly relevant to this aspect of education. The purpose of the present two-volume set is to summarize and interpret the existing research literature that deals with the various educational functions of illustrations.

In undertaking to produce an omnibus reference work on psychological and instructional issues surrounding illustrated learning material, our paramount aim has been to stimulate closer collaboration between researchers, producers, and users of educational text. The problems associated with moving the findings of educational research into the realm of everyday practice have been perennial ones. While many researchers and practitioners are interested in fundamentally similar questions, they typically speak dissimilar languages, read different journals, and carry out their work under disparate ideologies. Unlike some other professions, such as medicine, whose members are accustomed to keeping themselves apprised of the latest research, educators continue to be hampered by the expansive gap that exists between research and application. At present, it would appear that a great deal of instructional text design is guided by intuition, prior practice, trial-and-error approaches, and marketability considerations. Correspondingly, much empirical research is conceived of and carried out exclusive of the real world contexts that it ultimately seeks to improve.

If learning outcomes are to be optimized, it seems clear that researchers, producers, and consumers of educational text must interact with each other and engage in an ongoing process of reciprocal feedback. Authors, editors, and designers share a responsibility to inform their work by capitalizing upon the currently available knowledge base. Similarly, it is attendant upon theoreticians and researchers studying text-illustration arrangements to solicit input from publishers and practitioners alike. The goal of the present two-volume compendium is to encourage this alliance and to promote a mutually beneficial interchange of ideas.

Chapters in the first volume focus primarily on theoretical and empirical research issues in the psychological study of illustrated learning material. In doing so this volume brings together a wide range of research, all of which is concerned with some aspect of the instructional role of illustrations. The result is a reference work for researchers, students, and educators that delineates and examines significant research findings from the general field of inquiry.

W. Howard Levie, in Chapter 1, presents an overview of the voluminous and diverse literature on picture research. He discusses theoretical and research avenues emanating from a multiplicity of perspectives. Among these are semiotics, aesthetics, art criticism, advertising and information design, social psychology, visual perception, media research, art education, developmental psychology, cognitive psychology, memory, and human learning. The focus is on experimental research that yields promising implications for educational practice. A major purpose in surveying the relevant literature is to direct attention to important references in each research domain. Readers will find Levie's chapter especially informative in this regard. He concludes with a call for a unified psychology of pictorial learning that seeks to integrate the various disparate research approaches into a coherent field of inquiry.

There is a sizable body of research literature concerned with the effectiveness of pictures in promoting memory for factual information in text. In Chapter 2 Joel Levin, Gary Anglin, and Russell Carney consider this literature on "pictures in prose" from a functional perspective. Five functional classifications of pictures in prose learning (decoration, representation, organization, interpretation, and transformation) are described and illustrated. With the goal of assessing the degree of prose-learning facilitation promoted by these differing pictorial functions Levin, Anglin, and Carney report on a comprehensive meta-analysis of the "pictures-in-prose" literature that they carried out. The results of this major analysis, as well as the insights they garnered from it, serve as a basis for outlining a set of guiding principles—their *Ten Commandments*—for obtaining facilitative effects in prose-learning situations.

The efforts of cognitive researchers during the past decade have yielded substantial progress toward understanding how illustrations affect both comprehension and memory for prose. Recent studies of listening comprehension involving pictorially mediated oral prose learning have contributed much to our knowledge of how visual accompaniments to text promote or hinder children's learning. In Chapter 3, Michael Pressley and Gloria Miller examine the latest research dealing with the effects of illustrations on children's understanding and learning of oral prose material. After outlining theoretical and pragmatic motivations for studying illustration effects, Pressley and Miller discuss a variety of pertinent methodological issues. They then review recent empirical findings of significance before closing their chapter with some comments on future directions for related research.

Despite the widespread use of illustrations in textbooks very little basic research on the effects of such illustrations had been undertaken until the early 1970s. Since then, however, there has been a burgeoning interest in the role of illustrations (particularly pictures) in processing and remembering text. Fifteen very productive years of basic research have brought us much closer to understanding the factors that influence the educational effectiveness of pictures in text. In Chapter 4, Joan Peeck presents a comprehensive review of this literature. He examines the various roles of pictures in promoting comprehension and retention of textual information, and in enhancing readers' enjoyment and attention when reading. Peeck also considers these cognitive and affective/motivational roles of pictures in the context of a number of modulating influences, including reader and picture/text factors. In his conclusion, Peeck points out that despite recent productivity in this research domain, much yet remains to be done. He goes on to suggest some important directions for future research.

Volume 1 concludes with Bill Winn's chapter on charts, graphs, and diagrams in educational materials. In it he examines the salient characteristics of these graphic devices and how they endeavor to convey information. The chapter also looks at research on the instructional effectiveness of these kinds of visual aids in teaching factual content and in imparting knowledge of relationships or entire processes. Definitional issues are addressed at the outset. Physiological and cognitive mechanisms are discussed along with the general properties of the graphic forms themselves and the various ways by which they convey meaning through their differential utilization of space. These factors are considered in relation to students' abilities and the nature of the tasks that they are typically expected to perform in school settings. Cognitive models which seek to understand how people interact with and process graphic material are seen as essential for developing effective prescriptive principles of visualized instruction.

Volume 2 of this series is subtitled *Instructional Issues*. Accordingly, it concerns itself with historical and pragmatic considerations related to the use of pictures, graphs, charts, and diagrams in textbooks and other learning materials. The goal of this companion volume is twofold. One aim is to provide a handbook of practical value to all those who may be involved in developing, marketing, and purchasing illustrated educational materials. The second purpose is to inform researchers about practical matters related to the production and utilization of illustrated text.

In the first chapter of Volume 2, Patricia Mulcahy and S. Jay Samuels trace the history of illustration in American textbooks over a three-hundred-year period, culminating in the early part of the twentieth century. Although modern day textbooks make extensive use of illustration, such practice was relatively rare in previous eras. In describing and illustrating the changes that have occurred over the course of this time span, Mulcahy and Samuels point to the influences of a variety of factors (American history and educational practices, concepts of the child and attitudes toward childhood in general, and the values inherent in

American culture) as determinants of the nature and use of textbook illustration. Two factors that have exerted a particularly significant role in the more recent history of textbook illustration—the use of color and the move toward ethnicity and equality—are considered up to the present.

Chapter 2 by Evelyn Goldsmith addresses a difficulty that has long been faced by those interested in the psychology of illustration, be they concerned with research or instructional issues. This has been the lack of an adequate terminology to describe illustrations and their relation to textual information. In her recent book, *Research into Illustration: An Approach and a Review*, Goldsmith (1984) developed an analytical model incorporating a terminological framework to facilitate thinking and talking about illustrations. In her present chapter, Goldsmith presents a synopsis of this model. It is based on a combination of four visual factors (unity, location, emphasis, and text parallels) and three levels of communication (syntactic, semantic, and pragmatic). Using the resulting twelve elements of the model as an organizer, Goldsmith summarizes research on the perception and comprehension of illustration, focusing primarily on studies of the perceptual abilities of young children and on cross-cultural studies. Her review suggests a number of factors that should be taken into account in designing instructional illustrations. To further demonstrate the usefulness of her analytical model, Goldsmith concludes her chapter with a specific application of the model itself. In doing so she undertakes a critical analysis of the use of *emphasis* in double page spreads of instructional books designed for children.

One of the primary goals of this two-volume set on the psychology of illustration is to promote the development of illustrated learning materials that are both theoretically sound and practically useful. In the *Basic Research* volume the focus is on issues arising from the vast theory-based literature on illustrations in prose, with some speculation about educational implications. If such recommendations are ever to be implemented, theoreticians and researchers will need to learn about the practical side of instructional illustrations. In Chapter 3 of Volume 2, Mary Ann Evans, Catherine Watson, and Dale Willows present the results of an investigation into the development and use of illustrated educational materials. Their naturalistic inquiry includes a survey of both the producers (i.e., publishing companies) and the consumers (i.e., classroom teachers) of illustrated text. As well, the chapter contains a description of currently used materials themselves, based on quantitative and qualitative analyses of textbooks ranging across subject areas and grade levels. The results of their practical investigation of educational illustrations indicates a clear need for publishing companies, researchers, and educators to work more closely together.

There is both experimental and descriptive research to help evaluate factors that make text relatively easy or difficult to understand. Recent works in cognitive psychology, text linguistics, readability, educational psychology, and communication technology have contributed to a growing body of experimental research related to the effective design of instructional text. Regrettably, it appears that text researchers and text designers seldom collaborate. What seems to be needed is a theory of textbook design that incorporates knowledge about prose comprehension with knowledge about the role that graphic features can play in effective communication. The work of Barbara Hunter, Avon Crismore, and P. David Pearson (Chapter 4) on visual displays is a preliminary attempt to gather data that will assist in the construction and evaluation of improved theories of textbook design. Their chapter reports on the validation of a system for analyzing how effectively visual displays of information appearing in text are presented to students.

In Chapter 5, Malcolm Fleming provides some instructive insights into how research findings can be used to guide the way that text is structured and displayed in the "real world" of instructional design. Fleming presents a tutorial series of case studies wherein he analyzes, comments on, and revises a number of illustrations taken from actual textbooks. He is guided by a number of research-based design principles derived from the influential book he coauthored with Howard Levie, *Instructional Message Design: Principles from the Behavioral Sciences* (1978). In several of the case studies, these principles are operationalized through the manipulation of various design variables. The significance of Fleming's contribution lies in his admittedly speculative, but much-needed, attempt to transfer the findings of educational research into the realm of informed practice.

As computers have gained increased prominence in schools, computer graphics have introduced new dimensions to the roles of illustration in education. Dynamic, interactive graphics on video screens allow learners to create and modify their own educational illustrations. In the sixth and concluding chapter by Kathryn Alesandrini, the potential for computer graphics in learning and instruction is explored. In this rapidly developing field an extensive research literature has yet to emerge. A brief review of the few available studies directly concerned with the effects of computer graphics on learning and motivation is presented. Primary consideration is given to graphics application software (the visual equivalent of word processing software). The equipment and capabilities for generating computer graphics are described in some detail, and a preliminary report is presented on the classroom implementation of graphics application software in science education. Promising directions and future research needs are indicated.

Considered as an integral unit, the present two-volume set is designed to bring together significant findings, models, and insights emerging from recent research. As such, the component volumes are specifically intended to complement each other. Basic process, descriptive, and applied research (as well as theoretical and historical avenues) are considered in an effort to narrow the current gap between theory and practice. As the present chapters attest, research on illustrated prose is proceeding vigorously on a number of fronts. Accordingly, the publication of *The Psychology of Illustration* constitutes a timely supplement to the existing literature on illustrated text.

D.M.W.
H.A.H.

Contents

Preface	v
Contributors	xv

1. Research on Pictures: A Guide to the Literature 1
   W. Howard Levie

Introduction	1
Picture Perception	2
Theoretical Approaches to Picture Perception	2
Attention and Scanning	4
Interpreting Figures and Pictorial Cues	6
Perceiving Global Meaning	8
Memory for Pictures	9
Memory Models	10
Recognition Memory	12
Recall	14
Other Types of Memory Research	14
Learning and Cognition	15
The Acquisition of Knowledge	15
Problem Solving and Visual Thinking	17
The Acquisition of Cognitive Skills	19
Media Research	21
Affective Responses to Pictures	22
Arousal and Emotional Impact	23
Preferences	24
Attitudes	24
Aesthetic Responses	25
Final Comment	26
References and Selected Bibliography	27

2. On Empirically Validating Functions of Pictures in Prose 51
   Joel R. Levin, Gary J. Anglin, and Russell N. Carney

Introduction	51
What We Already Know: A Retrospective Sketch	52
On Pictures in Prose	52

xii Contents

        On Functions of Pictures in Prose 53
        On Empirically Validating Functions of Pictures in Prose 63
            Preliminary Remarks and Caveats About the Meta-Analysis 63
            A Meta-Analysis of Picture Functions 66
        An Analysis of the Meta-Analysis: Prescriptions and Proscriptions ... 73
            Ten Commandments of Picture Facilitation.......................... 73
            . . . And a Postscription 77
        References 78
        Appendix: Studies Included in the Meta-Analysis 80

3. **Effects of Illustrations on Children's Listening Comprehension and Oral Prose Memory** 87
   Michael Pressley and Gloria E. Miller

        Introduction 87
        Motivation for Studying Picture Effects 88
            Theoretical Concern 88
            Pragmatic Concerns 90
        Methodological Issues in Studying Picture Effects 91
        Recent Studies of Illustration Effects on Children's Prose Learning ... 93
            Effects Produced by Illustrations that Completely Match Prose 93
            Effects Produced by Illustrations that Do Not Completely Match Prose.... 96
        Discussion: Where to Go from Here?............................... 109
        References 111

4. **The Role of Illustrations in Processing and Remembering Illustrated Text** 115
   Joan Peeck

        Introduction 115
        Part 1: Roles and Effects of Illustrations 116
            Affective-Motivational and Cognitive Effects During Reading 117
            Affective-Motivational and Cognitive Effects After Reading 122
            Causes of Cognitive Effects 128
        Part 2: Factors Influencing Text–Illustration Effects 129
            Learner Characteristics... 130
            Picture, Picture/Text, and Text Variables........................ 137
        Part 3: Present Shortcomings and Future Avenues of Research 143
        References 145

5. **Charts, Graphs, and Diagrams in Educational Materials** 152
   Bill Winn

        Introduction 152
            Definitions 152
        Advantages of Graphic Forms...................................... 153
            Visual Argument 156
            Physiological Mechanisms 157
            Cognitive Mechanisms 158
            Summary 160

The Meaningful Use of Space 160
   Elements and Relationships 161
   Charts 162
   Graphs 163
   Diagrams 166
   Summary 167
Research on Instructional Effectiveness 168
   Characteristics of the Research 168
   Realism: The Descriptive Function 169
   Charts: The Organization of Information 175
   Spatial Visualization in Mathematics 180
   Diagrams and Science Instruction 184
   Graphics and Text Comprehension 187
Summary 190
Conclusions 191
References 193

Author Index 199
Subject Index 212

Contributors

Gary J. Anglin
 College of Education, University of Kentucky at Lexington, Lexington, Kentucky 40506, USA

Russell N. Carney
 Natchitoches Parish School System, Natchitoches, Louisiana 71458, USA

W. Howard Levie
 Audio-Visual Center, Indiana University, Bloomington, Indiana 47405, USA

Joel R. Levin
 Department of Educational Psychology, University of Wisconsin at Madison, Madison, Wisconsin 53706, USA

Gloria E. Miller
 Department of Psychology, University of South Carolina at Columbia, Columbia, South Carolina 29208, USA

Joan Peeck
 Department of Psychonomics, University of Utrecht, 3584 CS Utrecht, The Netherlands

Michael Pressley
 Department of Psychology, University of Western Ontario, London, Ontario, Canada N6A 5C2

Bill Winn
 College of Education, University of Washington, Seattle, Washington 98195, USA

1
Research on Pictures: A Guide to the Literature

W. HOWARD LEVIE

1. Introduction

Although the scientific study of human response to pictures is a relatively recent development, a substantial literature has already accumulated. The purpose of this chapter is to provide an overview of this literature, revealing its scope, diversity, and areas of emphasis and neglect.

The research is grouped into four broad topics: (a) picture perception—the process of interpreting pictures, (b) memory for pictures—factors that influence the mental representation and retention of pictures, (c) learning and cognition—research that is closely related to the uses of pictures in ordinary academic learning tasks, and (d) affective responses—emotional and aesthetic reactions to pictures. Within each area, the variables and theoretical issues that have been conspicuous in recent research are enumerated. Depth of analysis is sacrificed for breadth of coverage. The details of research findings and theory are described only to the extent necessary to epitomize the essential nature of the inquiry in each area.

Emphasis is given to experimental research in psychology and education that used representational pictures as stimulus material. Research on other visual nonverbal stimuli such as diagrams, graphs, symbols, and nonmeaningful shapes is mentioned only in passing. In a few cases, the research cited was conducted for the purpose of investigating some generic psychological process rather than to learn something about pictures per se. For example, some researchers who were interested in the effects of depth of processing on memory used pictures simply because they were convenient stimuli. When such research can contribute to our understanding of how pictures are processed or how they may be used in instruction, it is included in this survey. But in the vast majority of the research cited, the use of pictures as stimuli was central to, rather than incidental to, the investigator's purposes.

Selected bibliographies for each section of the chapter are provided at the end. These references were selected on the basis of recentness, significance, and availability (dissertations, convention papers, and low-circulation journals are not cited). Also, an attempt was made to sample from the range of issues and paradigms in the recent literature. Hence, one way to see what kind of research is being done in an area is to skim the titles of the articles listed under the appropriate heading in the bibliography.

2. Picture Perception

Picture perception is a process that begins with observing that a marked surface contains information about something other than itself—information about the depicted content. Then three major types of activity normally occur: (a) attention and scanning, (b) interpreting significant figures and cues, and (c) perceiving global meaning. Each of these topics has been the subject of extensive experimentation. But before this research is described, an overview of the major theoretical approaches to picture perception is provided to place the questions asked by researchers in context.

2.1. Theoretical Approaches to Picture Perception

How is perception of the world within a picture different from perception of the natural environment? How do pictures differ from other types of symbols? Is picture perception a process of extracting information from a stimulus or a process of conferring meaning upon a stimulus? Questions such as these have provoked conjecture from philosophers, psychologists, art historians, semioticians, educators, and computer scientists. Sometimes the answers are in clear disagreement; opposing views can be identified. In other cases authors simply speak different languages, and the positions are not really opposed, they are just different.

A logical place to begin is with the theory of linear perspective invented during the Renaissance by Brunelleschi (Lynes, 1980). As depicted in Figure 1.1, the perspective theory of pictorial representation is based on the equivalence of the pattern of light rays coming from a natural scene and from a picture of the same scene drawn in proper perspective. This was the starting point for J. J. Gibson's (1971) definition of "picture":

A picture is a surface so treated that a delimited optic array to a point of observation is made available that contains the same kind of information that is found in the ambient optic arrays of an ordinary environment. (p. 31)

According to Gibson (1971), picture perception is a stimulus-driven process in which information is picked up directly from the optic array. On the other hand, "constructivists" such as Gombrich (1969) and Gregory (1978) emphasize the role played by the perceiver. Pictures do not tell their own story; rather, the viewer constructs a meaning based on a rich heritage of conventions and expectations. As an example of the problems raised by these contrasting theories of picture perception, consider the question of what constitutes "realism" in pictures. For Gibson, realism is basically a function of the degree of resemblance between the information provided by two types of optic arrays. Constructivists, however,

1. Research on Pictures 3

FIGURE 1.1. Woodcut by Dürer of a draftsman drawing a reclining nude. Light rays from the scene converge at the station point determined by the pointed shaft in front of the artist's eye. The picture plane is determined by the window grid which cuts a cross section of these rays. The grid on the picture surface is used to reproduce the scene in accurate linear perspective. From *Complete Woodcuts of Albrecht Dürer* by W. Kurth (ed.), 1963. Copyright 1963 by Dover Publications. Reprinted by permission.

point out that judgments of pictorial realism are influenced heavily by our learned preconceptions of how such a picture *ought* to look. These preconceptions are often a considerable departure from the optical data available in nature and vary according to time and situation.

For Arnheim (1974), picture perception is neither an act of direct perception nor a process of decoding learned conventions. It is primarily a matter of responding to the basic forms and forces present in the picture that are isomorphic to psychological experience. The gestalt laws of organization are the primary conveyers of meaning.

A different approach to picture perception is symbol theory. The influential theory of symbols proposed by Goodman (1976) introduces a range of concepts that may be used to analyze and compare symbol systems such as words, drawings, graphs, diagrams, music, and number systems. For example, symbol systems differ in terms of notationality—the degree to which the elements of a system are distinct and combined according to precise rules. Number systems, for example, are high in notationality; each number is unique, and the rules of correspondence are exact. Drawings, on the other hand, are nonnotational. The elements of drawings are overlapping, confusing, and lacking in clear syntax. Goodman's approach suggests that attempts to develop a "grammar of picturing" are nonsensical. In another semiotic approach, Knowlton (1966) focuses on contrasts in the form and function of digital signs (words, numbers, etc.) and iconic signs (pictures, statues, etc.). He also distinguishes between realistic pictures (pictures that look like their referents), logical pictures (diagrammatic depictions of structures), and analogical pictures (depictions of nonphenomenal relationships).

Marr (1982) presents a computational theory of vision that yields another major approach to problems of picture perception. Using techniques of visual simulation by computer, Marr draws from psychophysics, neurophysiology, and artificial intelligence to show how knowledge about the visual world can be inferred from images of it and what assumptions about the real world are required to derive these relationships.

Other major contributors to this literature include Hagen, Hochberg, Kennedy, and Kolers. References to their work may be found in the bibliography. Also, the edited books listed in the "General References" section contain many excellent chapters on a wide variety of problems in the theory of picture perception.

2.2. Attention and Scanning

What factors influence the processes by which pictures are noticed and scanned? One research strategy for studying attention to pictures uses tests of learning as the dependent measure. For example, Beck (1984) and Jennings and Dwyer (1985) studied the effects of arrows and labels on learning the information shown in instructional illustrations. Differences in learning were attributed to differences in attention caused by the attention-directing cues in the study material. However, as measures of attentional behavior, these after-the-fact tests are rather insensitive. Accordingly, research of this kind will not be examined in this section. This section describes research involving the direct observation of viewing behavior in terms of (a) a general orienting response and (b) the deployment of selective attention within a picture.

Orienting responses are measured by simply recording the time a subject spends looking at a picture. In an example of this kind of research, Anderson and Levin (1976) placed a child in a furnished room that contained a variety of items including toys and a television set showing a *Sesame Street* program. The children's viewing behavior was matched to program content, permitting inferences about relationships between attention and program attributes. Other approaches are to give subjects control over how long they look at a picture (e.g., Russell, 1975, allowed viewers to control the slide advance mechanism on a projector) or to record which picture subjects look at most when given free choice from among two or more alternatives (Lewis, 1978). Stimulus variables that have been studied in such research include complexity, novelty, incongruity, familiarity, and pleasantness (Berlyne, 1960; Wohlwill, 1975).

Research on selective attention usually requires complex instrumentation that allows the researcher to monitor exactly where in a picture the viewer is looking at any given moment (Loftus, 1979). Within the visual field, fine discriminations can be made only in a small central area about 2° in diameter called the "fovea" (an area about the size of your thumb nail when held at arm's length). Pictures are scanned in brief fixations, normally lasting about 300 milliseconds each, separated by extremely rapid movements called saccades. The location of a foveal fixation influences how a picture is interpreted (see Figure 1.2a) and what is remembered about the picture (Nelson & Loftus, 1980). Although acuity falls off rapidly from the fovea, certain information can be picked up from peripheral vision. In fact, the gist of an entire picture usually can be understood even when it is presented for as little as 300 milliseconds. Thus, one research goal has been to understand the factors governing what can be seen in a single fixation (Biederman, 1981; Intraub, 1981; Loftus, 1981; Osaka, 1980; Williams, 1984, 1985).

Most research on selective attention concerns the pattern of eye movements by which the areas in a picture are fixated (Findlay, 1985; Gould, 1976; Parker, 1978) and then integrated into a meaningful whole (Pollatsek, Rayner, & Collins, 1984). Factors that influence which areas of a picture are fixated include a variety of stimulus variables (Antes, Singsaas, & Metzger, 1978; Phillips, 1977), viewer expectations (Biederman, Teitelbaum, & Mezzanotte, 1983), whether the viewer's purpose for looking is general exploration or task-related search (Yarbus, 1967), and viewer characteristics such as age (Mackworth & Bruner, 1970; Phillips, 1985), culture (Binnie-Dawson & Choi, 1982), and expertise in decoding the type of stimulus. (Next time you get a chest x-ray try not to think about the fact that error rates in the detection of tumors may be as high as 30% false negatives and 5% false positives. See Kundel and Nodine, 1978.)

Another research area concerns the degree of automaticity of the processes in picture perception. The Treisman and Gelade (1980) theory of attention stipulates that although pictorial features such as color and size can be perceived

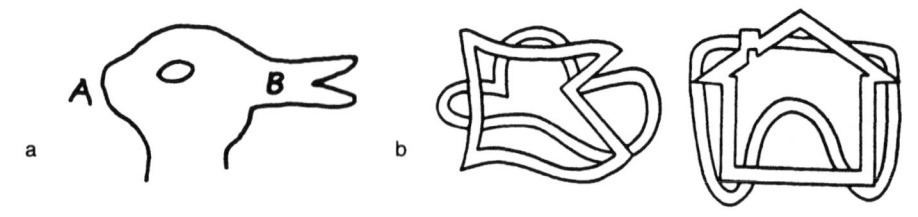

FIGURE 1.2. Where you look and why you look determines what you see. (a) Tsal and Kolbet (1985) found that interpretations of the ambiguous duck/rabbit figure depends on whether the viewer fixates at point A or point B. From "Disambiguating Ambiguous Figures by Selective Attention" by Y. Tsal and L. Kolbet, 1985, *The Quarterly Journal of Experimental Psychology, 37A*, p. 28. Copyright 1985 by Lawrence Erlbaum Associates, Ltd. Reproduced by permission. (b) Rock and Guttman (1981) showed college students overlapping figures of different colors (one red, one green) and asked them to rate the pleasingness of either the red or the green figure. Soon afterward, an unexpected recognition test for the figures was given. Recognition of the unrated figure was essentially nil, even when the figure was a meaningful shape, such as the house in the second pair shown above. From "The Effect of Inattention on Form Perception" by I. Rock and D. Guttman, 1981, *Journal of Experimental Psychology: Human Perception and Performance, 7*, pp. 276, 279. Copyright 1981 by American Psychological Association. Adapted by permission of the author.

automatically and in parallel, the figures in pictures are perceived one at a time in focused attention. Butler and McKelvie (1985), among others (see Figure 1.2b), show that the perception of shape and form requires conscious goal-directed attention. Current research concerns the identification of the perceptual processes that occur automatically during the "preattentive" stages and the determination of how these processes then combine with the more conscious cognitive operations involved in picture perception (Duncan, 1984; Intraub, 1985; Owen, 1985).

2.3. Interpreting Figures and Pictorial Cues

Pictures have a dual reality: they are objects themselves, and they act as surrogates for other objects. When a picture is used as a symbol, we know to disregard features of the picture-as-object such as the texture of the surface on which the picture appears, the border, and cues to flatness. We also know that certain aspects of pictures are not to be taken literally. We know that although a black and white photograph lacks color, the objects portrayed have color in real life. We know that a close-up of a fly does not betoken a 100 pound insect and that a portrait is not intended to represent a disembodied head. When we view a picture from an oblique angle, we do not conclude that the objects shown are tall and thin; we compensate for our station point and perceive the scene in correct perspective. We have also learned that in this culture we hold the convention that a picture represents a scene as it appears from a single point of view. We endow simple lines in an outline drawing with many meanings, depending on the context (see Figure 1.3). Thus, a broad range of complex skills is required in picture perception.

One stage in interpreting a picture is the identification of the significant figures. Figure–ground discrimination appears to be a fundamental operation of the visual system—although the ease with which a figure is identified can be affected by attributes of the figure (Ostergaard & Davidoff, 1985), the background (Biederman, 1981; Wong & Weisstein, 1983), and a wide range of viewer expectations. But shape alone is all that is usually needed (Hoffman & Richards, 1984). Pictures of familiar objects are recognized easily by young children (Hochberg & Brooks, 1962) and by people in remote cultures who have had at least some experience in looking at pictures (Hagen & Jones, 1978). Even chimpanzees demonstrate this ability (Cabe, 1980). Attempts are underway to program computers to perform as well as chimps (Sabbah, 1985).

Decoding the pictorial cues that provide information about the relationships among figures can be a more difficult task. The interpretation of depth cues has been the subject of extensive research (Berbaum, Tharp, & Mroczek, 1983; Haber, 1980). Several researchers have studied implied motion cues in line drawings (Brooks, 1977; Friedman & Stevenson, 1980) and in photographs (Freyd, 1983). Others have studied the comprehension of picture sequences (as in cartoon frames) by young children (Gelman, Bullock, & Meck, 1980) and by adults from non-Western cultures (Fussell & Haaland, 1978).

There is also an extensive literature about the perception of more elemental aspects of representation such as shapes (Kolers, 1983), contours (Koenderink, 1984), boundaries (Grossberg & Mingolla, 1985), lines (Bower & Glass, 1976), line fragments (Eijkman, 1984), and truncation of the visual field (Hagen, Jones, & Reed, 1978). Additional research concerns the perception of information about the nature of surfaces, such as texture (Caelli, 1982), curvature (Todd & Mingolla, 1984), glossiness (Beck & Prazdny, 1981), and shadows (Yonas, Goldsmith, & Hallstrom, 1978).

Overall, research on interpreting pictorial cues and features demonstrates that although some fundamental skills such as object recognition are essentially innate, young children and adults without ample picture-viewing experience have

FIGURE 1.3. Lines can be used to depict edges, boundaries, textures, color changes, and objects such as wires and ropes. A rare use of line shown in this drawing is the depiction of a change in illumination—the shadows. From "Arnheim, Gestalt Theory and Pictures" by J. M. Kennedy, 1985, *Visual Arts Research*, *11*, p. 27. Copyright 1985 by University of Illinois Press. Reproduced by permission.

trouble decoding pictorial information that is abstract, complex, or represented in culture-bound conventions—especially when the objects and concepts shown are unfamiliar. Instructional designers who wish to communicate to these audiences should field test their messages (see Figure 1.4). Because we acquired our ability to interpret pictures largely without intent or awareness, we may be misled into supposing that our mode of picturing is truly the universal language. In fact, pictures are heavily laden with culture-bound conventions that must be learned if they are to be understood. Overviews of the research in this area have been provided by Hagen and Jones (1978), Levie (1978), Serpell and Deregowski (1980), and Sigel (1978).

2.4. Perceiving Global Meaning

Two types of information can be extracted from pictures: "specific feature" information and "holistic" information. Specific feature information consists of the particular objects and cues shown in a complex picture. The nature of holistic information is a bit vague, but generally the concept refers to the schema, gist, or global meaning of a picture that can be perceived somewhat independent of the specific details. Loftus and his associates (1975, 1983) have shown that in memory experiments, either type of information can be used as the basis for storage and retrieval. Navon (1977) made a similar distinction between "local features" and "global features," and produced evidence showing that global features are processed prior to local features. Navon's global precedence hypothesis received support from Palmer (1977), who proposed a memory model in which visual forms are represented hierarchically, beginning with the global form, going down through intermediate forms and finally ending with the detailed

FIGURE 1.4. Pretesting this cartoon strip on adults in rural Botswana revealed several communication problems. Some villagers believed the character was meant to be a ghost, and the sweat was sometimes perceived as blood, rain, or tears. Most villagers did not understand that the three frames were meant to show the same character at different times. From "Research and Testing Nonformal Education Materials: A Multi-media Extension Project in Botswana" by M. Byram and C. Garforth, 1980, *Educational Broadcasting International*, *13*, p. 190. Copyright 1980 by Peter Peregrinus Ltd. Reprinted by permission.

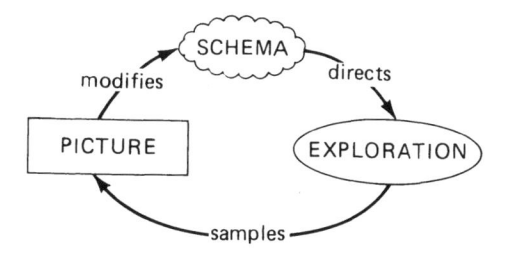

FIGURE 1.5. Modification of Neisser's perceptual cycle. An anticipatory schema directs exploration and sampling from the information available in the picture. The resulting sample is used to modify the schema. The modified schema directs further exploration. From *Cognition and Reality* (p. 21) by U. Neisser, 1976, San Francisco: W. H. Freeman. Copyright 1976 by W. H. Freeman. Adapted by permission.

features of the simplest elements. Antes and Mann (1984), however, found that the order in which global versus local information is processed may depend on factors such as the size of the image and the semantic relationship between key local features and global meaning.

A model describing the relationships among global meaning, local information, and eye movements has been proposed by Neisser (1976) (see Figure 1.5). The driving force in this model is the viewer's changing hypothesis about the scene's global meaning, represented as a schema. "Because we can see only what we know how to look for, it is these schemata (together with the information actually available) that determine what will be perceived" (Neisser, 1976, p. 20). The impact of an anticipatory schema on what is seen has been demonstrated repeatedly (Antes & Metzger, 1980; Becklen & Cervone, 1983; Friedman, 1979; Palmer, 1975) and related to diverse areas such as understanding works of art (Machotka & Spiegel, 1979) and viewing television (Luke, 1985).

The organization of scenic pictures has been the focus of several kinds of research. The perception of impossible arrangements of real-world objects as compared to "grammatically correct" scenes has been studied by Biederman, Mezzanotte, and Rabinowitz (1982) and Mandler and Johnson (1976). Mandler and Robinson (1978) showed that scene organization is more critical for young children than for adults. The ability to perceive parts and wholes in drawings also develops with age (Elkind, Koegler, & Go, 1964; Smith, 1977).

Finally, the potential contribution of work in perceptual organization should be noted (Kubovy & Pomerantz, 1981). An example is the current research related to the global minimum principle—the idea that when we are given a stimulus array capable of more than one interpretation, we tend to perceive the simplest alternative organization (Hatfield & Epstein, 1985; Peterson & Hochberg, 1983).

3. Memory for Pictures

The research cited in this section examines episodic memory, the retention of the particular pictures presented in the study phase of a memory experiment. Often the results of this research are contrasted with memory for verbal stimuli. A recurrent finding is that memory for pictures is better than memory for words, a general outcome known as the "pictorial superiority effect." Picture–word comparisons have also been central to speculation about the internal representation of pictures in long-term memory.

3.1. Memory Models

Are pictures and words encoded and stored in separate memory systems or in a single underlying mental representation? The dual-code model (Paivio, 1971, 1978) proposes a verbal system specialized for processing and storing linguistic information and a separate nonverbal system for spatial information and mental imagery. The two systems can function independently, but they are also interconnected so that, for example, a person looking at a picture might engage in covert verbalization. When a concept is registered in both memory systems, it is said to be dual coded. Paivio argues that dual coding is more likely to occur with pictures than words, and since two memory traces are better than one, dual coding explains the pictorial superiority effect. Paivio (1983) describes 10 types of research evidence that may be interpreted as support for the dual-code model.

Advocates of the single-code approach do not regard data such as the pictorial superiority effect as evidence for separate systems, but only as evidence of different activations of a common system in which all information is coded as abstract propositions. Although debate on this issue is subsiding, some of the recent protagonists are Anderson (1978), Kieras (1978), Kosslyn (1980, 1981), Pylyshyn (1981), and Shepard (1978).

Another influential model is the sensory–semantic model (Nelson, 1979). It was devised to account for differences in processing pictures and words such as the data that semantic judgments can be made more rapidly with pictures (e.g., deciding whether two items belong to the same general category such as furniture or clothing), whereas words are more readily accessible to phonemic (name) information (Potter & Faulconer, 1975). In this model, the pictorial superiority effect is attributed to a more distinctive sensory code for pictures (Nelson, Reed, & Walling, 1976) or to a greater likelihood that pictures will be processed semantically (Smith & Magee, 1980) (see Figure 1.6). Durso and his associates (1980, 1983) offer a generic–specific model in which the mental representations of pictures contain information specific to each picture, whereas semantic information of a more generic nature is encoded for words. Snodgrass (1984) proposes a multilevel model in which information from separate verbal and nonverbal systems is passed on to a single propositional store. Other researchers feel that even dual-code models are too narrow. For example, Deffenbacher, Carr, and Leu (1981) provide evidence that human faces constitute a special class of stimuli that might be handled by yet a third memory system. Furthermore, as Kolers and Brison (1984) argue, it is doubtless the case that knowledge can be represented in a variety of ways, depending on the task, the modality, and the mental operations involved.

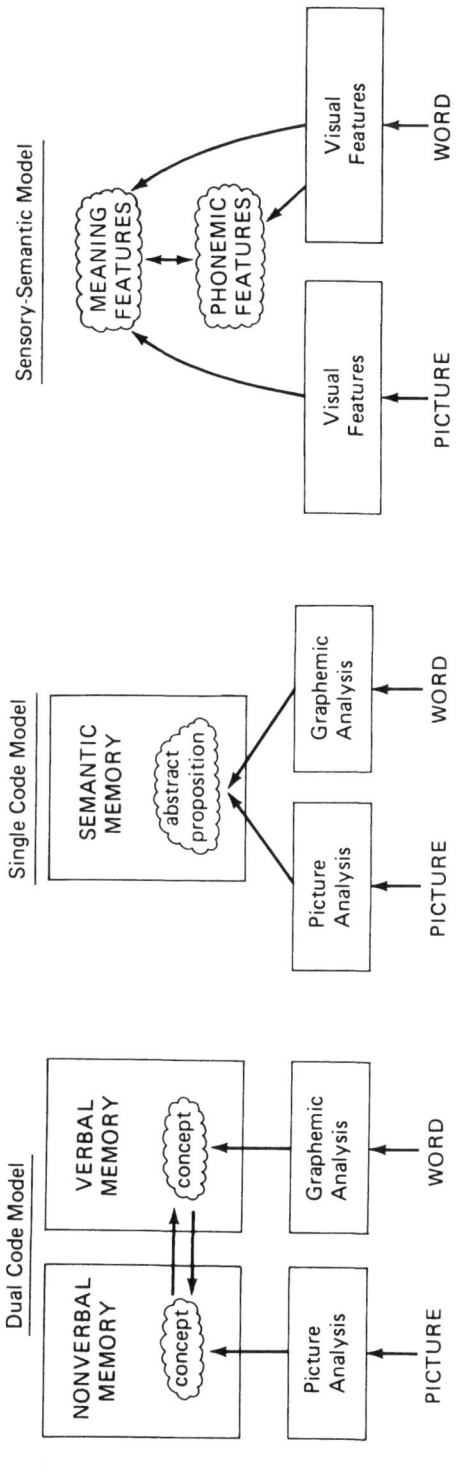

FIGURE 1.6. Three prominent models of encoding words and pictures. From "Picture–Word Differences in Decision Latency: A Test of Common-Coding Assumptions" by J. te Linde, 1982, *Journal of Experimental Psychology: Learning, Memory, and Cognition*, 8, p. 585, 586. Copyright 1982 by American Psychological Association. Adapted by permission. Also from "Learning to Order Pictures and Words: A Model of Sensory and Semantic Encoding" by D. L. Nelson, V. S. Reed, and C. L. McEvoy, 1977, *Journal of Experimental Psychology: Human Learning and Memory*, 3, p. 486. Copyright 1977 by the American Psychological Association. Adapted by permission.

3.2. Recognition Memory

Recognition memory for pictures is the largest body of picture research. In a typical experiment, subjects are shown a series of study pictures at a controlled rate and then tested using one of two basic types of procedure. In forced-choice tests, a test item consists of one study picture paired with one or more distracters. In single-item tests, study pictures and distracters are shown singly, and subjects respond *old* or *new* to each picture.

Our ability to recognize that we have seen a picture before is quite extraordinary. In an early study that attracted wide attention, Shepard (1967) showed subjects a series of 612 pictures culled from sources such as magazine advertisements. Performance on a two-alternative forced-choice test was 98.5%. Even after showing subjects 10,000 slides over a 5 day period, Standing (1973) reported recognition accuracy of 83%. In fact, under normal conditions, picture recognition is so good that researchers must go to some lengths to avoid ceiling effects. Even so, a wide variety of factors have been shown to affect picture recognition memory.

Pictorial stimulus variables that have a positive effect on recognition memory include meaningfulness (Wiseman & Neisser, 1974), distinctiveness (Courtois & Mueller, 1981), figure–ground clarity (Franken, 1977), complexity (Pezdek & Chen, 1982), color (Borges, Stepanowsky, & Holt, 1977), movement (Goldstein, Chance, Hoisington, & Buescher, 1982), and degree of heterogeneity within the picture set (Kiphart, Sjogren, Loomis, & Cross, 1985). The addition of verbal labels or descriptions is usually helpful, but a variety of other effects have also been observed. For example, Jörg and Hörmann (1978) showed that calling a picture a "flower" or a "tulip" affects recognition for particular aspects of the picture. Haber and Myers (1982) showed that memory for a picture–word combination (see Figure 1.7a) was superior to memory for words alone or pictures alone.

Several issues concerning the ways in which pictures are processed have received attention. The study of encoding strategy is one focus. Within the general levels-of-processing framework, researchers have manipulated depth of encoding (Emmerich & Ackerman, 1979), distinctiveness of encoding (Parkin & Hayward, 1983), spread of encoding (Kunen, Green, & Waterman, 1979), encoding effort (Kellogg, Cocklin, & Bourne, 1982), and degree of encoding elaboration (d'Ydewalle, Delhaye, & Goessens, 1985). Hampson and Cutting (1985) found that college students are good at judging the relative effectiveness of a range of strategies for remembering pictures, and Justice (1985) found developmental improvement in elementary school children's ability to judge the value of picture memory strategies.

Another research focus concerns the possibility that some sort of visual rehearsal of pictures occurs that is analogous to the verbal rehearsal of word stimuli. It is well established that picture memory improves when the amount of blank time between successive pictures is lengthened (Kallman, 1984), indicating that something must occur following the presentation of a picture that adds to the memory trace. Additionally, retention is better if subjects are instructed to

FIGURE 1.7. (a) Haber and Myers found better recognition memory for pictograms than for outline drawings or normally printed words. From "Memory for Pictograms, Pictures, and Words Separately and All Mixed Up" by R. N. Haber and B. L. Myers, 1982, *Perception, 11*, p. 59. Copyright 1982 by Pion Ltd., London. Reproduced by permission. (b) Goodman demonstrated that the nature of what is remembered about the objects in a picture depends on the relevance of the objects to the central theme of the picture. In this figure, schema-relevant objects such as the bookcase were recalled better than objects low in relevance such as the bird. On the other hand, recognition memory for detailed appearance was better for the low-relevance objects. From "Picture Memory: How the Action Schema Affects Retention" by G. S. Goodman, 1980, *Cognitive Psychology, 12*, p. 475. Copyright 1980 by Academic Press. Reprinted by permission. (c) In a paired-associate learning study involving the names of companies and their product or service, pictures depicting the two items in interaction (in this figure "Arrow Pest Control" exterminators) were very helpful. From "Cognitive Strategy in Advertising Design" by K. L. Alesandrini, 1983, in M. Pressley and J. R. Levin (eds.), *Cognitive Strategy Research: Psychological Foundations*, p. 207. Copyright 1983 by Springer-Verlag NY.

imagine, visualize, or simply "think about" pictures after they have been removed from view (Watkins & Graefe, 1981; Watkins, Peynircioglu, & Brems, 1984). But even without instructions, rehearsal of some sort often appears to occur. Furthermore, this process seems not to be just a matter of implicit naming of the objects pictured (Intraub, 1979) or the selection of specific detail information for additional processing (Weaver & Stanny, 1984). One technique for studying such issues involves following the presentation of pictures with masks designed to disrupt perceptual or conceptual processing (Intraub, 1984; Loftus and Ginn, 1984). Levin, Ghatala, DeRose, and Makoid (1977) demonstrated use of a remarkably effective rehearsal strategy in discrimination learning. After looking at an item, subjects were instructed to turn their heads to one side and trace the imagined outline of the to-be-remembered picture in the air with their fingers.

Subject variables that have been studied in connection with picture recognition memory include age (Morrison, Haith, & Kagan, 1980; Park & Puglisi, 1985), culture (Klich & Davidson, 1983), imagery ability (McKelvie, 1984), verbal ability (Ernest, 1983), field dependence (Chatterjea & Paul, 1981), impulsivity (Siegel, Babich, & Kirasic, 1974), extroversion (Stelmack, Wieland, Wall, &

Plouffe, 1984), and experience with the stimulus (Peeck & Zwarts, 1983). Closely related to research on picture recognition are the substantial literatures on eyewitness research (E. F. Loftus, 1979) and memory for faces (Davies, Ellis, & Shepherd, 1981).

3.3. Recall

Many of the issues and variables that have been studied in recognition memory have also been studied in recall experiments. Researchers have investigated the effects of pictorial stimulus variables (Coulter, Coulter, & Glover, 1984; Tabachnick & Brotsky, 1976), encoding strategies (Ackerman, 1985; Ghatala & Levin, 1982; Intraub & Nicklos, 1985), and rehearsal processes (Bray, Hersh, & Turner, 1985; Tversky & Sherman, 1975). Recall experiments have also dealt with variables such as the effects of organizing the series of items into categories (Dick & Engle, 1984; Ritchey, 1982) and showing items more than once (Topping & DiGeorge, 1984).

Several problems concerning differences between recall and recognition have received attention. For example, Goodman (1980) studied the role of picture schema and object distinctiveness on the recall and recognition of objects in pictures. In pictures that depict activities such as reading a book (Figure 1.7b), objects with high relevance to the "reading schema" (the bookcase, the book on the floor) were recalled well, whereas recognition memory for the appearance of these objects was poor. On the other hand, recall of objects with low relevance to the schema (the flower pot, the bird) was poor, while recognition was good. Basic differences between recognition and recall appear to occur during retrieval. Gillund and Shiffrin (1981) offer a model to describe retrieval processes in the recall of pictures and words.

3.4. Other Types of Memory Research

Several researchers have compared the effects of pictures and words in paired-associate learning. Best learning occurs when a pair consists of a pictorial stimulus that is to be associated with a verbal response (Brainerd, Desrochers, & Howe, 1981), a finding that has implications for vocabulary learning (Lippman & Shanahan, 1973). When both items in the pair are presented as pictures, research usually shows that learning is better if the two items are shown in interaction (Figure 1.7c). Recently, however, Biron and McKelvie (1984) failed to replicate this finding. Research on the bizarreness of the depicted interaction has also produced mixed results (Kee & Nakayama, 1982; O'Brien & Wolford, 1982).

In research on memory for presentation order, picture–word experiments show that serial recall is better for words than pictures (R. E. Anderson, 1976; Paivio, Philipchalk, & Rowe, 1975). Other research concerning sequential/temporal factors includes that by Brown and Brown (1982), Hicks (1980), Ledger and Ryan (1982), Poulsen, Kintsch, Kintsch, and Premack (1979), and Somerville, Haake, and Wellman (1984). Hintzman and Stern (1984) report that subjects have good memory for the frequency with which a given picture appears in a series of pictures.

In another line of research, subjects are shown a series of pictures and asked to recall as many as they can. After a delay, the subjects are asked to recall them once more. Surprisingly, the number of pictures recalled increases with repeated testing, a phenomenon known as "hypermnesia." Hypermnesia has been demonstrated for recall of pictures but not words (Erdelyi & Kleinbard, 1978; Madigan & Lawrence, 1980) and for recognition of pictures (Erdelyi & Stein, 1981). Several explanations for the effect have been offered (Erdelyi, 1982; Roediger, Payne, Gillespie, & Lean, 1982).

After a picture is removed from view, information from the image is held for a fraction of a second in a fast-decaying sensory store. Loftus, Shimamura, and Johnson (1985) show that, for about 100 milliseconds, as much information can be extracted from the icon (the stimulation that remains following stimulus offset) as from the picture itself. The nature and locus of this icon, however, are unclear. Some evidence suggests that the icon is primarily a matter of visible persistence located in the eye, and other evidence suggests that it is a form of memory located deeper in the nervous system (iconic memory). The topic has been a focus of much study and debate (Bowling & Lovegrove, 1982; Coltheart, 1980; Haber, 1983; Long, 1980).

4. Learning and Cognition

The research considered in this section employed dependent measures that are closely related to typical academic learning tasks. The first category consists of research on the uses of pictures in teaching facts, concepts, and procedures. The second category, problem solving and visual thinking, deals with higher-level learning objectives. The third category, the acquisition of cognitive skills, focuses on skills that are primarily spatial or perceptual in nature. The final category, media research, examines the issues that have historically clustered around film, television, and other forms of pictorial media.

4.1. The Acquisition of Knowledge

How can pictures be useful in teaching factual knowledge? One important type of research in this area has examined the effects of pictures on learning the information presented in accompanying written or oral prose. Some of the most prominent investigators in this field are authors of other chapters in this volume. They can speak for themselves; text illustrations and pictures with oral prose will not be discussed here.

The most prolific researcher on the effects of pictures on learning factual knowledge is Dwyer (1978, 1982–83). He and his associates have conducted over 200 studies based on a 2,000 word text and a set of illustrations of the human heart (see Peeck, this volume, p. 139). These illustrations have been presented by a variety of formats (e.g., booklets, television, slide-audiotape presentation, and computers) to study a wide range of issues in facilitating the attainment of instructional objectives such as teaching facts and definitions and the comprehension of processes. One general finding of Dwyer's research is that pictures are most helpful in achieving objectives that entail visual discriminations (such as identifying the parts of the heart). In research comparing the relative effectiveness of the different versions of the pictures, the line drawings are generally more effective in presentation formats where the learner's study time is fixed and limited (such as television), whereas the more realistic versions are sometimes more effective in presentation formats where unlimited study time is allowed.

Another substantial research program on the use of pictures in teaching facts has been led by Levin and Pressley. They observe that mnemonic learning techniques such as the keyword method are ineffective if learners, such as young children, are unable to generate useful mental imagery (Pressley & Levin, 1978). In a series of studies, they have shown that pictures that provide such imagery ("mnemonic pictures") can be used effectively in tasks such as learning the attributes of minerals, the capitals of states, the order of the U.S. presidents, and word definitions (Levin, McCormick, & Dretzke, 1981; Levin, McCormick, Miller, Berry, & Pressley, 1982; Peters, Levin, McGivern, & Pressley, 1985; Scruggs, Mastropieri, Levin, & Gaffney, 1985).

The use of pictures in teaching concepts has received sporadic attention. Some early research by Hollenberg (1970) seemed to indicate that pictures, because of their concreteness, might be a hindrance in teaching abstract concepts. Dixon and Saltz (1977), however, found that pictures and words were equally effective in teaching functional concepts (e.g., things that are containers) and that pictures were superior in teaching perceptual concepts (e.g., things that are pointed). Tennyson (1978) demonstrated that adding pictures to verbal instruction will help if the pictures draw attention to the critical attributes of a concept. Research on the effects of stimulus variables has shown that the number and variation of examples presented affect concept acquisition (Carnine, 1980a, 1980b; King & Newman, 1982). The rapidly developing area of research on the formation of real-world concepts (Medin & Smith, 1984) has made extensive use of pictorial stimuli. Such research includes the study of how people identify and classify pictures of objects (Jolicoeur, Gluck, & Kosslyn, 1984; Murphy & Smith, 1982) and how people acquire family-resemblance concepts based on stimuli such as impressionist paintings (Hartley & Homa, 1981) and schematic faces (Nelson, 1984).

Procedural tasks are the focus of another developing body of picture research. Kieras and Bovair (1984) showed that learning how to operate a mechanical device can be facilitated by providing a pictorial model that helps learners understand how the device works. Murphy and Wood (1981) observed that young children who were asked to construct a block pyramid made various uses of a series of illustrations and that the way the pictures were used was related to differences in task performance. Picture prompts have been used successfully to train retarded children in a variety of procedural tasks (Frank, Wacker, Berg, &

McMahon, 1985; Wacker & Berg, 1983). Stone and Glock (1981) found that fewer errors were made in assembling a model when the directions included illustrations, and Bieger and Glock (1984/85) studied the kinds of information that can be depicted effectively in procedural illustrations (e.g., information on the location, orientation, and composition of objects). The difficulties involved in unambiguously portraying actions such as flipping a switch or turning a knob have been studied by Marcel and Barnard (1979), Smith (1981), and Szlichcinski (1979). Smillie (1985) provides a set of general recommendations for the design of illustrated job performance aids.

Research on the effects of pictorial stimulus variables in teaching facts has been somewhat disappointing. This may be attributed in part to the diverse and intractable nature of these variables—which can sometimes be described only in terms of prototypes rather than by distinct attributes that researchers would prefer in defining independent variables. Generally, research based on instructional functions has been more productive than research based on surface-level features (see Chapter 2 in this volume). Nevertheless, the instructional effects of a wide range of pictorial design variables have been studied, including color (for reviews see Christ, 1975; Dwyer & Lamberski, 1982–83), the amount of figural detail (Borg & Schuller, 1979; Haring & Fry, 1979), the addition of close-up views of critical information (Hannafin, 1983), and the use of attention-directing devices such as arrows and visual embellishments (see Dwyer, 1978, for a review).

A logical speculation is that caricature-like drawings that exaggerate the critical features of an object and deemphasize irrelevant features might be more effective than photographs or accurate detailed drawings. In a widely cited study, Ryan and Schwartz (1956) found that cartoon drawings that "distorted the figure to emphasize the essential spatial relationships involved" were perceived more rapidly than photographs or line drawings (see Figure 1.8a). A different kind of evidence supporting this conjecture was provided by Murray and Szymczyk (1978) who showed that incomplete drawings that preserve the distinctive features of an object are easier to identify than incomplete drawings that contain few distinctive features (see Figure 1.8b). More recently, however, Hagen and Perkins (1983) and Tversky and Baratz (1985) found that in a variety of tasks, facial caricatures designed to be "superfaithful" carriers of facial information were no better than or poorer than photographs. Several other aspects of style in illustrations are discussed by Ashwin (1979) and Newton (1984).

Researchers who recently have offered general advice on how to design instructionally effective pictures include Fleming (1986), Haber (1981), Levin (1983), Perkins (1980), Twyman (1985), Winn (1982), Zimmerman and Perkin (1982).

4.2. Problem Solving and Visual Thinking

Research on the uses of pictures in higher-level cognitive processes such as reasoning, critical thinking, and problem solving has been sparse. Such research, however, has often implicated various forms of mental imagery.

One type of problem solving in which pictures can be useful involves analogical reasoning. Mayer (1983), Rigney and Lutz (1976), and Royer and Cable (1976)

18   W. Howard Levie

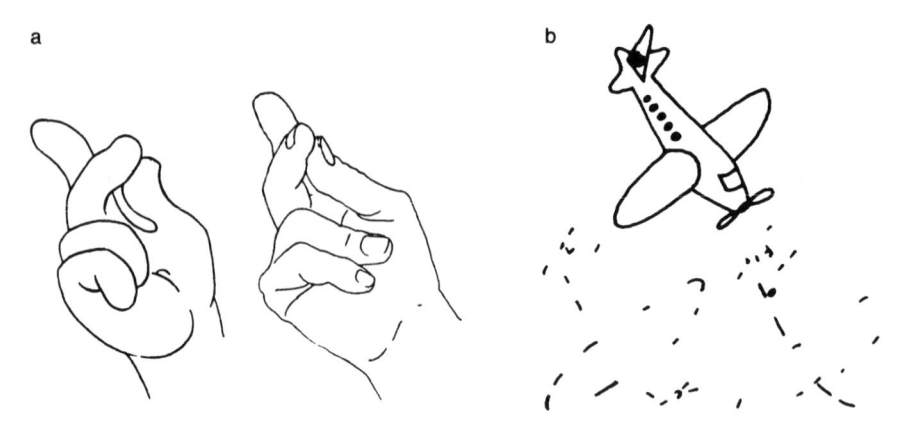

a   b

FIGURE 1.8. The perception of line drawings is facilitated by designs that emphasize an object's critical cues and contours. (a) Cartoons exaggerating the relevant cues and reducing unnecessary detail were identified more rapidly than realistic line drawings. From "Speed of Perception as a Function of Mode of Representation" by T. A. Ryan and C. B. Schwartz, 1956, *American Journal of Psychology, 69*, p. 66. Copyright 1956 by the University of Illinois Press. Reprinted by permission. (b) The fragmented drawing of the airplane on the left retains a higher proportion of the distinctive features of the object (the wings, propeller, and vertical stabilizer) than the fragmented drawing on the right. The drawing with more distinctive features was much easier to identify. From "Effects of Distinctive Features on Recognition of Incomplete Pictures" by F. S. Murray and J. M. Szymcyzyk, 1978, *Developmental Psychology, 14*, p. 358. Copyright 1978 by American Psychological Association. Reproduced by permission.

have shown that pictorial analogies can facilitate learning, due probably to making abstract information more concrete and imaginable. Gick (1985) studied the use of diagrams to help students grasp the nature of the problem and solution in an analogical problem-solving task. Moyer, Sowder, Threadgill-Sowder, and Moyer (1984), Reed (1985), and Threadgill-Sowder, Sowder, Moyer, and Moyer (1985) have shown that graphic presentation of mathematical story problems can lead to improved performance. Metaphoric reasoning with pictures has been studied by Gentner (1977) and Honeck, Voegtle, and Sowry (1981). Indeed, the meanings of pictures sometimes depend on regarding them as visual metaphors (see Figure 1.9).

A line of research with a rather long history concerns imaginal processes in syllogistic reasoning. DeSoto, London, and Handel (1965) asked subjects to solve linear syllogisms such as: If A is taller than B, and C is shorter than B, who is tallest? They proposed that a "spatial paralogic" in which the three terms are arrayed in mental imagery underlies the ability to solve such problems. Subsequent researchers proposed alternative linguistic strategies (Sternberg, 1980), and Egan and Grimes-Farrow (1982) claim that most people can be classified reliably according to which type of strategy they use. On the other hand, research in a related reasoning task called sentence–picture verification (deciding if the sentence "Star is above plus" accurately describes the simple picture "$\overset{*}{+}$") shows

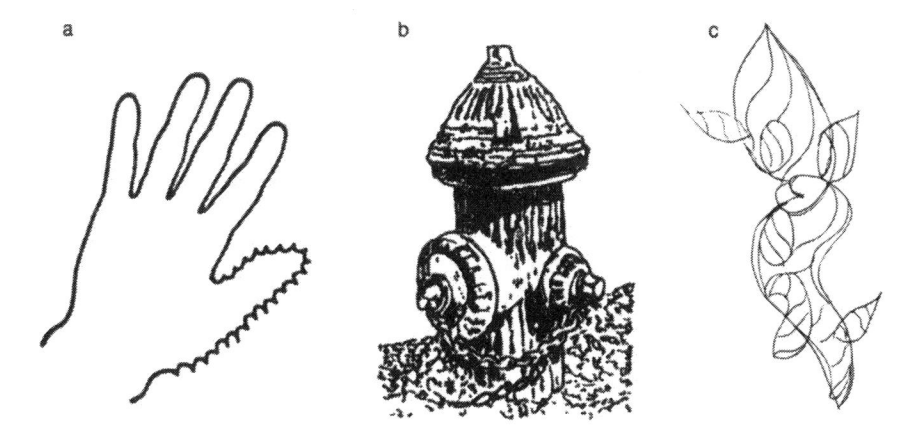

FIGURE 1.9. Visual metaphors. (a) The sawtooth outline of the thumb may be regarded as a metaphoric pictorial device depicting pain. From "For Each Kind of Figure of Speech There Is a Pictorial Metaphor: A Figure of Depiction" by J. M. Kennedy and W. Simpson, 1982, *Visual Arts Research*, 8, p. 7. Copyright 1982 by the University of Illinois Press. Reproduced by permission. (b) Based on a pencil drawing titled "Androgyny" by Feinstein. From "Meaning and Visual Metaphor" by H. Feinstein, 1982, *Studies in Art Education*, 23, p. 52. Copyright 1982 by the National Art Education Association. Reproduced by permission of the author. (c) Drawing by an anonymous college student representing the concept "good marriage." From *Visual Thinking* (p. 125) by R. Arnheim, 1969, Berkeley: University of California Press. Copyright 1969 by University of California Press. Reproduced by permission.

that subjects can adopt a spatial strategy or a linguistic strategy depending on task requirements or experimenter directions (Mathews, Hunt, & MacLeod, 1980). Kaufmann (1985) reviews evidence suggesting that task familiarity may be a determinant of the problem-solving mode used, with imagery being particularly useful in novel situations. For example, imagery appears to be particularly crucial in invention and discovery (Hadamard, 1954).

Thus, "visual thinking" appears to be an important mode of cognition in problem solving. It is, however, an elusive concept. Arnheim (1985), the foremost advocate of teaching visual thinking, contrasts the enigmatic nature of intuition (thought to be a component of visual thinking) with the comparatively discernible chain of intellectual operations involved in verbal reasoning. "Intuition is much less easily understood because we know it mostly by its achievements whereas its mode of operation tends to elude awareness. It is like a gift from nowhere" (p. 79). Yet creative problem solving appears to require both modes: "Good reasoning depends crucially on the vigorous exercise of imagination" (Perkins, 1985, p. 25).

4.3. The Acquisition of Cognitive Skills

Since the uses of pictures in the acquisition of linguistic skills are covered elsewhere in this volume, the following discussion is limited to skills that are spatial in nature. The skills that are related most directly to pictures are those that are required to detect and decode pictorial information.

Most picture perception skills are acquired without special instruction in the normal course of exposure to pictorial media (Cassidy & Knowlton, 1983). For example, young children typically have opportunity to interact with picture books extensively and in a wide range of unstructured ways (Kiefer, 1983). However, many of the skills involved in extracting information from pictures can also be taught directly. Modest amounts of instruction can improve children's responsiveness to pictorial cues depicting texture (Seefeldt, 1979), shading (Yonas, Kuskowski, & Sternfels, 1979), and depth (Leach, 1978; Nicholson, Seddon, & Worsnop, 1977). Brief training procedures can improve young children's ability to encode left–right orientation in pictures (Fisher & Braine, 1981) and to read pictograph sentences (Ledger & Ryan, 1985). In a more ambitious project, Higgins (1979) developed and validated a 16 unit training program to improve children's ability to draw inferences from pictures. Other researchers have demonstrated training effects with adult subjects in skills such as map reading (Barsam & Simutis, 1984), processing visual art (Koroscik, 1984), and improving the ability to discriminate and recognize faces of people from another racial group—thereby reducing the "they all look alike to me" effect (Goldstein & Chance, 1985).

A large body of related literature concerns the development of spatial abilities and spatial cognition (Olson & Bialystok, 1983; Pellegrino, Alderton, & Shute, 1984). Researchers have demonstrated training or practice effects in perspective-taking ability (Cox, 1978), doing mental rotations of three-dimensional structures (Seddon, Tariq, & Dos Santos Veiga, 1984), performance on standard tests of visual–spatial skill (Stericker & LeVesconte, 1982), and improvement on several measures of mental imagery ability (Kosslyn, Brunn, Cave, & Wallach, 1984). Simple exposure to media visualization techniques such as zooming in on the critical details in pictures can affect a variety of spatial skills such as the ability to single out details, change points of view, visualize rotations in space, and identify embedded figures (Salomon, 1979). The process of acquiring mental skills may, however, be one of gradual cultivation during prolonged media exposure. The potential impact of heavy television viewing on cognitive skills, particularly with reference to schooling and verbal literacy, has been the subject of much research and speculation (Lonner, Thorndike, Forbes, & Ashworth, 1985; Salomon, 1983; Shannon & Fernie, 1985; Williams, Haertel, Haertel, & Walberg, 1982).

Cognitive skills can be affected by the act of producing pictures as well as perceiving pictures. Researchers have shown that mental representations and skills can be influenced by making drawings (Lansing, 1984), taking photographs (Seidman & Beilin, 1984), and filmmaking (Tidhar, 1984). The substantial literature on children's drawings is much more concerned with the cognitive act of seeing than with the motor act of producing visual representations (Freeman, 1980; Gardner, 1980).

4.4. Media Research

Media research has a troubled past and an uncertain future. The advent of each new teaching technology has spawned an outbreak of research hoping to demonstrate the superiority of the new medium to "conventional" instruction. Repeatedly, these hopes have been dashed. With but few exceptions, research comparing normal classroom teaching with instruction by radio, filmstrips, motion pictures, programmed instruction, or television has failed to produce differences in learning—or in any measure of instructional importance (Campeau, 1974; Jamison, Suppes, & Wells, 1974). A recent meta-analysis of research comparing conventional college instruction with various forms of visual-based instruction (e.g., motion pictures, still projection, and educational television) produced the same outcome. Overall, student achievement was only 1.5% better with visual-based instruction, and no differences were observed in student drop out rate, attitudes, or aptitude–achievement correlations (Cohen, Ebeling, & Kulik, 1981). Moreover, severe methodological problems with this approach preclude the possibility of ever producing interpretable data. The treatments are too grossly defined, and they are confounded with differences in content, instructional strategy, and the novelty effects of newer media (Clark & Salomon, 1986). If, however, the competing treatments in an experiment of this kind were well controlled, the conceptual problems would then become apparent. If the only difference between treatments were the medium, it would become clear that "media are mere vehicles that deliver instruction but do not influence student achievement any more than the truck that delivers groceries causes changes in our nutrition" (Clark, 1983, p. 445). Nevertheless, the conviction that the medium should make a difference has persisted.

When might the choice of medium make a difference in instructional effectiveness? If a medium has the potential to present information of a particular kind (e.g., the potential to show objects in motion), and if this potential is used when the information is relevant to an instructional objective, then using that medium might be more effective than using a medium that lacks this potential. Such reasoning led to the suggestion that media effects should be studied in terms of media attributes (Levie & Dickie, 1973). Some research of this kind has been productive. For example, useful data about the circumstances in which the attribute of motion is helpful have been provided by Blake (1977), Collins, Adams, and Pew (1978), and Spangenberg (1973). It might be observed, however, that research on media attributes is essentially indistinguishable from research on instructional methods (e.g., research on the effects of advance organizers and the effects of adjunct questions), leading one to question whether the concept of media attributes serves to clarify or confuse our understanding of media effects.

Another approach to media research has been proposed by Salomon (1979). He argues that although media differ in terms of their technologies of transmission, their situations of use, and their contents, the differences among media that are critical to problems of learning and cognition are the differences in the symbol systems they employ. Symbol systems, the means by which meaning is encoded, determine the kinds of messages a medium can carry and the kinds of mental skills that are activated in decoding these messages. Some media are best characterized as a blend of symbol systems. For example, Kjorup (1977) describes motion pictures as a meeting place of multiple codes. An example of recent research based on this perspective has been the attempt to identify the characteristic differences in processing and remembering story narratives presented by film/television as compared to presentation in verbal form (Baggett & Ehrenfeucht, 1982; Beagles-Roos & Gat, 1983; Meringoff, 1980; Pezdek, Lehrer, & Simon, 1984).

Historically, media research has been organized according to the particular medium that is dominant at any particular moment. The earliest substantial body of such research was the government-sponsored film research that began during World War II and lasted through the mid-1950s. This was followed by a decade of educational television research. Typical research programs concerned broad instructional problems such as the instructional effects of repetition, providing summaries, and note-taking. Other research focused on more narrow media-specific problems such as the effects of camera angles and animation techniques (Chu & Schramm, 1967; Reid & MacLennan, 1976). More recently, research on children's television, particularly with reference to attentional factors, has formed the basis for another coherent body of media research (Bryant & Anderson, 1983). Other recent topics of film/television research include the processing and retention of audio versus video information (Hayes & Kelly, 1984; Pezdek & Stevens, 1984) and the effects of various editing techniques (Smith, Anderson, & Fischer, 1985; Wright et al., 1984). Research reviews have focused on the uses of film and television in education (Leifer, 1976; Nadaner, 1983), on the effects of production variables on learning from film (Marchant, 1977) and broadcast television (Gunter, Berry, & Clifford, 1982), and on semiotic approaches to film (Carroll, 1982). Other media-specific research has concerned multi-image presentation (Goldstein, 1975; Kreszock & Moore, 1981-82; Whiteside, 1983-84), maps (Atkins, 1981; Kulhavy, Lee, & Caterino, 1985; Potash, 1977), and photographs (Kose, 1985; McIsaac, Mosley, & Story, 1984).

In suggesting directions for future research on media in teaching, Clark and Salomon (1986) stress the role of learner perceptions in media effects. For example, Salomon (1984) reports that students perceive that their ease and efficacy in learning from television is quite different from their ease and efficacy in learning from print. These perceptions have consequences for the amount of mental effort students invest in learning from these media, which in turn affects the amount learned. The effects of the medium and the learner are reciprocal.

5. Affective Responses to Pictures

Compared to the large bodies of research in the first three areas, research on affective responses to pictures has been sparse. Some of this neglect might be attributed to the presence of methodological problems. Dependent measures in the affective domain are typically less well developed than cognitive measures, and affective responses to the picture design variables of interest are sometimes difficult to separate from responses to the subject matter of pictures. Also, many of the key concepts in this area lack a clear and accepted definition. Even so, there are firm foundations for several kinds of further research in this domain.

5.1. Arousal and Emotional Impact

Photographs of piles of corpses from Hitler's death camps, television footage of starving children in Africa—we hardly need controlled experimentation to be convinced that pictures such as these can elicit strong emotional reactions. Nevertheless, several kinds of experimental evidence have been produced. In a study dealing with the effects of fear appeals on attitude change, Rogers and Mewborn (1976) showed that gruesome pictures of automobile accidents produced high levels of arousal. Emotional reactions to film and television have been documented repeatedly. For example, Lagerspetz and Engblom (1979) documented children's expressions of fear and tenseness when watching violent films, and Efran and Spangler (1979) studied when and why adult film viewers cry. Berlyne (1960) demonstrated that pictures providing various types of uncertainty can influence arousal and exploratory behavior. Such pictures could be said to possess motivational qualities.

There is little evidence, however, to support the simple proposition that pictures are necessarily more evocative than words. Culbertson (1974) compared the emotional ratings of newspaper photographs with matter-of-fact descriptions. Overall, there was little difference between the two, although words sometimes produced stronger reactions when abstract issues were paramount, and pictures sometimes produced stronger reactions when the visual appearance of the people shown in the photographs was important. It might be argued, however, that pictures can elicit emotions more rapidly. Cupchik and Berlyne (1979) showed that subjects can detect the arousal value of a picture in less than a second. They suggest that such rapidly established tensions may serve as a background against which further pictorial information is perceived.

One type of emotional response that has received a fair amount of attention is humor. Such research has dealt with mode of presentation (Sheppard, 1983), the effects of captions (McKay & McKay, 1982), and the social facilitation of group viewing (Butcher & Whissell, 1984). Other research on arousal and emotion concerns developmental issues in the perception of emotion (Wilson & Cantor, 1985; Wiggers & van Lieshout, 1985), the effects of stimulus emotionality on memory for pictures (Evans & Denny, 1978), the effects of curiosity-arousing pictures on learning (Paradowski, 1967), and affective reactions to color versus black and white pictures (Winn & Everett, 1979).

5.2. Preferences

Do students prefer learning from illustrated materials or nonillustrated materials? Apparently the answer is so obvious that the question has received very little study. Preference for illustrated materials, however, has been demonstrated by a few researchers (Baker & Popham, 1965; Samuels, Biesbrock, & Terry, 1974; Sewell & Moore, 1980).

Quite a bit of research has been done on preferences for various pictorial design features. Children prefer realistic pictures for instructional illustrations (Myatt & Carter, 1979), although interactions have been found with type of subject matter (Ramsey, 1982) and learner characteristics (Stewig, 1975). Degree of realism also appears to be important in preferences for painting style (Hardiman & Zernich, 1982), although less so with recent art (Bell & Bell, 1979). Other stimulus variables that have been studied include color (D'Hondt & Vanderwiele, 1983; Holmes & Buchanan, 1984), complexity (Chevrier & DeLorme, 1980; Frost & Lindauer, 1980), and ambiguity (Heinrichs, 1984; Nicki, Lee, & Moss, 1981). The features of simple shapes that are associated with judgments of beauty have been studied by Boselie (1983), Boselie and Leeuwenberg (1985), McManus (1980), and Plug (1980).

5.3. Attitudes

There have been numerous demonstrations that messages presented by pictorial media such as film and television can affect attitudes (Simonson, 1980; Simonson, Thies, & Burch, 1979). Obviously, pictorial media, like any communication channel, can carry messages containing attitude-relevant information. But do pictures have any special advantages in attitude change? Taylor and Thompson (1982) reasoned that pictures might have particular persuasive impact due to their "vividness." They reviewed four studies dealing with the effects of still pictures and 13 studies comparing videotape with written or oral presentation. Although videotapes were more effective in certain limited situations, the overall results indicate that persuasion is not necessarily facilitated by the use of pictures.

On the other hand, there is some evidence that pictures can enhance the believability of information. Ryan (1975) showed that on a television news program, stories were judged to be more believable when news film taken on location was shown. Oliver and Griffitt (1976) found that in a simulated personal injury trial, mock jurors awarded higher monetary damages when the evidence included a color photograph of the accident. Whalen and Blanchard (1982) produced similar evidence with a color photograph but not a black and white photograph and attributed the effect of the color photo to heightened emotional arousal. O'Connor, Beilin, and Kose (1981) report that 6-year-old children believe that photographs are inherently more truthful than drawings.

Another role that pictures can play in attitude change involves the effects on source credibility. It is well established that when the source of a persuasive message is perceived as being trustworthy and also an expert on the topic, attitude change will be enhanced. A variety of photographic techniques can be used to manipulate the portrayal of the source (Baggaley, 1980). For example, Duck and Baggaley (1975) showed that the evaluation of a speaker on television can be influenced by interspersing cutaways that show members of the audience reacting to the speaker in positive or negative ways. Pictures may also be used advantageously if they serve to heighten the salience of a high-credibility communicator. A pictorial presentation that keeps reminding the viewer that the message is coming from a high-credibility source may be superior to nonpictorial presentation (Andreoli & Worchel, 1978).

From time to time the possibility of persuasion via some subliminal technique is raised (Kelly, 1979; Vokey & Read, 1985). Although there are reasons to believe that stimuli are sometimes perceived without awareness (Henley, 1984), there is no evidence that such stimuli can influence attitudes or attitude-relevant behavior (George & Jennings, 1975; Hovespian & Quatman, 1978). In a similar vein, some authors believe that visual persuasion might be particularly effective because the intent to persuade might be less obvious with pictures than with words. Thus, Margolin (1979) offers an analysis of "the visual rhetoric of propaganda," and Medhurst and DeSousa (1981) discuss special techniques used in "graphic persuasion." Finally, it should be noted that school media as well as mass media can play a role in attitude formation regarding a wide range of topics. For example, the stereotypic portrayal of sex roles in television and textbooks has been a matter of considerable concern (Huston, Greer, Wright, Welch, & Ross, 1984; Kolbe & LaVole, 1981; Scott, 1980; Zuckerman, Singer, & Singer, 1980).

5.4. Aesthetic Responses

Well made pictures have aesthetic properties. Perceiving these properties is a learned ability, the rewards of which are a stimulating, satisfying experience and the acquisition of a special "mode of knowing" (Eisner, 1985). Although many aspects of aesthetic literacy are not yet well enough defined to permit empirical investigation, a field of experimental aesthetics is beginning to emerge (Boyer, 1983).

What constitutes an aesthetic response? One approach to the question has been to ask subjects to rate pictures on semantic differential scales (e.g., beautiful–ugly and simple–complex) and factor analyze the results. Based on several studies, Berlyne (1971, 1974) identified a factor he called Hedonic Value, which emphasizes judgments of pleasingness, goodness, and beauty. Biaggio and Supplee (1983) add scales such as interestingness and complexity to this factor. Arguing that aesthetic response has a high emotional component, Hoege (1984) showed that subjects' emotional mood when viewing pictures can have an impact on their aesthetic judgments.

Sensitivity to style and expressive quality is another aspect of aesthetic response. Researchers have studied subjects' ability to classify works of art according to a variety of criteria such as the broad stylistic characteristics of the baroque, neoclassic, and romantic eras (Hasenfus, Martindale, & Birnbaum, 1983), the styles of different French impressionists (Rush & Sabers, 1981), and dimensions of line variation contained in specially prepared drawings (O'Hare &

Westwood, 1984). Taunton (1984) studied young children's ability to match paintings with expressive terms such as happy, fearful, and dreamy.

Much of the research in this area has focused on tracing developmental trends. Preschool children often respond to visual art in creative and enthusiastic ways, but their sensitivity to aesthetic features is usually minimal. Aesthetic development has been documented in a variety of skills such as the ability to use stylistic features in the classification of paintings (Hardiman & Zernich, 1985) and the ability to provide logical explanations for artistic judgments (D'Onofrio & Nodine, 1981). A major source of such research has been Harvard's Project Zero. (The project name refers to the founders' estimate of the amount of reliable knowledge in the area when the project was begun in 1966.) This group has championed a cognitive perspective on the study of aesthetic development (Gardner, 1973, 1982; Winner, 1982; Wohlwill, 1985). Although the approach has dominated the experimental literature, it has failed to gain wide acceptance among art educators (Lovano-Kerr & Rush, 1982). For commentary on current approaches to research on teaching aesthetics and visual arts, see Jones and McFee (1986).

Final Comment

It is clear that "research on pictures" is not a coherent field of inquiry. An aerial view of the picture research literature would look like a group of small topical islands with only a few connecting bridges in between. Most researchers refer to a narrow range of this literature in devising their hypotheses and in discussing their results. Similarly, authors of picture memory models, for example, take little notice of theories of picture perception. Although there have been a few efforts at integration across topics—work relating eye movements to picture recognition memory is one example—research generally is conducted within contexts that divide research on pictures into isolated groups. Those doing picture research usually are allied to some field such as developmental psychology, perception, communications, art education, or educational psychology and tend to focus on the literature in their own traditional area. Indeed, researchers' primary concerns usually are defined even more narrowly focusing on some process such as divided attention, short-term memory, concept learning, or problem solving. Thus, most picture research is embedded within separate areas usually identified by the mental processes evoked by stimuli rather than by surface-level features of the stimuli themselves.

In these days when cognitive psychology holds center stage, it might seem to be a myopic perspective to suggest that a field of inquiry should be based on a type of stimulus. However, there could be benefits from taking a stimulus-oriented approach. Attempts to integrate separate areas of picture research might reveal mutual implications that lead to new research questions. Efforts toward a "psychology of pictorial learning" might also make picture research more accessible to practitioners who design instructional illustrations. Surely there is room for multiple perspectives. Granted it is important that pictures be viewed in context by both researchers and educational practitioners. But an additional approach that brings together data and ideas from separate contexts could contribute much to our understanding of this pervasive, versatile mode of communication.

References and Selected Bibliography

2. PICTURE PERCEPTION

General References

Hagen, M. A. (Ed.). (1980). *The perception of pictures, Vol. 1. Alberti's window: The projective model of pictorial information*. New York: Academic Press.
Hagen, M. A. (Ed.). (1980). *The perception of pictures, Vol. 2. Dürer's devices: Beyond the projective model of pictures*. New York: Academic Press.
Kennedy, J. M. (1974). *A psychology of picture perception*. San Fransciso: Jossey-Bass.
Kolers, P. A. (1983). Perception and representation. *Annual Review of Psychology, 34*, 129–166.
Nodine, C. F., & Fisher, D. F. (Eds.). (1979). *Perception and pictorial representation*. New York: Praeger.
Perkins, D. N., Leondar, B. (Eds.). (1977). *The arts and cognition*. Baltimore, MD: Johns Hopkins University Press.

2.1 THEORETICAL APPROACHES TO PICTURE PERCEPTION

Arnheim, R. (1974). *Art and visual perception: A psychology of the creative eye* (rev. ed.). Berkeley, CA: University of California Press.
Blinder, D. (1983). The controversy over conventionalism. *Journal of Aesthetics and Art Criticism, 41*, 253–264.
Carrier, D. (1983). Gombrich on art historical explanations. *Leonardo, 16*, 91–96.
Gibson, J. J. (1971). The information available in pictures. *Leonardo, 4*, 27–35.
Gibson, J. J. (1979). *The ecological approach to visual perception*. Boston, MA: Houghton Mifflin.
Gombrich, E. H. (1969). *Art and illusion: A study in the psychology of pictorial representation*. Princeton, NJ: Princeton University Press.
Gombrich, E. H. (1982). *The image and the eye: Further studies in the psychology of pictorial representation*. Ithaca, NY: Cornell University Press.
Goodman, N. (1976). *Languages of art: An approach to a theory of symbols* (2nd ed.). Indianapolis, IN: Hackett Publishing.
Gregory, R. L. (1978). *Eye and brain* (3rd ed.). New York: McGraw-Hill.
Gregory, R. L. (1981). Questions of pattern and object perception by man and computer. In J. Long & A. Baddeley (Eds.), *Attention and performance IX* (pp. 97–116). Hillsdale, NJ: Erlbaum.
Hochberg, J. (1983). Problems of picture perception. *Visual Arts Research, 9*(2), 7–24.
Katz, S. (1983). R. L. Gregory and others: The wrong picture of the picture theory of perception. *Perception, 12*, 269–279.
Kennedy, J. M. (1985). Arnheim, Gestalt theory and pictures. *Visual Arts Research, 11*, 23–44.
Kennedy, J. M., & Ostry, D. J. (1976). Approaches to picture perception: Perceptual experience and ecological optics. *Canadian Journal of Psychology, 30*(1), 90–98.

Knowlton, J. Q. (1966). On the definition of "picture." *AV Communication Review, 14,* 157–183.

Kolers, P. A., & Smythe, W. E. (1984). Symbol manipulation: Alternatives to the computational view of mind. *Journal of Verbal Learning and Verbal Behavior, 23,* 289–314.

Lynes, J. A. (1980). Brunelleschi's perspectives reconsidered. *Perception, 9,* 87–99.

Marr, D. (1982). *Vision: A computational investigation into the human representation and processing of visual information.* San Francisco: W. H. Freeman.

Mitchell, W. J. T. (Ed.). (1980). *The languages of images.* Chicago: University of Chicago Press.

Salomon, G. (1979). Media and symbol systems as related to cognition and learning. *Journal of Educational Psychology, 71,* 131–148.

Veltrusky, J. (1976). Some aspects of the pictorial sign. In L. Matejka & I. R. Titunik (Eds.), *Semiotics of art* (pp. 245–264). Cambridge, MA: The MIT Press.

2.2. ATTENTION AND SCANNING

Anderson, D. R., & Levin, S. R. (1976). Young children's attention to "Sesame Street." *Child Development, 47,* 806–811.

Antes, J. R., Singsaas, P. A., & Metzger, R. L. (1978). Components of pictorial informativeness. *Perceptual and Motor Skills, 47,* 459–464.

Beck, C. R. (1984). Visual cueing strategies: Pictorial, textual, and combinational effects. *Educational Communication and Technology Journal, 32,* 207–216.

Berlyne, D. E. (1960). *Conflict, arousal, and curiosity.* New York: McGraw-Hill.

Biederman, I. (1981). On the semantics of a glance at a scene. In M. Kubovy & J. R. Pomerantz (Eds.), *Perceptual organization* (pp. 213–253). Hillsdale, NJ: Erlbaum.

Biederman, I., Teitelbaum, R. C., & Mezzanotte, R. J. (1983). Scene perception: A failure to find a benefit from prior expectancy or familiarity. *Journal of Experimental Psychology: Learning, Memory, and Cognition, 9,* 411–429.

Binnie-Dawson, J. L. M., & Choi, P. P. (1982). A study of perceptual and cultural cues in Chinese and Western paintings. *Psychologia, 25,* 18–31.

Buswell, G. T. (1935). *How people look at pictures.* Chicago: University of Chicago Press.

Butler, L., & McKelvie, S. J. (1985). Processing of form: Further evidence for the necessity of attention. *Perceptual and Motor Skills, 61,* 215–221.

Byram, M., & Garforth, C. (1980). Research and testing nonformal education materials: A multi-media extension project in Botswana. *Educational Broadcasting International, 13,* 25–31.

Duncan, J. (1984). Selective attention and the organization of visual information. *Journal of Experimental Psychology: General, 113,* 501–517.

Findlay, J. M. (1985). Saccadic eye movements and visual cognition. *L'Annee Psychologique, 85,* 101–136.

Fisher, D. F., Monty, R. A., & Senders, J. W. (Eds.). (1981). *Eye movements: Cognition and visual perception.* Hillsdale, NJ: Erlbaum.

Goldstein, E. B., & Fink, S. I. (1981). Selective attention in vision: Recognition memory for superimposed line drawings. *Journal of Experimental Psychology: Human Perception and Performance, 7,* 954–967.

Gould, J. D. (1976). Looking at pictures. In R. A. Monty & J. W. Senders (Eds.), *Eye movements and psychological processes* (pp. 323–343). Hillsdale, NJ: Erlbaum.

Intraub, H. (1981). Rapid conceptual identification of sequentially presented pictures. *Journal of Experimental Psychology: Human Perception and Performance, 7,* 604–610.

Intraub, H. (1985). Visual dissociation: An illusory conjunction of pictures and forms. *Journal of Experimental Psychology: Human Perception and Performance, 11,* 431-442.

Jennings, T., & Dwyer, F. (1985). The instructional effect of differential cueing strategies in facilitating student achievement of different educational objectives. *International Journal of Instructional Media, 12,* 8-20.

Kundel, H. L., & Nodine, C. F. (1978). Studies of eye movements and visual search in radiology. In J. W. Senders, D. F. Fisher, & R. A. Monty (Eds.), *Eye movements and the higher psychological functions* (pp. 317-328). Hillsdale, NJ: Erlbaum.

Lewis, M. (1978). Attention and verbal labeling behavior in preschool children: A study in the measurement of internal representations. *The Journal of Genetic Psychology, 133,* 191-202.

Loftus, G. R. (1979). On-line eye movement recorders: The good, the bad, and the ugly. *Behavior Research Methods & Instrumentation, 11,* 188-191.

Loftus, G. R. (1981). Tachistoscopic simulations of eye fixations on pictures. *Journal of Experimental Psychology: Human Learning and Memory, 7,* 369-376.

Mackworth, N. H., & Bruner, J. S. (1970). How adults and children search and recognize pictures. *Human Development, 13,* 149-177.

Nelson, W. W., & Loftus, G. R. (1980). The functional visual field during picture viewing. *Journal of Experimental Psychology: Human Learning and Memory, 6,* 391-399.

Nodine, C. F., & McGinnis, J. J. (1983). Artistic style, compositional design, and visual scanning. *Visual Arts Research, 9*(1), 1-9.

Osaka, N. (1980). Effect of peripheral visual field size upon visual search in children and adults. *Perception, 9,* 451-455.

Owen, L. A. (1985). Dichoptic priming effects on ambiguous picture processing. *British Journal of Psychology, 76,* 437-447.

Parker, R. E. (1978). Picture processing during recognition. *Journal of Experimental Psychology: Human Perception and Performance, 4,* 284-293.

Phillips, P. E. (1985). A developmental study of the selective viewing of paintings. *Visual Arts Research, 11*(2), 40-53.

Phillips, P. E. (1977). Selective attention theory and its application to visual arts research: A review of theory and supporting research. *Review of Research in Visual Arts Education, 6,* 13-33.

Pollatsek, A., Rayner, K., & Collins, W. E. (1984). Integrating pictorial information across eye movements. *Journal of Experimental Psychology: General, 113,* 426-442.

Rock, I., & Guttman, D. (1981). The effect of inattention on form perception. *Journal of Experimental Psychology: Human Perception and Performance, 7,* 275-285.

Russell, A. (1975). Interrelations among response frequency, looking time and rated interest with visual stimuli. *Australian Journal of Psychology, 27,* 251-256.

Senders, J. W., Fisher, D. F., & Monty, R. A. (Eds.). (1978). *Eye movements and the higher psychological functions.* Hillsdale, NJ: Erlbaum.

Treisman, A., & Gelade, G. (1980). A feature integration theory of attention. *Cognitive Psychology, 12,* 97-136.

Tsal, Y., & Kolbet, L. (1985). Disambiguating ambiguous figures by selective attention. *The Quarterly Journal of Experimental Psychology, 37A,* 25-37.

Williams, L. J. (1984). Information processing in near peripheral vision. *The Journal of General Psychology, 111,* 201-207.

Williams, L. J. (1985). Tunnel vision induced by a foveal load manipulation. *Human Factors, 27,* 221-227.

Wohlwill, J. F. (1975). Children's responses to meaningful pictures varying in diversity: Exploration time vs. preference. *Journal of Experimental Child Psychology, 20,* 341-351.

Yarbus, A. L. (1967). *Eye movements and vision.* New York: Plenum Press.

2.3. INTERPRETING FIGURES AND PICTORIAL CUES

Beck, J., & Prazdny, S. (1981). Highlights and the perception of glossiness. *Perception & Psychophysics, 30,* 407-410.

Bengston, J. K., Stergios, J. C., Ward, J. L., & Jester, R. E. (1980). Optic array determinants of apparent distance and size in pictures. *Journal of Experimental Psychology: Human Perception and Performance, 6,* 751-759.

Berbaum, K., Tharp, D., & Mroczek, K. (1983). Depth perception of surfaces in pictures: Looking for conventions of depiction in Pandora's box. *Perception, 12,* 5-20.

Biederman, I. (1981). Do background depth gradients facilitate object identification? *Perception, 10,* 573-578.

Bower, G. H., & Glass, A. L. (1976). Structural units and the reintegrative power of picture fragments. *Journal of Experimental Psychology: Human Learning and Memory, 2,* 456-466.

Brooks, P. H. (1977). The role of action lines in children's memory for pictures. *Journal of Experimental Child Psychology, 23,* 98-107.

Butler, D. L. (1982). Predicting the perception of three-dimensional objects from the geometrical information in drawings. *Journal of Experimental Psychology: Human Perception and Performance, 8,* 674-692.

Byram, M., & Garforth, C. (1980). Research and testing nonformal education materials: A multi-media extension project in Botswana. *Educational Broadcasting International,* Vol. 13, 190-194.

Cabe, P. A. (1980). Picture perception in nonhuman subjects. In M. A. Hagen (Ed.), *The perception of pictures* (Vol. 2, pp. 305-345). New York: Academic Press.

Caelli, T. (1982). On discriminating visual textures and images. *Perception & Psychophysics, 31,* 149-159.

Cohen, S. R. (1985). The development of constraints on symbol-meaning structure in notation: Evidence from production, interpretation, and forced-choice judgements. *Child Development, 56,* 177-195.

Deregowski, J. B. (1976). On seeing a picture for the first time. *Leonardo, 9,* 19-23.

Eijkman, E. G. J. (1984). Perturbing line pictures for identification of visual features and their syntax. *Perception, 13,* 675-686.

Freyd, J. J. (1983). The mental representation of movement when static stimuli are viewed. *Perception & Psychophysics, 33,* 575-581.

Friedman, S. L., & Stevenson, M. B. (1980). Perception of movement in pictures. In M. A. Hagen (Ed.), *The perception of pictures* (Vol. 1, pp. 225-255). New York: Academic Press.

Fussell, D., & Haaland, A. (1978). Communicating with pictures in Nepal: Results of practical study used in visual education. *Educational Broadcasting International, 11,* 25-31.

Gelman, R., Bullock, M., & Meck, E. (1980). Preschoolers' understanding of simple object transformations. *Child Development, 51,* 691-699.

Greene, R. (1983). Determining the preferred viewpoint in linear perspective. *Leonardo, 16,* 97-102.

Grossberg, S., & Mingolla, E. (1985). Neural dynamics of form perception: Boundary completion, illusory figures, and neon color spreading. *Psychological Review, 92,* 173-211.

Haber, R. H. (1980). How we see depth from flat pictures. *American Scientist, 68,* 370-380.

Hagen, M. A., & Jones, R. K. (1978). Cultural effects on pictorial perception: How many words is one picture really worth? In R. D. Walk & H. L. Pick, Jr. (Eds.), *Perception and experience* (pp. 171-212). New York: Plenum Press.

Hagen, M. A., Jones, R. K., & Reed, E. S. (1978). On a neglected variable in theories of pictorial perception: Truncation of the visual field. *Perception & Psychophysics, 23,* 326-330.

Higgins, L. C. (1980). Literalism in the young child's interpretation of pictures. *Educational Communication and Technology Journal, 28,* 99-119.

Hochberg, J., & Brooks, V. (1962). Pictorial recognition as an unlearned ability: A study of one child's performance. *American Journal of Psychology, 75,* 624-628.

Hoffman, D. D., & Richards, W. A. (1984). Parts of recognition. *Cognition, 18,* 65-96.

Koenderink, J. J. (1984). What does the occluding contour tell you about solid shape? *Perception, 13,* 321-330.

Kolers, P. A. (1983). Some features of visual form. *Computer Vision, Graphics, and Image Processing, 23,* 15-41.

Levie, W. H. (1978). A prospective for instructional research on visual literacy. *Educational Communication and Technology Journal, 26,* 25-36.

Ostergaard, A. L., & Davidoff, J. B. (1985). Some effects of color on naming and recognition of objects. *Journal of Experimental Psychology: Learning, Memory, and Cognition, 11,* 579-587.

Palmer, S., Rosch, E., & Chase, P. (1981). Canonical perspective and the perception of objects. In J. Long & A. Baddeley (Eds.), *Attention and performance IX* (pp. 135-151). Hillsdale, NJ: Erlbaum.

Pillow, B. H., & Flavell, J. H. (1985). Intellectual realism: The role of children's interpretations of pictures and perceptual verbs. *Child Development, 56,* 664-670.

Pratt, F. (1979). The contribution of colour to three-dimensional ambiguities in paintings and drawings. *Perception, 8,* 157-173.

Rose, S. A., Gottfried, A. W., & Bridger, W. H. (1983). Cross-modal transfer from solid objects to their graphic representations. *Child Development, 54,* 686-694.

Sabbah, D. (1985). Computing with connections in visual recognition of Origami objects. *Cognitive Science, 9,* 25-50.

Serpell, R., & Deregowski, J. B. (1980). The skill of pictorial perception: An interpretation of cross-cultural evidence. *International Journal of Psychology, 15,* 145-180.

Sigel, I. E. (1978). The development of pictorial comprehension. In B. S. Randhawa & W. E. Coffman (Eds.), *Visual learning, thinking, and communication* (pp. 93-111). New York: Academic Press.

Sorce, J. F. (1980). The role of operative knowledge in picture comprehension. *Journal of Genetic Psychology, 136,* 173-183.

Todd, J. T., & Mingolla, E. (1984). Simulation of curved surfaces from patterns of optical texture. *Journal of Experimental Psychology: Human Perception and Performance, 10,* 734-739.

Wong, E., & Weisstein, N. (1983). Sharp targets are detected better against a figure, and blurred targets are detected better against a background. *Journal of Experimental Psychology: Human Perception and Performance, 9,* 194-202.

Yonas, A., Goldsmith, L. T., & Hallstrom, J. L. (1978). Development of sensitivity to information provided by cast shadows in pictures. *Perception, 7*, 333-341.

2.4. Perceiving Global Meaning

Antes, J. R., & Mann, S. W. (1984). Global-local precedence in picture processing. *Psychological Research, 46*, 247-259.

Antes, J. R., & Metzger, R. L. (1980). Influence of picture context on object recognition. *Acta Psychologica, 44*, 21-30.

Becklen, R., & Cervone, D. (1983). Selective looking and the noticing of unexpected events. *Memory & Cognition, 11*, 601-608.

Biederman, I., Mezzanotte, R. J., & Rabinowitz, J. C. (1982). Scene perception: Detecting and judging objects undergoing relational violations. *Cognitive Psychology, 14*, 143-177.

Elkind, D., Koegler, R. R., & Go, E. (1964). Studies in perceptual development. II. Part-whole perception. *Child Development, 35*, 81-90.

Freedman, J., & Haber, R. N. (1974). One reason why we rarely forget a face. *Bulletin of the Psychonomic Society, 3*, 107-109.

Friedman, A. (1979). Framing pictures: The role of knowledge in automatized encoding and memory for gist. *Journal of Experimental Psychology: General, 108*, 316-355.

Hatfield, G., & Epstein, W. (1985). The status of the minimum principle in the theoretical analysis of visual perception. *Psychological Bulletin, 97*, 155-186.

Hock, H. S., & Schmelzkopf, K. F. (1980). The abstraction of schematic representations from photographs of real-world scenes. *Memory & Cognition, 8*, 543-554.

Kubovy, M., & Pomerantz, J. R. (Eds.). (1981). *Perceptual organization*. Hillsdale, NJ: Erlbaum.

Loftus, G. R., & Bell, S. M. (1975). Two types of information in picture memory. *Journal of Experimental Psychology: Human Learning and Memory, 1*, 103-113.

Loftus, G. R., & Ginn, M. (1984). Perceptual and conceptual masking of pictures. *Journal of Experimental Psychology: Learning, Memory, and Cognition, 10*, 435-441.

Loftus, G. R., Nelson, W. W., & Kallman, H. J. (1983). Differential acquisition rates for different types of information from pictures. *Quarterly Journal of Experimental Psychology, 35A*, 187-198.

Luke, C. (1985). Television discourse processing: A schema theoretic approach. *Communication Education, 34*, 91-105.

Machotka, P., & Spiegel, J. P. (1979). Construction of pictorial meaning. *Studies in the Anthropology of Visual Communication, 5*, 115-131.

Mandler, J. M., & Johnson, N. S. (1976). Some of the thousand words a picture is worth. *Journal of Experimental Psychology: Human Learning and Memory, 2*, 529-540.

Mandler, J. M., & Robinson, C. A. (1978). Developmental changes in picture recognition. *Journal of Experimental Child Psychology, 26*, 122-136.

Metzger, R. L., & Perlmutter, M. (1984). Specific and global processing by preschool children and college adults. *Bulletin of the Psychonomic Society, 22*, 333-336.

Navon, D. (1977). Forest before trees: The precedence of global features in visual perception. *Cognitive Psychology, 9*, 353-383.

Neisser, U. (1976). *Cognition and reality*. San Francisco: W. H. Freeman.

Palmer, S. E. (1975). The effects of contextual scenes on the identification of objects. *Memory & Cognition, 3*, 519-526.

Palmer, S. E. (1977). Hierarchical structure in perceptual representation. *Cognitive Psychology, 9*, 441-474.

Peterson, M. A., & Hochberg, J. (1983). Opposed-set measurement procedure: A quantitative analysis of the role of local cues and intention in form perception. *Journal of Experimental Psychology: Human Perception and Performance, 9,* 183–193.

Reynolds, R. I. (1985). The role of object-hypotheses in the organization of fragmented figures. *Perception, 14,* 49–52.

Smith, J. D. (1977). Perceptual decentering in EMR and nonretarded children. *American Journal of Mental Deficiency, 81,* 499–501.

3. MEMORY FOR PICTURES

General References

Kobayashi, S. (1985). An updated bibliography of picture-memory studies. *Perceptual and Motor Skills, 61,* 91–122.

Paivio, A. (1971). *Imagery and verbal processes.* New York: Holt, Rinehart & Winston.

Paivio, A. (1986). *Mental representations.* New York: Oxford University Press.

Snodgrass, J. G., & Vanderwart, M. (1980). A standardized set of 260 pictures: Norms for name agreement, image agreement, familiarity, and visual complexity. *Journal of Experimental Psychology: Human Learning and Memory, 6,* 174–215.

Spoehr, K. T., & Lehmkuhle, S. W. (1982). *Visual information processing.* San Francisco: W. H. Freeman.

Yuille, J. C. (Ed.). (1983). *Imagery, memory, and cognition.* Hillsdale, NJ: Erlbaum.

3.1. MEMORY MODELS

Anderson, J. R. (1978). Arguments concerning representations for mental imagery. *Psychological Review, 85,* 249–277.

Carr, T. H., McCauley, C., Sperber, R. D., & Parmelee, C. M. (1982). Words, pictures, and priming: On semantic activation, conscious identification, and the automaticity of information processing. *Journal of Experimental Psychology: Human Perception and Performance, 8,* 757–775.

Deffenbacher, K. A., Carr, T. H., & Leu, J. R. (1981). Memory for words, pictures, and faces: Retroactive interference, forgetting, and reminiscence. *Journal of Experimental Psychology: Human Learning and Memory, 7,* 299–305.

Durso, F. T., & Johnson, M. K. (1980). The effects of orienting tasks on recognition, recall, and modality confusion of pictures and words. *Journal of Verbal Learning and Verbal Behavior, 19,* 416–429.

Durso, F. T., & O'Sullivan, C. S. (1983). Naming and remembering proper and common nouns and pictures. *Journal of Experimental Psychology: Learning, Memory, and Cognition, 9,* 497–510.

Farah, M. J. (1985). Psychophysical evidence for a shared representational medium for mental images and percepts. *Journal of Experimental Psychology: General, 114,* 91–103.

Finke, R. A. (1985). Theories relating mental imagery to perception. *Psychological Bulletin, 98,* 236–259.

Kelter, S., Grotzbach, H., Freiheit, R., Hohle, B., Wutzig, S., & Diesch, E. (1984). Object identification: The mental representation of physical and conceptual attributes. *Memory & Cognition, 12,* 123–133.

Kieras, D. (1978). Beyond pictures and words: Alternative information processing models for imagery effects in verbal memory. *Psychological Bulletin, 85,* 532–554.

Kolers, P. A., & Brison, S. J. (1984). Commentary: On pictures, words, and their mental representation. *Journal of Verbal Learning and Verbal Behavior, 23*, 105-113.

Kosslyn, S. M. (1980). *Image and mind.* Cambridge, MA: Harvard University Press.

Kosslyn, S. M. (1981). The medium and the message in mental imagery: A theory. *Psychological Review, 88*, 46-66.

Kroll, J. F., & Potter, M. C. (1984). Recognizing words, pictures, and concepts: A comparison of lexical, object, and reality decisions. *Journal of Verbal Learning and Verbal Behavior, 23*, 39-66.

Nelson, D. L. (1979). Remembering pictures and words: Appearance, significance, and name. In L. S. Cermak & F. I. M. Craik (Eds.), *Levels of processing in human memory* (pp. 45-76). Hillsdale, NJ: Erlbaum.

Nelson, D. L., & Castano, D. (1984). Mental representations for pictures and words: Same or different? *American Journal of Psychology, 97*, 1-15.

Nelson, D. L., Reed, V. S., & Walling, J. R. (1976). The pictorial superiority effect. *Journal of Experimental Psychology: Human Learning and Memory, 2*, 523-528.

Paivio, A. (1978). A dual coding approach to perception and cognition. In H. L. Pick, Jr. & E. Saltzman (Eds.), *Modes of perceiving and processing information* (pp. 39-51). Hillsdale, NJ: Erlbaum.

Paivio, A. (1983). The empirical case for dual coding. In J. C. Yuille (Ed.), *Imagery, memory and cognition* (pp. 307-332). Hillsdale, NJ: Erlbaum.

Pinker, S. (1984). Visual cognition: An introduction. *Cognition, 18*, 1-63.

Potter, M. C., & Faulconer, B. A. (1975). Time to understand pictures and words. *Nature, 253*, 437-438.

Pylyshyn, Z. W. (1981). The imagery debate: Analogue media versus tacit knowledge. *Psychological Review, 88*, 16-45.

Shepard, R. N. (1978). The mental image. *American Psychologist, 33*, 125-137.

Smith, M. C., & Magee, L. E. (1980). Tracing the time course of picture-word processing. *Journal of Experimental Psychology: General, 109*, 373-392.

Snodgrass, J. G. (1984). Concepts and their surface representations. *Journal of Verbal Learning and Verbal Behavior, 23*, 3-22.

te Linde, J. (1982). Picture-word differences in decision latency: A test of common-coding assumptions. *Journal of Experimental Psychology: Learning, Memory and Cognition, 8*, 584-598.

3.2. Recognition Memory

Bartlett, J. C., Till, R. E., & Fields, W. C., III (1980). Effects of label distinctiveness and label testing on recognition of complex pictures. *American Journal of Psychology, 93*, 505-527.

Borges, M. A., Stepanowsky, M. A., & Holt, L. H. (1977). Recall and recognition of words and pictures by adults and children. *Bulletin of the Psychonomic Society, 9*, 113-114.

Chatterjea, R. G., & Paul, B. (1981). Field dependency, recognition capacity and extraversion. *Psychologia, 24*, 217-222.

Courtois, M. R., & Mueller, J. H. (1981). Target and distractor typicality in facial recognition. *Journal of Applied Psychology, 66*, 639-645.

Davies, G., Ellis, H., & Shepherd, J. (Eds.). (1981). *Perceiving and remembering faces.* New York: Academic Press.

d'Ydewalle, G., Delhaye, P., & Goessens, L. (1985). Structural, semantic, and self-reference processing of pictorial advertisements. *Human Learning, 4*, 29-38.

Emmerich, H. J., & Ackerman, B. P. (1979). The effect of orienting activity on memory for pictures and words in children and adults. *Journal of Experimental Child Psychology, 28*, 449-515.

Ernest, C. H. (1983). Imagery and verbal ability and recognition memory for pictures and words in males and females. *Educational Psychology, 3*, 277-244.

Franken, R. E. (1977). Picture-recognition memory as a function of picture organization and age. *Perceptual and Motor Skills, 44*, 1151-1154.

Goldstein, A. G., Bailis, K., & Chance, J. E. (1983). Do students remember pictures in psychology textbooks? *Teaching of Psychology, 10*, 23-26.

Goldstein, A. G., Chance, J. E., Hoisington, M., & Buescher, K. (1982). Recognition memory for pictures: Dynamic vs. static stimuli. *Bulletin of the Psychonomic Society, 20*, 37-40.

Graefe, T. M., & Watkins, M. J. (1980). Picture rehearsal: An effect of selectively attending to pictures no longer in view. *Journal of Experimental Psychology: Human Learning and Memory, 6*, 156-162.

Haber, R. N., & Myers, B. L. (1982). Memory for pictograms, pictures, and words separately and all mixed up. *Perception, 11*, 57-64.

Hampson, P. J., & Cutting, V. (1985). Subjects' assessment of the processing demands of a series of orienting tasks. *Acta Psychologica, 58*, 17-29.

Intraub, H. (1979). The role of implicit meaning in pictorial encoding. *Journal of Experimental Psychology: Human Learning and Memory, 5*, 78-87.

Intraub, H. (1984). Conceptual masking: The effects of subsequent visual events on memory for pictures. *Journal of Experimental Psychology: Learning, Memory and Cognition, 10*, 115-125.

Jörg, S., & Hörmann, H. (1978). The influence of general and specific verbal labels on the recognition of labeled and unlabeled parts of pictures. *Journal of Verbal Learning and Verbal Behavior, 17*, 445-454.

Justice, E. M. (1985). Categorization as a preferred memory strategy: Developmental changes during elementary school. *Developmental Psychology, 21*, 1105-1110.

Kallman, H. J. (1984). Effect of blank time on picture recognition. *American Journal of Psychology, 97*, 399-406.

Kellogg, R. T., Cocklin, T., & Bourne, L. E., Jr. (1982). Conscious attentional demands of encoding and retrieval from long-term memory. *American Journal of Psychology, 95*, 183-198.

Kiphart, M. J., Sjogren, D. D., & Cross, H. A. (1984). Some factors involved in complex-picture recognition. *Bulletin of the Psychonomic Society, 22*, 197-199.

Kiphart, M. J., Sjogren, D. D., Loomis, R. J., & Cross, H. A. (1985). Recognition of homogeneous and heterogeneous pictures as a function of viewing context. *Bulletin of the Psychonomic Society, 23*, 109-112.

Klich, L. Z., & Davidson, G. R. (1983). A cultural difference in visual memory: On le voit, on ne le voit plus. *International Journal of Psychology, 18*, 189-201.

Kunen, S., Green, D., & Waterman, D. (1979). Spread of encoding effects within the nonverbal visual domain. *Journal of Experimental Psychology: Human Learning and Memory, 5*, 574-584.

Levin, J. R., Ghatala, E. S., DeRose, T. M., & Makoid, L. A. (1977). Image tracing: An analysis of its effectiveness in children's pictorial discrimination learning. *Journal of Experimental Child Psychology, 23*, 78-83.

Loftus, E. F. (1979). *Eyewitness testimony.* Cambridge, MA: Harvard University Press.

Loftus, G. R., & Ginn, M. (1984). Perceptual and conceptual masking of pictures. *Journal of Experimental Psychology: Learning, Memory, and Cognition, 10*, 435-441.

McKelvie, S. J. (1984). Reported visual imagery for faces and facial recognition memory. *Perceptual and Motor Skills, 59*, 825-826.

Morrison, F. J., Haith, M. M., & Kagan, J. (1980). Age trends in recognition memory for pictures: The effects of delay and testing procedure. *Bulletin of the Psychonomic Society, 16*, 480-483.

Nelson, T. O., Metzler, J., & Reed, D. A. (1974). Role of details in the long-term recognition of pictures and verbal descriptions. *Journal of Experimental Psychology, 102*, 184-186.

Park, D. C., & Puglisi, J. T. (1985). Older adults' memory for the color of pictures and words. *Journal of Gerontology, 40*, 198-204.

Parkin, A. J., & Hayward, C. (1983). The influence of trait and physical-feature-based orienting strategies on aspects of facial memory. *British Journal of Psychology, 74*, 71-82.

Peeck, J., & Zwarts, J. (1983). Recognition memory for pictures of birds in relation to bird-watching skill. *American Journal of Psychology, 96*, 553-566.

Pezdek, K., & Chen, H. (1982). Developmental differences in the role of detail in picture recognition memory. *Journal of Experimental Child Psychology, 33*, 207-215.

Shepard, R. N. (1967). Recognition memory for words, sentences, and pictures. *Journal of Verbal Learning and Verbal Behavior, 6*, 156-163.

Siegel, A. W., Babich, J. M., & Kirasic, K. C. (1974). Visual recognition memory in reflective and impulsive children. *Memory & Cognition, 2*, 379-384.

Standing, L. (1973). Learning 10,000 pictures. *Quarterly Journal of Experimental Psychology, 25*, 207-222.

Stelmack, R. M., Wieland, L. D., Wall, M. U., & Plouffe, L. (1984). Personality and the effects of stress on recognition memory. *Journal of Research in Personality, 18*, 164-178.

Tulving, E. (1981). Similarity relations in recognition. *Journal of Verbal Learning and Verbal Behavior, 20*, 479-496.

Watkins, M. J., & Graefe, T. M. (1981). Delayed rehearsal of pictures. *Journal of Verbal Learning and Verbal Behavior, 20*, 532-539.

Watkins, M. J., Peynircioglu, Z. F., & Brems, D. J. (1984). Pictorial rehearsal. *Memory & Cognition, 12*, 553-557.

Weaver, G. E., & Stanny, C. J. (1984). The role of detail information in the recognition of complex pictorial stimuli. *The Journal of General Psychology, 111*, 185-199.

Wiseman, S., MacLeod, C. M., & Lootsteen, P. J. (1985). Picture recognition improves with subsequent verbal information. *Journal of Experimental Psychology: Learning, Memory, and Cognition, 11*, 588-595.

Wiseman, S., & Neisser, U. (1974). Perceptual organization as a determinant of visual recognition memory. *American Journal of Psychology, 87*, 675-681.

3.3. RECALL

Ackerman, B. P. (1985). The effects of specific and categorical orienting on children's incidental and intentional memory for pictures and words. *Journal of Experimental Child Psychology, 39*, 300-325.

Baumeister, A. A., & Smith, S. (1979). Thematic elaboration and proximity in children's recall, organization, and long-term retention of pictorial materials. *Journal of Experimental Child Psychology, 28*, 132-148.

Bray, N. W., Hersh, R. E., & Turner, L. A. (1985). Selective remembering during adolescence. *Developmental Psychology, 21*, 290-294.

Brimer, R. W., & Mueller, J. H. (1979). Immediate and final recall of pictures and words with written or oral tests. *American Journal of Psychology, 92,* 437–447.

Carroll, W. R., Carroll, R. W., & Rogers, C. A. (1979). Effect of varying picture–sentence congruence on children's free recall. *Perceptual and Motor Skills, 48,* 419–423.

Coulter, R. G., Coulter, M. L., & Glover, J. A. (1984). Details and picture recall. *Bulletin of the Psychonomic Society, 22,* 327–329.

Dick, M. B., & Engle, R. W. (1984). The effect of instruction with relational and item-specific elaborative strategies on young children's organization and free recall. *Journal of Experimental Child Psychology, 37,* 282–302.

Ghatala, E. S., & Levin, J. R. (1982). Orienting versus learning instructions in children's free recall: New evidence. *Journal of Experimental Child Psychology, 33,* 504–513.

Gillund, G., & Shiffrin, R. M. (1981). Free recall of complex pictures and abstract words. *Journal of Verbal Learning and Verbal Behavior, 20,* 575–592.

Goodman, G. S. (1980). Picture memory: How the action schema affects retention. *Cognitive Psychology, 12,* 473–495.

Howe, M. L., & Hunter, M. A. (1985). Adult age differences in storage–retrieval processes: A stages-of-learning analysis of developmental interactions in concreteness effects. *Canadian Journal of Psychology, 39,* 130–150.

Intraub, H., & Nicklos, S. (1985). Levels of processing and picture memory: The physical superiority effect. *Journal of Experimental Psychology: Learning, Memory, and Cognition, 11,* 284–298.

Kirkpatrick, E. A. (1894)! An experimental study of memory. *Psychological Review, 1,* 602–609.

Nickerson, R. S., & Adams, M. J. (1979). Long-term memory for a common object. *Cognitive Psychology, 11,* 287–307.

Paivio, A., & Csapo, K. (1973). Picture superiority in free recall: Imagery or dual coding? *Cognitive Psychology, 5,* 176–206.

Puff, C. R., Tyrrell, D. J., Heibeck, T. H., & Van Slyke, D. A. (1984). Encoding activities and free recall of categorized and noncategorized pictures by young children. *Bulletin of the Psychonomic Society, 22,* 389–392.

Ritchey, G. H. (1982). Pictorial detail and recall in adults and children. *Journal of Experimental Psychology: Learning, Memory, and Cognition, 8,* 139–141.

Tabachnick, B., & Brotsky, S. J. (1976). Free recall and complexity of pictorial stimuli. *Memory & Cognition, 4,* 466–470.

Toppino, T. C., & DiGeorge, W. (1984). The spacing effect in free recall emerges with development. *Memory & Cognition, 12,* 118–122.

Tversky, B., & Sherman, T. (1975). Picture memory improves with longer on time and off time. *Journal of Experimental Psychology, 104,* 114–118.

3.4. OTHER TYPES OF MEMORY RESEARCH

Alesandrini, K. L. (1983). Cognitive strategies in advertising design. In M. Pressley & J. R. Levin (Eds.), *Cognitive strategy research: Psychological foundations* (pp. 203–220). New York: Springer-Verlag.

Anderson, R. E. (1976). Short-term retention of the where and when of pictures and words. *Journal of Experimental Psychology: General, 105,* 378–402.

Biron, J., & McKelvie, S. J. (1984). Effects of interactive and noninteractive imagery on recall of advertisements. *Perceptual and Motor Skills, 59,* 799–805.

Bowling, A., & Lovegrove, W. (1982). Iconic memory: Fallacies persist (?). *Perception & Psychophysics, 31,* 194-198.

Brainerd, C. J., Desrochers, A., & Howe, M. L. (1981). Stages-of-learning analysis of picture–word effects in associative memory. *Journal of Experimental Psychology: Human Learning and Memory, 7,* 1-14.

Brown, R. M., & Brown, N. L. (1982). Factors underlying primacy and recency in the pictorial memory of school-aged children. *Journal of General Psychology, 106,* 251-262.

Cantor, D. S., Andreassen, C., & Waters, H. S. (1985). Organization in visual episodic memory: Relationships between verbalized knowledge, strategy use, and performance. *Journal of Experimental Child Psychology, 40,* 218-232.

Coltheart, M. (1980). Iconic memory and visible persistence. *Perception & Psychophysics, 27,* 183-228.

Erdelyi, M. H. (1982). A note on the level of recall, level of processing and imagery hypothesis of hypermnesia. *Journal of Verbal Learning and Verbal Behavior, 21,* 656-661.

Erdelyi, M. H., & Kleinbard, J. (1978). Has Ebbinghaus decayed with time?: The growth of recall (hypermnesia) over days. *Journal of Experimental Psychology: Human Learning and Memory, 4,* 275-289.

Erdelyi, M. H., & Stein, J. B. (1981). Recognition hypermnesia: The growth of recognition memory (d') over time with repeated testing. *Cognition, 9,* 23-33.

Haber, R. N. (1983). The impending demise of the icon: A critique of the concept of iconic storage in visual information processing. *The Behavioral and Brain Sciences, 6,* 1-11.

Hicks, C. (1980). The ITPA visual sequential memory task: An alternative interpretation and the implications for good and poor readers. *British Journal of Educational Psychology, 50,* 16-25.

Hintzman, D. L., & Stern, L. D. (1984). A comparison of forgetting rates in frequency discrimination and recognition. *Bulletin of the Psychonomic Society, 22,* 409-412.

Kee, D. W., & Nakayama, S. Y. (1982). Children's noun-pair retention: Assessment of pictorial elaboration and bizarreness effects. *Journal of Educational Psychology, 74,* 351-359.

Ledger, G. W., & Ryan, E. B. (1982). The effects of semantic integration training on memory for pictograph sentences. *Journal of Experimental Child Psychology, 33,* 39-54.

Lippman, M. Z., & Shanahan, M. W. (1973). Pictorial facilitation of paired-associate learning: Implications for vocabulary training. *Journal of Educational Psychology, 64,* 216-222.

Loftus, G. R., Shimamura, A. P., & Johnson, C. A. (1985). How much is an icon worth? *Journal of Experimental Psychology: Human Perception and Performance, 11,* 1-13.

Long, G. M. (1980). Iconic memory: A review and critique of the study of short-term visual storage. *Psychological Bulletin, 88,* 785-820.

Madigan, S., & Lawrence, V. (1980). Factors affecting item recovery and hypermnesia in free recall. *American Journal of Psychology, 93,* 489-504.

Nelson, T. O., & Chaiklin, S. (1980). Immediate memory for spatial location. *Journal of Experimental Psychology: Human Learning and Memory, 6,* 529-545.

O'Brien, E. J., & Wolford, C. R. (1982). Effect of delay in testing on retention of plausible versus bizarre mental images. *Journal of Experimental Psychology: Learning, Memory, and Cognition, 8,* 148-152.

Paivio, A., Philipchalk, R., & Rowe, E. J. (1975). Free and serial recall of pictures, sounds, and words. *Memory & Cognition, 3,* 586-590.

Poulsen, D., Kintsch, E., Kintsch, W., & Premack, D. (1979). Children's comprehension and memory for stories. *Journal of Experimental Child Psychology, 28,* 379–403.

Roediger, H. L., Payne, D. G., Gillespie, G. L., & Lean, D. S. (1982). Hypermnesia as determined by level of recall. *Journal of Verbal Learning and Verbal Behavior, 21,* 635–655.

Schmidt, C. R., Paris, S. G., & Stober, S. (1979). Inferential distance and children's memory for pictorial sequences. *Developmental Psychology, 15,* 395–405.

Somerville, S. C., Haake, R. J., & Wellman, H. M. (1984). Spatial and temporal determinants of serial position effects in young children and adults. *Genetic Psychology Monographs, 109,* 19–51.

4. Learning and Cognition

General References

Dwyer, F. M. (1978). *Strategies for improving visual learning.* State College, PA: Learning Services.

Gage, N. L. (Ed.). (1976). *Psychology of teaching methods. Seventy-fifth yearbook of the National Society for the Study of Education.* Chicago: University of Chicago Press.

Goldsmith, E. (1984). *Research into illustration: An approach and a review.* Cambridge, England: Cambridge University Press.

Olson, D. R. (Ed.). (1974). *Media and symbols: The forms of expression, communication, and education. Seventy-third yearbook of the National Society for the Study of Education.* Chicago: University of Chicago Press.

Randhawa, B. S., & Coffman, W. E. (1978). *Visual learning, thinking, and communication.* New York: Academic Press.

Salomon, G. (1979). *Interaction of media, cognition, and learning: An exploration of how symbolic forms cultivate mental skills and affect knowledge acquisition.* San Francisco: Jossey-Bass.

Sless, D. (1981). *Learning and visual communication.* New York: Wiley.

4.1. The Acquisition of Knowledge

Ashwin, C. (1979). The ingredients of style in contemporary illustration: A case study. *Information Design Journal, 1,* 51–67.

Bieger, G. R., & Glock, M. D. (1984/85). The information content of picture–text instructions. *Journal of Experimental Education, 53*(2), 68–76.

Borg, W. R., & Schuller, C. F. (1979). Detail and background in audiovisual lessons and their effect on learners. *Educational Communication and Technology Journal, 27,* 31–38.

Canelos, J., Taylor, W., & Dwyer, F. (1985). The effects of recall cue and cognitive trace compatibility when learning from visualized instruction: An application of encoding specificity. *International Journal of Instructional Media, 12,* 167–178.

Carnine, D. (1980). Relationships between stimulus variation and the formation of misconceptions. *Journal of Educational Research, 74,* 106–110. (a)

Carnine, D. (1980). Three procedures for presenting minimally different positive and negative instances. *Journal of Educational Psychology, 72,* 452–456. (b)

Christ, R. E. (1975). Review and analysis of color coding research for visual displays. *Human Factors, 17,* 542–570.

Dixon, D., & Saltz, E. (1977). The role of imagery on concept acquisition in lower-SES children. *Child Development, 48,* 288-291.

Dwyer, F. M. (1982-83). The program of systematic evaluation—a brief review. *International Journal of Instructional Media, 10,* 23-39.

Dwyer, F. M., & Lamberski, R. J. (1982-83). A review of the research on the effects of the use of color in the teaching-learning process. *International Journal of Instructional Media , 10,* 303-327.

Fleming, M. L. (1986). Displays and communication. In R. M. Gagne (Ed.), *Instructional technology: Foundations.* Hillsdale, NJ: Erlbaum.

Frank, A. R., Wacker, D. P., Berg, W. K., & McMahon, C. M. (1985). Teaching selected microcomputer skills to retarded students via picture prompts. *Journal of Applied Behavior Analysis, 18,* 179-185.

Fulton, J. L., & Fulton, O. (1980). Sequential development of modes of response in the concept learning of elementary students. *Contemporary Educational Psychology, 5,* 83-89.

Haber, R. N. (1981). The power of visual perceiving. *Journal of Mental Imagery, 5*(2), 1-16.

Hagen, M. A., & Perkins, D. (1983). A refutation of the hypothesis of the superfidelity of caricatures relative to photographs. *Perception, 12,* 55-61.

Hannafin, M. J. (1983). The effects of instructional stimulus loading on the recall of abstract and concrete prose. *Educational Communication and Technology Journal, 31,* 103-109.

Haring, M. J., & Fry, M. A. (1979). Effect of pictures on children's comprehension of written text. *Educational Communication and Technology Journal, 27,* 185-190.

Hartley, J., & Homa, D. (1981). Abstraction of stylistic concepts. *Journal of Experimental Psychology: Human Learning and Memory, 7,* 33-46.

Hollenberg, C. K. (1970). Functions of visual imagery in the learning and concept formation of children. *Child Development, 41,* 1003-1015.

Jolicoeur, P., Gluck, M. A., & Kosslyn, S. M. (1984). Pictures and names: Making the connection. *Cognitive Psychology, 16,* 243-275.

Kieras, D. E., & Bovair, S. (1984). The role of a mental model in learning to operate a device. *Cognitive Science, 8,* 255-273.

King, D. L., & Newman, L. A. (1982). Concept learning: Similarity and number of exemplars, category number information, and description of prototypical features. *Psychological Record, 32,* 109-120.

Levin, J. R. (1983). Pictorial strategies for school learning: Practical illustrations. In M. Pressley & J. R. Levin (Eds.), *Cognitive Strategy Research: Educational Applications* (pp. 213-237). New York: Springer-Verlag.

Levin, J. R., McCormick, C. B., & Dretzke, B. J. (1981). A combined pictorial mnemonic strategy for ordered information. *Educational Communication and Technology Journal, 29,* 219-225.

Levin, J. R., McCormick, C. B., Miller, G. E., Berry, J. K., & Pressley, M. (1982). Mnemonic versus nonmnemonic vocabulary-learning strategies for children. *American Educational Research Journal, 19,* 121-136.

Marcel, T., & Barnard, P. (1979). Paragraphs of pictographs: The use of non-verbal instructions for equipment. In P. A. Kolers, M. F. Wrolstad, & H. Bouma (Eds.), *Processing of visible language* (Vol. 1, pp. 501-518). New York: Plenum Press.

Medin, D. L., & Smith, E. E. (1984). Concepts and concept formation. *Annual Review of Psychology, 35,* 113-138.

Murphy, C. M., & Wood, D. J. (1981). Learning from pictures: The use of pictorial information by young children. *Journal of Experimental Child Psychology, 32*, 279-297.

Murphy, G. L., & Smith, E. E. (1982). Basic-level superiority in picture categorization. *Journal of Verbal Learning and Verbal Behavior, 21*, 1-20.

Murray, F. S., & Szymczyk, J. M. (1978). Effects of distinctive features on recognition of incomplete pictures. *Developmental Psychology, 14*, 356-362.

Nelson, D. G. K. (1984). The effect of intention on what concepts are acquired. *Journal of Verbal Learning and Verbal Behavior, 23*, 734-759.

Newton, D. P. (1984). A way of classifying and measuring some aspects of the illustration style of textbooks. *Programmed Learning and Educational Technology, 21*, 21-27.

Perkins, D. N. (1980). Pictures and the real thing. In P. A. Kolers, M. F. Wrolstad, & H. Bouma (Eds.), *Processing of visible language* (Vol. 2, pp. 259-278). New York: Plenum Press.

Peters, E. E., Levin, J. R., McGivern, J. E., & Pressley, M. (1985). Further comparison of representational and transformational prose-learning imagery. *Journal of Educational Psychology, 77*, 129-136.

Pressley, M., & Levin, J. R. (1978). Developmental constraints associated with children's use of the keyword method of foreign language vocabulary learning. *Journal of Experimental Child Psychology, 26*, 359-373.

Ryan, T. A., & Schwartz, C. B. (1956). Speed of perception as a function of mode of representation. *American Journal of Psychology, 69*, 60-69.

Scruggs, T. E., Mastropieri, M. A., Levin, J. R., & Gaffney, J. S. (1985). Facilitating the acquisition of science facts in learning disabled students. *American Educational Research Journal, 22*, 575-586.

Smillie, R. J. (1985). Design strategies for job performance aids. In T. M. Duffy & R. Waller (Eds.), *Designing usable texts* (pp. 213-243). New York: Academic Press.

Smith, S. L. (1981). Exploring compatibility with words and pictures. *Human Factors, 23*, 305-315.

Stone, D. E., & Glock, M. D. (1981). How do young adults read directions with and without pictures? *Journal of Educational Psychology, 73*, 419-426.

Szlichcinski, K. P. (1979). Telling people how things work. *Applied Ergonomics, 10*, 2-8.

Tennyson, R. D. (1978). Pictorial support and specific instructions as design variables for children's concept and rule learning. *Educational Communication and Technology Journal, 26*, 291-299.

Travers, R. M., & Alvarado, V. (1970). The design of pictures for teaching children in elementary school. *AV Communication Review, 18*, 47-64.

Tversky, B., & Baratz, D. (1985). Memory for faces: Are caricatures better than photographs? *Memory & Cognition, 13*, 45-49.

Twyman, M. (1985). Using pictorial language: A discussion of the dimensions of the problem. In T. M. Duffy & R. Waller (Eds.), *Designing usable texts* (pp. 245-312). New York: Academic Press.

Wacker, D., & Berg, W. (1983). Effects of picture prompts on the acquisition of complex vocational skills by mental retarded adolescents. *Journal of Applied Behavior Analysis, 16*, 417-433.

Winn, W. (1982). Visualization in learning and instruction: A cognitive approach. *Educational Communication and Technology Journal, 30*, 3-25.

Zimmerman, M. L., & Perkin, G. W. (1982). Instructing through pictures: Print materials for people who do not read. *Information Design Journal, 3*, 119-134.

4.2. PROBLEM SOLVING AND VISUAL THINKING

Arnheim, R. (1969). *Visual thinking*. Berkeley: University of California Press.
Arnheim, R. (1985). The double-edged mind: Intuition and the intellect. In E. Eisner (Ed.), *Learning and teaching the ways of knowing. Eighty-fourth yearbook of the National Society for the Study of Education* (pp. 77-96). Chicago: University of Chicago Press.
Coscarelli, W. C., & Schwen, T. M. (1979). Effects of three algorithmic representations on critical thinking, laboratory efficiency, and final grade. *Educational Communication and Technology Journal*, 27, 58-64.
DeSoto, C. B., London, M., & Handel, S. (1965). Social reasoning and spatial paralogic. *Journal of Personality and Social Psychology*, 2, 513-521.
Egan, D. E., & Grimes-Farrow, D. D. (1982). Differences in mental representations spontaneously adopted for reasoning. *Memory & Cognition*, 10, 297-307.
Feinstein, H. (1982). Meaning and visual metaphor. *Studies in Art Education*, 23(2), 45-55.
Gentner, D. (1977). Children's performance on a spatial analogies task. *Child Development*, 48, 1034-1039.
Gick, M. L. (1985). The effect of a diagram retrieval cue on spontaneous analogical transfer. *Canadian Journal of Psychology*, 39, 460-466.
Hadamard, J. (1954). *The psychology of invention in the mathematical field*. New York: Dover Publications.
Honeck, R. P., Voegtle, K., & Sowry, B. M. (1981). Figurative understanding of pictures and sentences. *Journal of Psycholinguistic Research*, 10, 135-153.
Kaufmann, G. (1985). A theory of symbolic representation in problem solving. *Journal of Mental Imagery*, 9, 51-70.
Kennedy, J. M., & Simpson, W. (1982). For each kind of figure of speech there is pictorial metaphor: A figure of depiction. *Visual Arts Research*, (16), 1-11.
LaChapelle, J. R. (1983). Creativity research: Its sociological and educational limitations. *Studies in Art Education*, 24, 131-139.
Levine, M., Jankovic, I. N., & Palij, M. (1982). Principles of spatial problem solving. *Journal of Experimental Psychology: General*, 111, 157-175.
Liu, I. (1981). Common and specific features in pictorial analogies. *Memory & Cognition*, 9, 515-523.
Marschark, M., Katz, A. N., & Paivio, A. (1983). Dimensions of metaphor. *Journal of Psycholinguistic Research*, 12, 17-40.
Mathews, N. N., Hunt, E. B., & MacLeod, C. M. (1980). Strategy choice and strategy thinking in sentence-picture verification. *Journal of Verbal Learning and Verbal Behavior*, 19, 531-548.
Mayer, R. E. (1983). Can you repeat that? Qualitative effects of repetition and advance organizers on learning from science prose. *Journal of Educational Psychology*, 75, 40-49.
Moyer, J. C., Sowder, L., Threadgill-Sowder, J., & Moyer, M. B. (1984). Story problem formats: Drawn versus verbal versus telegraphic. *Journal for Research in Mathematics Education*, 15, 342-351.
Perkins, D. (1985). Reasoning as imagination. *Interchange*, 16, 14-26.
Presson, C. C. (1982). Strategies in spatial reasoning. *Journal of Experimental Psychology: Learning, Memory, and Cognition*, 8, 243-251.
Reed, S. K. (1985). Effect of computer graphics on improving estimates to algebra word problems. *Journal of Experimental Psychology*, 77, 285-298.

Rigney, J. W., & Lutz, K. A. (1976). Effect of graphic analogies of concepts in chemistry on learning and attitude. *Journal of Educational Psychology, 68,* 305-311.

Royer, J. M., & Cable, G. W. (1976). Illustrations, analogies, facilitative transfer in prose learning. *Journal of Educational Psychology, 68,* 205-209.

Sternberg, R. J. (1980). Representation and process in linear syllogistic reasoning. *Journal of Experimental Psychology: General, 109,* 355-362.

Threadgill-Sowder, J., Sowder, L., Moyer, J. C., & Moyer, M. B. (1985). Cognitive variables and performance on mathematical story problems. *Journal of Experimental Education, 54,* 56-62.

4.3. ACQUISITION OF COGNITIVE SKILLS

Barsam, H. F., & Simutis, Z. M. (1984). Computer-based graphics for terrain visualization training. *Human Factors, 26,* 659-665.

Caplan, P. J., MacPherson, G. M., & Tobin, P. (1985). Do sex-related differences in spatial abilities exist? *American Psychologist, 40,* 786-799.

Cassidy, M. F., & Knowlton, J. Q. (1983). Visual literary: A failed metaphor? *Educational Communication and Technology Journal, 31,* 67-90.

Cox, M. V. (1978). Perspective ability: A training program. *Journal of Educational Research, 71,* 127-133.

Fisher, C. B., & Braine, L. G. (1981). Children's left-right concepts: Generalization across figure and location. *Child Development, 52,* 451-456.

Freeman, N. H. (1980). *Strategies of representation in young children: Analysis of spatial skills and drawing processes.* London: Academic Press.

Gardner, H. (1980). *Artful scribbles: The significance of children's drawings.* New York: Basic Books.

Goldstein, A. G., & Chance, J. E. (1985). Effects of training on Japanese face recognition: Reduction of the other-race effect. *Bulletin of the Psychonomic Society, 23,* 211-214.

Higgins, L. C. (1979). Effects of strategy-oriented training on children's inference drawing from pictures. *Educational Communication and Technology Journal, 27,* 265-280.

Hodapp, T. V. (1977). Children's ability to learn problem solving strategies from television. *Albert Journal of Educational Research, 23,* 171-177.

Kiefer, B. (1983). The responses of children in a combination first/second grade classroom to picture books in a variety of artistic style. *Journal of Research and Development in Education, 16*(3), 14-20.

Koroscik, J. S. (1984). Cognition in viewing and talking about art. *Theory into Practice, 23,* 330-334.

Kosslyn, S. M., Brunn, J., Cave, K. R., & Wallach, R. W. (1984). Individual differences in mental imagery ability: A computational analysis. *Cognition, 18,* 195-243.

Kyllonen, P. C., Lohman, D. F., & Snow, R. E. (1984). Effects of aptitudes, strategy training, and task facets on spatial task performance. *Journal of Educational Psychology, 76,* 130-145.

Lansing, K. M. (1984). The effect of drawing on the development of mental representations: A continuing study. *Studies in Art Education, 25,* 167-175.

Leach, M. L. (1978). Pictorial depth and space: Procedural, instrumental, cultural, and experiential factors contributing to their perception by Shona children. *Journal of Cross-Cultural Psychology, 9,* 417-438.

Ledger, G. W., & Ryan, E. B. (1985). Semantic integration: Effects of imagery, enaction, and sentence repetition training on prereaders' recall for pictograph sentences. *Journal of Experimental Child Psychology, 39,* 531-545.

Lonner, W. J., Thorndike, R. M., Forbes, N. E., & Ashworth, C. (1985). The influence of television on measured cognitive abilities. A study with native Alaskan children. *Journal of Cross-Cultural Psychology, 16*, 255-380.

McGee, M. G. (1979). Human spatial abilities: Psychometric studies and environmental, genetic, hormonal, and neurological influences. *Psychological Bulletin, 86*, 889-918.

Nicholson, J. R., Seddon, G. M., & Worsnop, J. G. (1977). Teaching the understanding of pictorial spatial relationships to Nigerian secondary school students. *Journal of Cross-Cultural Psychology, 8*, 401-414.

Olson, D. R., & Bialystok, E. (Eds.). (1983). *Spatial cognition: The structure and development of mental representations of spatial relations.* Hillsdale, NJ: Erlbaum.

Pellegrino, J. W., Alderton, D. L., & Shute, V. J. (1984). Understanding spatial ability. *Educational Psychologist, 19*, 239-253.

Salomon, G. (1983). Television watching and mental effort: A social psychological view. In J. Bryant & D. R. Anderson (Eds.), *Children's understanding of television* (pp. 181-198). New York: Academic Press.

Seddon, G. M., Tariq, R. J., & Dos Santos Veiga, J. (1984). The transferability of two pictorial scientific tasks between different spatial dimensions. *British Journal of Educational Psychology, 54*, 276-283.

Seefeldt, C. (1979). The effects of a program designed to increase young children's perception of texture. *Studies in Art Education, 20*(2), 40-44.

Seidman, S., & Beilin, H. (1984). Effects of media on picturing by children and adults. *Developmental Psychology, 20*, 667-672.

Shannon, P., & Fernie, D. E. (1985). Print and television: Children's use of the medium is the message. *The Elementary School Journal, 85*, 663-672.

Silver, R. A. (1976). Using art to evelute and develop cognitive skills. *American Journal of Art Therapy, 16*, 11-19.

Stericker, A., & LeVesconte, S. (1982). Effect of brief training on sex-related differences in visual-spatial skill. *Journal of Personality and Social Psychology, 43*, 1018-1029.

Tidhar, C. E. (1984). Children communicating in cinematic codes: Effects on cognitive skills. *Journal of Educational Psychology, 76*, 957-965.

Williams, P. A., Haertel, E. H., Haertel, G. D., & Walberg, H. J. (1982). The impact of leisure-time television on school learning. *American Educational Research Journal, 19*, 19-50.

Yonas, A., Kuskowski, M., & Sternfels, S. (1979). The role of frames of reference in the development of responsiveness to shading information. *Child Development, 50*, 495-500.

4.4. Media Research

Atkins, C. L. (1981). Introducing basic map and globe concepts to young children. *Journal of Geography, 80*, 228-233.

Baggett, P., & Ehrenfeucht, A. (1982). Information in content equivalent movie and text stories. *Discourse Processes, 5*, 73-99.

Beagles-Roos, J., & Gat, I. (1983). Specific impact of radio and television on children's story comprehension. *Journal of Educational Psychology, 75*, 128-137.

Blake, T. (1977). Motion in instructional media: Some subject-display mode interactions. *Perceptual and Motor Skills, 44*, 975-985.

Bryant, J., & Anderson, D. R. (Eds.). (1983). *Children's understanding of television: Research on attention and comprehension.* New York: Academic Press.

Campeau, P. L. (1974). Selective review of results of research on the use of audiovisual media to teach adults. *AV Communication Review, 22*, 5-40.
Carroll, J. M. (1982). Structure in visual communication. *Semiotica, 40*, 371-392.
Chu, G. C., & Schramm, W. (1967). *Learning from television: What the research says.* Washington, DC: National Association of Educational Broadcasters.
Clark, R. E. (1983). Reconsidering research on learning from media. *Review of Educational Research, 53*, 445-459.
Clark, R. E., & Salomon, G. (1986). Media in teaching. In M. C. Wittrock (Ed.), *Handbook of research on teaching* (3rd ed., pp. 464-478). New York: Macmillan.
Cohen, P. A., Ebeling, B. J., & Kulik, J. A. (1981). A meta-analysis of outcome studies of visual-based instruction. *Educational Communication and Technology Journal, 29*, 26-36.
Collins, A., Adams, M. J., & Pew, R. W. (1978). Effectiveness of an interactive map display in tutoring geography. *Journal of Educational Psychology, 70*, 1-7.
Field, D. E., & Anderson, D. R. (1985). Instruction and modality effects on children's television attention and comprehension. *Journal of Educational Psychology, 77*, 91-100.
Goldstein, E. B. (1975). The perception of multiple images. *AV Communication Review, 23*, 34-68.
Gunter, B., Berry, C., & Clifford, B. (1982). Remembering broadcast news: The implications of experimental research for production technique. *Human Learning, 1*, 13-29.
Hayes, D. S., & Kelly, S. B. (1984). Young children's processing of television: Modality differences in the retention of temporal relations. *Journal of Experimental Child Psychology, 38*, 505-514.
Heidt, E. U. (1980). Differences between media and differences between learners: Can we relate them? *Instructional Science, 9*, 365-391.
Howe, M. J. A. (Ed.). (1983). *Learning from television: Psychological and educational research.* New York: Academic Press.
Jamison, D., Suppes, P., & Wells, S. (1974). The effectiveness of alternative instructional media: A survey. *Review of Educational Research, 44*, 1-67.
Kjorup, S. (1977). Film as a meetingplace of multiple codes. In D. Perkins & B. Leondar (Eds.), *The arts and cognition* (pp. 20-47). Baltimore, MD: Johns Hopkins University Press.
Kose, G. (1985). Children's knowledge of photography: A study of the developing awareness of a representational medium. *British Journal of Developmental Psychology, 3*, 373-384.
Kreszock, C. M., & Moore, D. M. (1981-82). Affective and cognitive responses of college students to single and multi-image presentations. *International Journal of Instructional Media, 9*, 281-292.
Kulhavy, R. W., Lee, J. B., & Caterino, L. C. (1985). Conjoint retention of maps and related discourse. *Contemporary Educational Psychology, 10*, 28-37.
Leifer, A. D. (1976). Teaching with television and film. In N. L. Gage (Ed.), *The psychology of teaching methods. Seventy-fifth yearbook of the National Society for the Study of Education* (pp. 302-334). Chicago: University of Chicago Press.
Levie, W. H., & Dickie, K. E. (1973). The analysis and application of media. In R. M. W. Travers (Ed.), *Second handbook of research on teaching* (pp. 858-882). Chicago: Rand McNally.
Marchant, H. (1977). Increasing the effectiveness of educational films: A selected review of research. *British Journal of Educational Technology, 8*, 89-96.

McIsaac, M. S., Mosley, M. L., & Story, N. (1984). Identification of visual dimensions in photographs using multidimensional scaling techniques. *Educational Communication and Technology Journal, 32*, 169-179.

Meringoff, L. K. (1980). Influence of the medium on children's story apprehension. *Journal of Educational Psychology, 72*, 240-249.

Nadaner, D. (1983). Toward an analysis of the educational value of film and television. *Interchange, 14*, 43-55.

Owens, R. D., & Coldevin, G. O. (1977). Effects of varied temporal visual overlapping in multi-image tape-slide presentations. *Programmed Learning and Educational Technology, 14*, 36-42.

Pezdek, K., Lehrer, A., & Simon, S. (1984). The relationship between reading and cognitive processing of television and radio. *Child Development, 55*, 2072-2082.

Pezdek, K., & Stevens, E. (1984). Children's memory for auditory and visual information on television. *Developmental Psychology, 20*, 212-218.

Potash, L. M. (1977). Design of maps and map-related research. *Human Factors, 19*, 139-150.

Reid, J. C., & MacLennan, D. W. (1976). *Research in instructional television and film.* Washington, DC: U.S. Office of Education, Department of Health, Education, and Welfare.

Salomon, G. (1984). Television is "easy" and print is "tough": The differential investment of mental effort in learning as a function of perceptions and attributions. *Journal of Educational Psychology, 76*, 647-658.

Smith, R., Anderson, D. R., & Fischer, C. (1985). Young children's comprehension of montage. *Child Development, 56*, 962-971.

Spangenberg, R. (1973). The motion variable in procedural learning. *AV Communication Review, 21*, 419-436.

Whiteside, C. (1983-84). The effects of presentation rates on visual recognition memory and eye movement patterns in a multi-image presentation. *International Journal of Instructional Media, 11*, 295-304.

Wright, J. C., Huston, A. C., Ross, R. P., Calvert, S. L., Rolandelli, D., Weeks, L. A., Raeissi, P., & Potts, R. (1984). Pace and continuity of television programs: Effects on children's attention and comprehension. *Developmental Psychology, 20*, 653-666.

5.1. Arousal and Emotional Impact

Berlyne, D. E. (1960). *Conflict, arousal, and curiosity.* New York: McGraw-Hill.

Butcher, J., & Whissell, C. (1984). Laughter as a function of audience size, sex of the audience, and segments of the short film "Duck Soup." *Perceptual and Motor Skills, 59*, 949-950.

Culbertson, H. M. (1974). Words vs. pictures: Perceived impact and connotative meaning. *Journalism Quarterly, 51*, 226-237.

Cupchik, G. C., & Berlyne, D. E. (1979). The perception of collative properties in visual stimuli. *Scandinavian Journal of Psychology, 20*, 93-104.

DeKosky, S. T., Heilman, K. M., Bowers, D., & Valenstein, E. (1980). Recognition and discrimination of emotional faces and pictures. *Brain and Language, 9*, 206-214.

Efran, J. S., & Spangler, T. J. (1979). Why grown-ups cry: A two-factor theory and evidence from "The Miracle Worker." *Motivation and Emotion, 3*, 63-78.

Evans, T., & Denny, M. R. (1978). Emotionality of pictures and the retention of related and unrelated phrases. *Bulletin of the Psychonomic Society, 11*, 149–152.

Farley, F. H., & Grant, A. P. (1976). Arousal and cognition: Memory for color versus black and white multimedia presentation. *Journal of Psychology, 94*, 147–150.

Hengen, N. (1970). The perception of danger in action illustrations. *AV Communication Review, 18*, 250–262.

Lagerspetz, K. M. J., & Engblom, P. (1979). Immediate reactions to TV-violence by Finnish pre-school children of different personality types. *Scandinavian Journal of Psychology, 20*, 43–53.

McKay, T. D., & McKay, M. E. (1982). Captioned and non-captioned cartoons: Effects of structural properties on ratings of humor. *Perceptual and Motor Skills, 54*, 143–146.

Paradowski, W. (1967). Effect of curiosity on incidental learning. *Journal of Educational Psychology, 58*, 50–55.

Rogers, R. W., & Mewborn, C. R. (1976). Fear appeals and attitude change: Effects of a threat's noxiousness, probability of occurrence, and the efficacy of coping responses. *Journal of Personality and Social Psychology, 34*, 54–61.

Sheppard, A. (1983). Effect of mode of representation on visual humor. *Psychological Reports, 52*, 299–305.

Wiggers, M., & van Lieshout, C. F. M. (1985). Development of recognition of emotions: Children's reliance on situational and facial expressive cues. *Developmental Psychology, 21*, 338–349.

Wilson, B. J., & Cantor, J. (1985). Developmental differences in empathy with a television protagonist's fear. *Journal of Experimental Child Psychology, 39*, 284–299.

Winn, W., & Everett, R. J. (1979). Affective rating of color and black-and-white pictures. *Educational Communication and Technology Journal, 27*, 148–156.

5.2 Preferences

Baker, E. L., & Popham, W. J. (1965). Value of pictorial embellishments in tape-slide instructional program. *AV Communication Review, 13*, 397–404.

Bell, R., & Bell, G. (1979). Individual differences in children's preferences among recent paintings. *British Journal of Educational Psychology, 49*, 182–187.

Boselie, F. (1983). Ambiguity, beauty, and interestingness of line drawings. *Canadian Journal of Psychology, 37*, 287–292.

Boselie, F., & Leeuwenberg, E. (1985). Birkhoff revisited: Beauty as a function of effect and means. *American Journal of Psychology, 98*, 1–39.

Chevrier, J., & DeLorme, A. (1980). Aesthetic preferences: Influence of perceptual ability, age, and complexity of stimulus. *Perceptual and Motor Skills, 50*, 839–849.

D'Hondt, W., & Vanderwiele, M. (1983). Colors and figures in Senegal. *Perceptual and Motor Skills, 56*, 971–978.

Ellis, A. W., & Miller, D. (1981). Left and wrong in adverts: Neuropsychological correlates of aesthetic preference. *British Journal of Psychology, 72*, 225–229.

Frost, A. G., & Lindauer, M. S. (1980). Preferences for figural complexity as a function of cognitive style. *Bulletin of the Psychonomic Society, 16*, 221–224.

Hardiman, G. W., & Zernich, T. (1977). Preferences for the visual arts: A review of recent studies. *Perceptual and Motor Skills, 44*, 455–463.

Hardiman, G. W., & Zernich, T. (1982). The relative influence of parts and wholes in shaping preference responses to paintings. *Studies in Art Education, 23*(2), 31–38.

Heinrichs, R. W. (1984). Verbal responses to human figure paintings: A test of the uncertainty hypothesis. *Canadian Journal of Psychology, 38,* 512-518.

Holmes, C. B., & Buchanan, J. A. (1984). Color preference as a function of the object described. *Bulletin of the Psychonomic Society, 22,* 423-425.

McManus, I. C. (1980). The aesthetics of simple figures. *British Journal of Psychology, 71,* 505-524.

McManus, I. C., Edmondson, D., & Roger, J. (1985). Balance in pictures. *British Journal of Psychology, 76,* 311-324.

Myatt, B., & Carter, J. M. (1979). Picture preferences of children and young adults. *Educational Communication and Technology Journal, 27,* 45-53.

Nicki, R. M., Lee, P. L., & Moss, V. (1981). Ambiguity, Cubist works of art, and preference. *Acta Psychologia, 49,* 27-41.

Plug, C. (1980). The golden section hypothesis. *American Journal of Psychology, 93,* 467-487.

Ramsey, I. L. (1982). Effect of art style on children's picture preferences. *Journal of Educational Research, 75,* 237-240.

Samuels, S. J., Beisbrock, E., & Terry, P. R. (1974). The effect of pictures on children's attitudes toward presented stories. *Journal of Educational Research, 67,* 243-246.

Savarese, J. M., & Miller, R. J. (1979). Artistic preferences and cognitive-perceptual style. *Studies in Art Education, 20*(2), 45-51.

Sewell, E. H., Jr., & Moore, R. L. (1980). Cartoon embellishments in informative presentations. *Educational Communication and Technology Journal, 28,* 39-46.

Stewig, J. W. (1975). Assessing visual elements preferred in pictures by young children. *Reading Improvement, 12,* 94-97.

5.3. ATTITUDES

Andreoli, V., & Worchel, S. (1978). Effects of media communicator, and message position on attitude change. *Public Opinion Quarterly, 42,* 59-70.

Baggaley, J. (1980). *Psychology of the TV image.* Westmead, Farnborough, Hants., England: Grower Publishing.

Duck, S. W., & Baggaley, J. (1975). Audience reaction and its effect on perceived expertise. *Communication Research, 2,* 79-85.

Espe, H. (1985). A cross-cultural investigation of the graphic differential. *Journal of Psycholinguistic Research, 14,* 97-111.

George, S. G., & Jennings, L. B. (1975). Effect of subliminal stimuli on consumer behavior: Negative evidence. *Perceptual and Motor Skills, 41,* 847-854.

Henley, S. H. A. (1984). Unconscious perception re-revisited: A comment on Merikle's (1982) paper. *Bulletin of the Psychonomic Society, 22,* 121-124.

Hovespian, W. (1978). Effects of subliminal stimulation on masculinity–femininity ratings of a male model. *Perceptual and Motor Skills, 46,* 155-161.

Huston, A. C., Greer, D., Wright, J. C., Welch, R., & Ross, R. (1984). Children's comprehension of televised formal features with masculine and feminine connotations. *Developmental Psychology, 20,* 707-716.

Kari, J. (1980). Affective elements in teaching materials: An empirical study. *Scientia Paedagogica Experimentalis, 17,* 168-189.

Kelly, J. S. (1979). Subliminal embeds in print advertising: A challenge to advertising ethics. *Journal of Advertising, 8,* 20-24.

Kolbe, R., & LaVole, J. (1981). Sex-role stereotyping in preschool children's picture books. *Social Psychology Quarterly, 44,* 369-374.

Margolin, V. (1979). The visual rhetoric of propaganda. *Information Design Journal, 1*, 107-122.
Medhurst, M. J., & DeSousa, M. A. (1981). Political cartoons as rhetorical form: A taxonomy of graphic discourse. *Communication Monographs, 48*, 197-236.
O'Connor, J., Beilin, H., & Kose, G. (1981). Children's belief in photographic fidelity. *Developmental Psychology, 17*, 859-865.
Oliver, E., & Griffitt, W. (1976). Emotional arousal and "objective" judgment. *Bulletin of the Psychonomic Society, 8*, 399-400.
Osgood, C. E. (1981). The cognitive dynamics of synesthesia and metaphor. *Review of Research in Visual Art Education, 14*, 56-82.
Ryan, M. (1975). The impact of television news film on perceived media credibility. *Journal of Applied Communications Research, 3*, 69-75.
Scott, K. P. (1980). Sexist and nonsexist materials: What impact do they have? *Elementary School Journal, 81*, 47-52.
Seiler, W. (1971). The effects of visual materials on attitudes, credibility and retention. *Speech Monographs, 38*, 331-334.
Simonson, M. R. (1980). Media and attitudes: A bibliography, part 2. *Educational Communication and Technology Journal, 28*, 47-61.
Simonson, M. R., Thies, P., & Burch, G. (1979). Media and attitudes: A bibliography, part 1. *Educational Communication and Technology Journal, 27*, 217-236.
Taylor, S. E., & Thompson, S. C. (1982). Stalking the elusive "vividness" effect. *Psychological Review, 89*, 155-181.
Vokey, J. R., & Read, J. D. (1985). Subliminal messages: Between the devil and the media. *American Psychologist, 40*, 1231-1239.
Whalen, D. H., & Blanchard, F. A. (1982). Effects of photographic evidence on mock juror judgement. *Journal of Applied Social Psychology, 12*, 30-41.
Zuckerman, D. M., Singer, D. G., & Singer, J. L. (1980). Children's television viewing, racial and sex-role attitudes. *Journal of Applied Social Psychology, 10*, 281-294.

5.4. AESTHETIC RESPONSES

Arnheim, R. (1982). *The power of the center: A study of composition in the visual arts.* Berkeley: University of California Press.
Berlyne, D. E. (1971). *Aesthetics and psychobiology.* New York: Appleton-Century-Crofts.
Berlyne, D. E. (Ed.). (1974). *Studies in the new experimental aesthetics: Steps toward an objective psychology of aesthetic appreciation.* New York: Wiley.
Biaggio, M. K., & Supplee, K. A. (1983). Dimensions of aesthetic perception. *Journal of Psychology, 114*, 29-35.
Boyer, B. A. (1983). An examination of experimental aesthetic research from 1970 to 1980 related to the visual perception of paintings with implications for art education. *Visual Arts Research, 9*(1), 34-40.
Carothers, T., & Gardner, H. (1979). When children's drawings become art: The emergence of aesthetic production and perception. *Developmental Psychology, 15*, 570-580.
Cupchik, G. C. (1983). The scientific study of artistic creativity. *Leonardo, 16*, 193-195.
Dawson, J. (1980). Measures of aesthetic sensitivity as predicators to performance in the visual arts. *Information Design Journal, 1*, 190-197.
D'Onofrio, A., & Nodine, C. F. (1981). Children's responses to paintings. *Studies in Art Education, 23*(1), 14-23.

Eisner, E. (1985). Aesthetic modes of knowing. In E. Eisner (Ed.), *Learning and teaching the ways of knowing. Eighty-fourth yearbook of the National Society for the Study of Education* (pp. 23-36). Chicago: University of Chicago Press.

Eysenck, H. J. (1983). A new measure of "good taste" in visual art. *Leonardo, 16*, 229-231.

Foss, S. K., & Radich, A. J. (1980). The aesthetic response to nonrepresentational art: A suggested model. *Review of Research in Visual Arts Education, 12*, 40-49.

Gardner, H. (1973). *The arts and human development.* New York: Wiley.

Gardner, H. (1982). *Art, mind, and brain: A cognitive approach to creativity.* New York: Basic Books.

Gombrich, E. H. (1979). *The sense of order: A study in the psychology of decorative art.* Ithaca, NY: Cornell University Press.

Hardiman, G. W., & Zernich, T. (1985). Discrimination of style in painting: A developmental study. *Studies in Art Education, 26*(3), 157-162.

Hasenfus, N., Martindale, C., & Birnbaum, D. (1983). Psychological reality of cross-media artistic styles. *Journal of Experimental Psychology: Human Perception and Performance, 9*, 841-863.

Hoege, H. (1984). The emotional impact on aesthetic judgments: An experimental investigation of a time-honored hypothesis. *Visual Arts Research, 10*(2), 37-48.

Ives, S. W. (1984). The development of expressivity in drawing. *British Journal of Educational Psychology, 54*, 152-159.

Jones, B. J., & McFee, J. K. (1986). Research on teaching arts and aesthetics. In M. C. Wittrock (Ed.), *Handbook of research on teaching* (3rd ed., pp. 906-991). New York: Macmillan.

Lovano-Kerr, J., & Rush, J. (1982). Project Zero: The evolution of visual arts research during the seventies. *Review of Research in Visual Arts Education,* Issue 15, 61-81.

McManus, I. C., Edmondson, D., & Rodger, J. (1985). Balance in pictures. *British Journal of Psychology, 76*, 311-324.

Nodine, C. F. (1982). Compositional design as a perceptual determinant of aesthetic judgment. *Visual Arts Research,* Issue 16, 43-54.

O'Hare, D., & Westwood, H. (1984). Features of style classification: A multivariate experimental analysis of children's responses to drawings. *Developmental Psychology, 20*, 150-158.

Peacock, J. (1984). From child to artist: A developmental perspective on perceptual patterning and symbolization. *Journal of Mental Imagery, 8*, 33-42.

Rush, J. C., & Sabers, D. L. (1981). The perception of artistic style. *Studies in Art Education, 23*(1), 24-32.

Taunton, M. (1982). Aesthetic responses of young children to the visual arts: A review of the literature. *Journal of Aesthetic Education, 16*, 93-109.

Taunton, M. (1984). Four-year-old children's recognition of expressive qualities in painting reproductions. *Journal of Research and Development in Education, 17*(4), 36-42.

Winner, E. (1982). *Invented worlds.* Cambridge, MA: Harvard University Press.

Winner, E., Blank, P., Massey, C., & Gardner, H. (1982). Children's sensitivity to aesthetic properties of line drawings. In D. Rogers & J. A. Sloboda (Eds.), *The acquisition of symbolic skills* (pp. 97-104). New York: Plenum Press.

Wohlwill, J. R. (1985). The Gardner-Winner view of children's visual-artistic development: Overview, assessment, and critique. *Visual Arts Research, 11*(1), 1-22.

2
On Empirically Validating Functions of Pictures in Prose

JOEL R. LEVIN, GARY J. ANGLIN, AND RUSSELL N. CARNEY

Introduction

Anyone who has ever leafed through the pages of children's reading books, textbooks, and other instructional materials will most surely have noticed variation in both the quantity and quality of pictures that are provided. Why do some authors choose to include illustrations or photographs in their books, whereas others do not? Why are particular pictures selected to illustrate particular text segments? What is a picture's purpose? And most importantly for our own purposes, is there a relationship—either imagined or real—between the kind of pictures provided and their instructional value?

This chapter focuses on the various "functions" served by pictures in prose materials. We begin with a look back at previous considerations of textbook illustrations and their impact on students' prose-learning performance in relation to their hypothesized functional significance. We then present the results of a fairly extensive investigation examining the empirical validity of these considerations. Finally, we capitalize on hints provided by the empirical investigation to speculate on conditions that are likely to differentiate between effective and ineffective instructional applications of prose-learning pictures.

Before embarking, however, it is necessary to make a few stage-setting remarks. As has been our custom in reviewing the evidence concerning the role of pictures in prose learning (e.g., Levin, 1981b, 1982, 1983; Levin & Lesgold, 1978), we wish to make clear from the outset exactly what we mean by both "prose learning" and "pictures." First, we are considering only the issue of learning *from* text—or what some have referred to as "reading to learn." We therefore are concerned here only with the effect of pictures on students' ability to remember prose *content*. Consideration of pictures in relation to students' acquisition of decoding and word-recognition *skills* per se (i.e., "learning to read") is another matter entirely, which yields fundamentally different prescriptive conclusions than those derived from the reading-to-learn literature (e.g., Levin, 1983; Willows, 1978, 1979).

Second, throughout our discussion we think it important to make distinctions regarding the specific prose and picture formats being considered. Regarding prose formats, in previous examinations of pictures-in-prose effects a distinction has been made between *written* and *oral* text presentations. Concerning picture formats, wherever possible we distinguish between pictures on the page (visual *illustrations*) and pictures in the head (visual *imagery*). One more potentially important specification relates to the nature of the subject population under consideration and, in particular, whether we are talking about normally functioning *adults* or *children*, or *educationally handicapped students*. As will be seen later, the effect of pictures on students' prose learning can be posited to vary as a function of these just-described format and subject-population characteristics.

What We Already Know: A Retrospective Sketch

On Pictures in Prose

The present volume is replete with accounts of text–illustration phenomena, beginning with the Samuels and Mulcahy historical perspective and progressing through a number of other interesting topics. As a point of departure for this chapter, we can summarize the literature on the effect of pictures on learning from prose in three general conclusions:

1. In cases where text-embedded *illustrations* are relevant to (i.e., largely overlapping or redundant with) the to-be-remembered content, moderate to substantial prose-learning gains can be expected.
2. In cases where text-embedded *illustrations* are not relevant to the to-be-remembered prose content (i.e., they depict unrelated—or worse, conflicting—text information), no prose-learning facilitation is to be expected.
3. In cases where "pictures" consist of self-generated *visual images* that are relevant to the to-be-remembered content, some positive effects can be expected, but these are much more modest and more variable than those associated with actual illustrations.

Each of these conclusions can be documented readily in reviews of the pictures-in-prose literature. Focusing on empirical studies in which *children listened to* prose passages, Levin and Lesgold (1978) provided evidence to support the claim of moderate to substantial learning benefits associated with text-relevant illustrations (Conclusion 1). The same conclusion was reached when later extended to include both children and adults in actual reading situations (Haring & Fry, 1979; Levie & Lentz, 1982; Readence & Moore, 1981; Schallert, 1980). Several empirical studies (some described in this volume) and the Levie and Lentz review provide evidence in support of the claim that text-irrelevant illustrations are not facilitative (Conclusion 2). Finally, the Levie and Lentz review, along with that of Levin (1981b), reveals the small and variable prose-learning benefits resulting from the use of relevant self-generated imagery (Conclusion 3).

Understanding the preceding discussion is critical if one hopes to understand both past accounts of pictures-in-prose effects, as well as the one to be developed here. For example, although the distinction between "learning to read" and "reading to learn" was recognized by Samuels (1970) in his widely cited review, very few reading-to-learn studies had been conducted at that time. Moreover, for the few that were available, the distinction between text-relevant and text-irrelevant pictures was not made. The mixed results stemming from that handful of reading-to-learn studies simply were amalgamated with findings derived from the learning-to-read studies, which consistently produced either negative or neutral picture effects. Thus, the general conclusion extracted from Samuels' review and cited for many years thereafter was: *Pictures in text are not beneficial and may even be harmful.* It is hoped that our brief historical account and associated comments will permanently eradicate this erroneous impression for the reading-to-learn situation, which at least as far as text-relevant illustrations are concerned indicates that: *Pictures in text consistently produce prose-learning benefits.*

On Functions of Pictures in Prose

In part as an attempt to clarify the muddied picture of prose-learning picture effects, Levin (1981b) proposed that not all *types* of picture are equally facilitative of prose learning. As an already-cited example, pictures that illustrate text-irrelevant content may be useful for a number of purposes (see below), but enhancing a student's recall of the text content is not one of them. In contrast, following directly from several different psychological theories of learning and memory, text-relevant illustrations *would be* expected to be beneficial. Along with making the basic distinction between text-relevant and text-irrelevant pictures, Levin argued that different types of text-embedded picture serve noticeably different prose-learning "functions." Five of these functions will be considered here (see also Duchastel & Waller, 1979, and Levie & Lentz, 1982, for alternative "functional" classifications of prose-learning pictures).

FIVE PICTURE FUNCTIONS

Decoration Function

This is the function associated with text-irrelevant pictures. In particular, when illustrations are selected to make a textbook look more attractive (rather than to support or supplement critical text information), then a decoration function is being served. For present purposes, this function also encompasses two other text-irrelevant functions proposed by Levin (1981b): the *remuneration* function (when illustrations are provided mainly to increase a publisher's sales) and the *motivation* function (when illustrations are provided to increase students' interest in the material). Naturally, text-relevant illustrations also can help to make a book more attractive, marketable, or engaging, but in this chapter pictures classified as "decorational" are those that have no direct connection with the prose content.

An example of a decorational picture is shown in Figure 2.1. Note that although selected recognizable figures appear in the illustration, the information and events described in the narrative do not. For example, Thumbelina does not

54 Joel R. Levin, Gary J. Anglin, and Russell N. Carney

Illustration   Text

...leaving Thumbelina crying, for she didn't want to live with the horrid toad, nor have her ugly son for a husband. But the little fish under the water had heard the old toad, and now thrust their heads out to see for themselves. No, Thumbelina was much too beautiful for a toad to carry off. So they all gathered...

FIGURE 2.1. Example of a decorational illustration. From *Thumbelina* by Hans Christian Andersen, 1939, New York: Holiday House. Copyright 1939 by Holiday House. Reprinted by permission.

Illustration   Text

13. SUSAN
He had promised to go to Meridian Hill after his examinations. It was the last thing Glasgow wanted to do, but he went.

The minute he got there he knew Commodore Porter had heard about his failure. The commodore led the way to his library and closed the door.

"What happened?"

Glasgow told him about the dust-up over Bottles, and Hatchet-Face. Then he flared. "But I'll not take this standing still! I'm going to the Secretary of the Navy! I'll demand they tell me in what way I was 'deficient in other respects'! And I'll demand I take the examination again under another board!"

FIGURE 2.2. Example of a decorational illustration. From *Anchor's aweigh: The story of David Glasgow Farragut* by J. L. Latham, 1968, New York: Harper & Row. Copyright 1968 by Harper & Row. Reprinted by permission.

appear to be crying, and the events associated with the old toad are not depicted. Another example is the sailing ship shown in Figure 2.2, which, despite supporting a nautical theme, bears no relationship at all to the information presented with it.

Representation Function

Whereas decorational pictures do not represent the actors, objects, and activities taking place in narrative passages, representational pictures do. That is, the pictures serve to reinforce the major narrative events. Illustrations that "tell" exactly the same story as the words are prototype representational pictures, and illustrations that overlap substantially with the text also fit the definition. Such illustrations appear in a good many children's reading books as, for example, in the *Mrs. Gaddy* and *Horton* excerpts in Figures 2.3 and 2.4, respectively. Note in each case that a good portion of the critical textual information is "represented" in the accompanying illustration.

Although reserved primarily for narrative passages (e.g., Bender & Levin, 1978), representational pictures also have been used to depict expository-text information (e.g., Anglin, in press). In our later-reported meta-analysis based on

Text

Mrs. Gaddy was a farmer.
She had a little old house
and a big old barn.
She had some fields of corn
and a vegetable garden.
She had a meadow
and some apple trees
She had a storm cellar to go in
if a tornado happened.
She had some chickens.
She had a cow and a mule.
It was a very nice farm.

Illustration

FIGURE 2.3. Example of a representational illustration. From *Mrs. Gaddy and the ghost* by W. Gage. Text copyright 1979 by Mary Q. Steele. Illustration copyright 1979 by Marylin Hafner. By permission of Greenwillow Books (a division of William Morrow).

Illustration	Text
	And the first thing he knew, they had built a big wagon With ropes on the front for the pullers to drag on. They dug up his tree and they put it inside, With Horton so sad that he practically cried. "We're off!" the men shouted. And off they all went With Horton unhappy, one hundred per cent.

FIGURE 2.4. Example of a representational illustration. From *Horton hatches the egg* by Dr. Seuss. Copyright 1940 and renewed 1968 by Dr. Seuss. Reprinted by permission of Random House, Inc.

the present five functional categories, representational pictures comprise more than half of the entries—with expository texts being used in several of those instances. An important functional distinction for our purposes is between expository-text pictures that basically overlap with well-organized, comprehensible text content, serving mainly to make that content more *concrete* (representational pictures), and pictures that make expository-text content more *coherent* or more *comprehensible* (organizational and interpretational pictures, whose descriptions follow).

Organization Function

As was just noted, pictures can be used to provide an organizational framework for a text, giving it greater coherence. In a social studies context, illustrated maps frequently are used to make geographical relationships more transparent (e.g., Dean & Kulhavy, 1981). "How-to-do-it" diagrams serve a similar function with respect to what are called *procedural texts*, such as how to assemble something (e.g., Stone & Glock, 1981) or how to perform cardiopulmonary resuscitation (see Figure 2.5). Passages that basically list the distinctive features of several characters or objects (e.g., Rusted & Coltheart, 1979) also usually lend themselves to a more coherent organization via pictorial representation—bringing to mind the overused "one picture is worth a thousand words" aphorism. That aphorism can readily be applied to the narrative listing of objects described in the Figure 2.6 excerpt.[1]

---

[1]Some might argue that because Figure 2.6 conveys the information of a narrative passage, it is a representational illustration (similar to Figures 2.3 and 2.4). However, we prefer to view Figure 2.6 as an organizational illustration because of its "map-like" quality, which serves to integrate a narrative passage that includes several spatial relationships and connections among objects.

2. On Empirically Validating Functions of Pictures in Prose   57

Text

Open the airway by placing one hand under victim's neck and the other on his or her forehead, tilting back the head to lift the tongue from the back of the throat. Remove any obstructions—solids, liquids, vomitus. If victim is not breathing, proceed to step 2.

To restart breathing, pinch nostrils closed, put your mouth over victim's to form tight seal, and inflate lungs with four quick, full breaths, without waiting between breaths. If no pulse is felt, proceed to step 4. Otherwise continue rescue breathing 12 times a minute until breathing resumes or help arrives.

If you have help, begin CPR in a 5 to 1 ratio—5 chest compressions to 1 lung inflation, without pause.

Illustration

If no pulse can be felt strike a sharp, quick single blow to the mid-chest with the fleshy portion of your fist, starting 8 to 12 inches above the chest. This must be done within 60 seconds of cessation of heartbeat.

Begin CPR. If alone, use 15 chest compressions (80 per minute) as shown in drawing 6, followed by 2 very quick inflations of victim's lungs as shown in drawing 3.

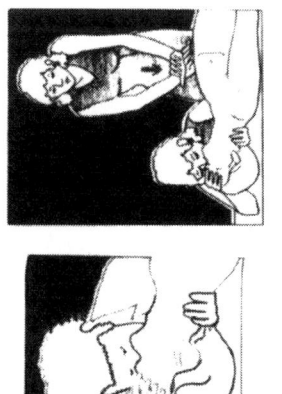

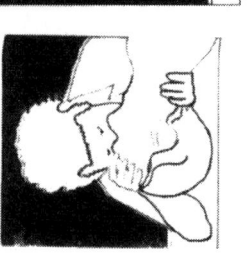

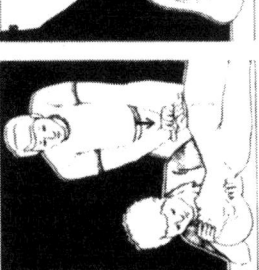

Effective cardiac compression in adult requires enough pressure to depress sternum (breast bone) at least 1½ inches. Hold fingers free of chest wall.

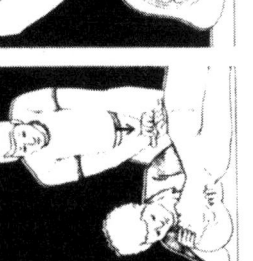

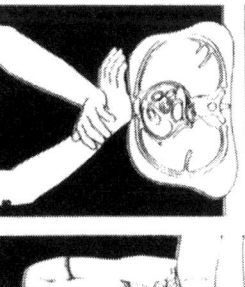

FIGURE 2.5. Example of an organizational illustration. From *Alive and well: Decisions in health* by A. Eisenberg and H. Eisenberg, 1979, New York: McGraw-Hill. Copyright 1979 by McGraw-Hill. Reprinted by permission.

58   Joel R. Levin, Gary J. Anglin, and Russell N. Carney

Illustration   Text

There was a round room downstairs and a round room up, but that was smaller and had a pointed roof; the windows were small and the front door narrow—it was the only door. The corkscrew staircase came up in the middle of the bedroom floor. The vinegar bottle was not exactly comfortable but the old woman did not mind. "There's no place like home," said the old woman.

In the sitting room downstairs she had a table and chair and a dresser set out with her bits of china. She had made a rag rug to go in front of the fire, and by it was her high-backed wooden rocking chair. Upstairs, for her bed she had made a patchwork quilt "from pieces of all the dresses I have ever had since I was seven." A wooden box that stood upright made a place to put her candlestick, and there were some useful pegs on which to hang her clothes.

Outside, on the bottle wall, a tin bath hung from a nail—the old woman had a bath every Saturday night; there was a pail for carrying water, a dustpan and a broom, and small black kettle that sang to itself on the hob all day long. "What more can a body want?" asked the old woman.

FIGURE 2.6. Example of an organizational illustration. From *The old woman who lived in a vinegar bottle* by Rumer Godden, 1972, New York: Viking Press. Copyright 1972 by Mcmillan & Co., Ltd., London and Basingstoke. Reprinted by permission.

Interpretation Function

Interpretational pictures clarify difficult-to-understand passages and abstract concepts within passages. Passages requiring Ausubelian "advance organizers" (e.g., Ausubel, 1963) are especially conducive to this type of stage-setting support (Levin & Pressley, 1981). Indeed, some investigators have capitalized on an interpretational-picture strategy to render comprehensible virtually incomprehensible narrative text (e.g., Arnold & Brooks, 1976). Other investigators have

▶

FIGURE 2.7. Example of an interpretational illustration. From *Animal ecology* (Fig. 7-6, p. 95) by S. Charles Kendeigh, 1961, Englewood Cliffs, NJ: Prentice-Hall. Copyright 1961 by Prentice-Hall, Inc. Reprinted by permission. (Adapted from "Ecological Study of the Peat Bogs of Eastern North America" by D. Dansereau and F. Segadas-Vianna, 1952, *Canadian Journal of Botany*, 30, 490–520. Copyright 1952 by the National Research Council of Canada. Adapted by permission.)

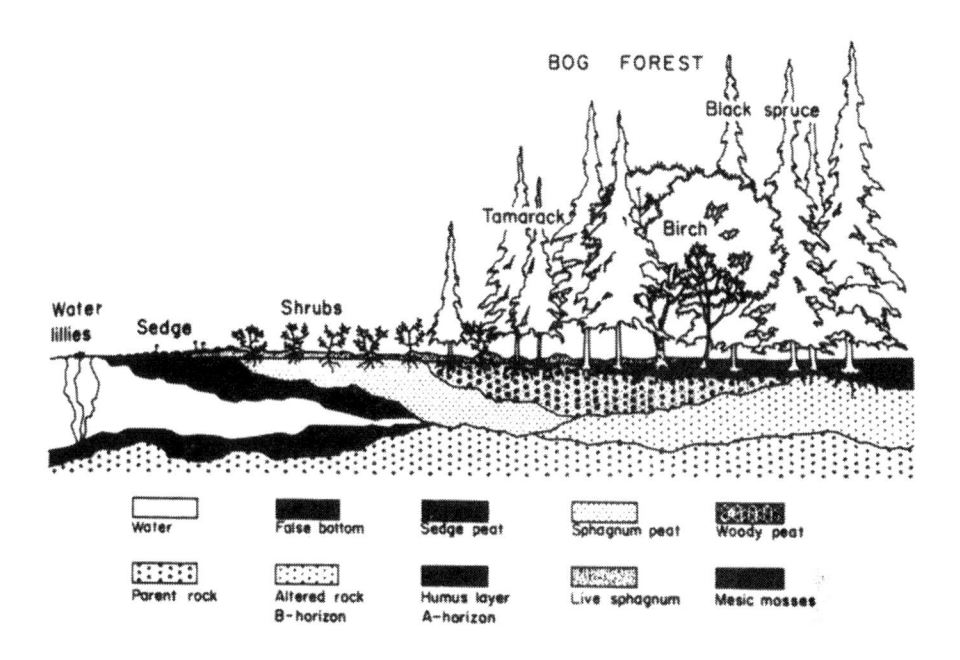

2. On Empirically Validating Functions of Pictures in Prose   59

[Figure: Bog forest cross-section diagram showing Water lillies, Sedge, Shrubs, Tamarack, Birch, Black spruce, and BOG FOREST zones. Legend: Water, False bottom, Sedge peat, Sphagnum peat, Woody peat, Parent rock B-horizon, Altered rock, Humus layer A-horizon, Live sphagnum, Mesic mosses.]

Text

The plant bog sere

In the early stages of development of the bog, organic detritus may accumulate mostly in the deepest portions (Potzger, 1956). As time goes on, however, a definite concentric-circle zonation of vegetation is established around the margin. As peat accumulates, each zone encroaches on the next inner; the inmost shrinks until all open water disappears. The area becomes finally covered with *climax forest* (Dachnowski, 1912).

In some bogs (Gates, 1942; Dansereau and Segadas-Vianna, 1952) the first plant stage may be composed of floating vegetation (*Nuphar, Nymphaea, Potamogeton, Sparganium*) but floating vegetation is often absent and the first stage is a *sedge-mat* composed of sedges, cottongrass, and buckbean. The rhizomes of the sedges grow out into the water and become so interlaced that they form a floating mat. At the water edge the mat may be very thin, but towards shore it may become as much as a meter thick. Since the mat floats on open water it jars easily, hence the name quaking bog—one must watch his step that he does not break through. Sphagnum moss is not essential for the formation of a mat, but it invades the mat quickly and helps bind it together. Sphagnum persists into the shrub and *bog-forest* stages following. Interesting insectivorous species such as the pitcher plant and sundew are common, as are various members of the orchid family.

The next plant stage is dominated by *low shrubs*, which encroach on the floating mat. The leatherleaf, bog rosemary, laurels, albrador tea, sweet gale, and cranberries are important species.

A *high-shrub* stage commonly follows the low shrubs at such time as the mat becomes thicker or grounded. Common shrub species are holly, willow, chokeberry, alders, and dwarf birch.

The first tree of the bog forest to invade the shrubs is commonly the tamarack, but this species is now less common than formerly because of fire, logging, and the depredations of the sawfly larvae *Lygaeonematus erichsonii*. Black spruce may either invade the shrubs directly or follow the tamarack. Later, the northern white-cedar may become dominant and persist for a very long time, but the ultimate fate of the bog, upon addition of upland soil or lowering of the water table, is to be covered with the climax forest of the region.

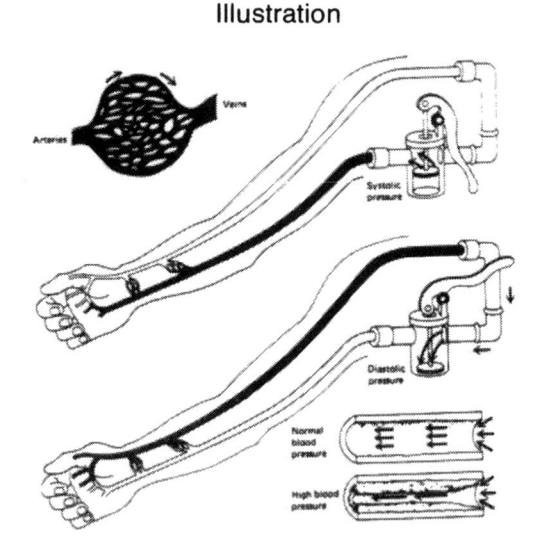

Illustration	Text

The mechanics of blood pressure. When the heart is pumping blood into the circulatory system, blood pressure is at its highest point and is called *systolic pressure.* When the heart is at rest and filling between pumping beats, blood pressure is at its lowest point and is called *diastolic pressure.*

High blood pressure (over 150 systolic and 95 diastolic in most people) occurs when the arteries become partially blocked, inflexible, or both, thereby increasing pressure in the arteries and making the heart work harder to pump blood through the system.

FIGURE 2.8. Example of an interpretational illustration. From *Alive and well: Decisions in health* by A. Eisenberg and H. Eisenberg, 1979, New York: McGraw-Hill. Copyright 1979 by McGraw-Hill. Reprinted by permission.

illustrated rather abstract or complex science and social studies concepts (e.g., Alesandrini & Rigney, 1981; Rasco, Tennyson, & Boutwell, 1975) in an effort to make them more readily understood. Examples of what we regard as good interpretational pictures appear in Figures 2.7 and 2.8. Figure 2.8 uses a pictorial analogy to make an abstract concept more concrete (see also Royer & Cable, 1976). Note that both figures share some of the coherence properties of organizational pictures. The basic difference, in our view, is that whereas the text associated with organizational pictures describes relatively easy-to-process text (because it focuses on simple or familiar concepts described in a straightforward fashion), the text associated with interpretational pictures describes more unfamiliar, difficult, concepts (e.g., technical terms and their associated characteristics).

All picture functions discussed so far are served more or less by "conventional" textbook illustrations. The major premise underlying the three text-relevant picture types (representational, organizational, and interpretational) is that their inclusion supplements the verbally presented text, thereby producing a positive effect on students' memory for the prose passage. As was noted earlier—and as can be gleaned from the theoretical literature on basic cognitive processes—the different picture types assumedly facilitate students' prose learning as a result of the operation of different underlying mechanisms: (a) representational pictures, from their added *concreteness* (i.e., memory for pictorial materials is superior to memory for their less concrete verbal counterparts); (b) organizational pictures, from their added *coherence* (i.e., memory for thematically organized materials exceeds memory for unorganized materials); and (c) interpretational pictures, from their added *comprehensibility* (i.e., materials that are initially well understood are remembered better than those that are more poorly understood).

Transformation Function

Transformational pictures represent a contrast to those just discussed. First, they are "unconventional" in the sense of their being conspicuously absent in the class of traditional textbook illustrations. Second, in contrast to the indirect effects on students' memory produced by the just-discussed types of picture, transformational pictures are designed to impact on students' memory directly. They do so by targeting the critical information to be learned and then (a) *recoding* it into a more concrete and memorable form, (b) *relating* in a well-organized context the separate pieces of that information, and (c) providing the student with a systematic means of *retrieving* the critical information when later asked for it. These three components have been dubbed the "three *R*s" of associative mnemonic (memory-enhancing) techniques (Levin, 1983) and have been analyzed both theoretically and empirically in a variety of learning-and-memory contexts (e.g., Bellezza, 1981; Levin, 1981a; Pressley, Levin, & Delaney, 1982)—including prose learning (e.g., Levin, 1982, 1985).

An example of a transformational prose-learning picture is presented in Figure 2.9, which mnemonically illustrates four important characteristics (*considerable wealth*, *abundant natural resources*, *advances in technology*, and *growing population*) of the fictional town *Fostoria*. Capitalizing on the other picture functions to render these four characteristics more concrete, coherent, and comprehensible, the predominant transformational quality of the picture results from its (a) recoding the unfamiliar, abstract town name *Fostoria* into the more familiar, concrete proxy *frost* (as pictorially represented by cold, snow, and icicles) and (b) relating that recoded proxy to the associated attributes in a thematically organized scene, thereby (c) providing a direct retrieval path from the town name (*Fostoria*) to the recoded proxy (*frost*) to the winter scene with the concretized interacting attributes.

Although mnemonically recoding a name may not be necessary in the case of having to remember only *one* town and its attributes, when a student is presented with a *large number* of towns and their attributes, such mnemonic transformations are extremely beneficial (Levin, Shriberg, & Berry, 1983). Thus, prose passages that describe a variety of factual information that would be otherwise difficult to remember lend themselves directly to the use of transformational pictures. Curriculum examples include social studies and science lessons, where prose passages instruct students in a variety of unfamiliar terms and their associated attributes, where passages compare and contrast the critical features of different constructs, and where historical or biographical passages detail a sequence of critical events or accomplishments. In short, transformational pictures would be expected to help students in situations that require relieving the memory burden. Figure 2.10 provides an example of a transformational illustration that was used effectively to teach poor-reading middle-school students how to construct their own visual images in order to remember the accom-

62   Joel R. Levin, Gary J. Anglin, and Russell N. Carney

FIGURE 2.9. Example of a transformational illustration. From "A Concrete Strategy for Remembering Abstract Prose" by J. R. Levin, L. K. Shriberg, and J. K. Berry, 1983, *American Educational Research Journal*, 20, p. 282. Copyright 1983 by the American Educational Research Association. Reprinted by permission.

plishments of famous people described in a series of nonfictional reading passages (Peters & Levin, 1986, Experiment 2). In the Figure 2.10 example, the critical information is that *Karl Jansky invented an antenna for improving the quality of telecommunications*. The transformational illustration recodes the unfamiliar name *Jansky* into the more concrete *jam* and then relates *jam* and *antenna* in an interactive scene.

FIGURE 2.10. Example of a transformational illustration. From "Effects of a Mnemonic Imagery Strategy on Good and Poor Readers' Prose Recall" by E. E. Peters and J. R. Levin, 1986, *Reading Research Quarterly*. Copyright by International Reading Association, Inc. Adapted by permission.

PICTURE FUNCTIONS AND ANTICIPATED PROSE-LEARNING BENEFITS

In addition to outlining the different functions served by prose-learning pictures, Levin (1981b) speculated that the different functions would be expected to produce different *degrees* of prose-learning facilitation. He did so on the basis of both a rudimentary analysis of the cognitive components associated with the various picture functions and the modest amount of relevant "pictures-in-prose" empirical data that were available at the time. At the extremes, for example, *little or no* prose-learning facilitation would be expected of text-irrelevant pictures (decoration function), whereas *substantial* prose-learning facilitation would be expected of pictures designed specifically with a mnemonic objective in mind (transformation function). Between these extremes were placed the three other text-relevant functions (representation, organization, and interpretation), with the representation function posited to produce *moderate* degrees of prose-learning facilitation and the organization and interpretation functions hypothesized to produce *moderate to substantial* facilitation, depending on particular picture, prose, and person characteristics.

To assess the empirical validity of the claim that different picture functions yield different degrees of prose-learning facilitation (in the manner just indicated), we have conducted a reasonably comprehensive meta-analysis of the "pictures-in-prose" literature. Also examined in this synthesis is Levin's (1981b) suggestion that different function-related facilitation profiles would be associated with "pictures" defined as experimenter-provided *visual illustrations* on the one hand and as subject-generated *visual imagery* on the other. Present page limitations preclude our providing a complete account of the findings, and so we stick to the highlights.

On Empirically Validating Functions of Pictures in Prose

Preliminary Remarks and Caveats About the Meta-Analysis

In any empirical investigation, the quality of one's conclusions depends on the quality of the constituent data on which those conclusions are based. This is certainly a relevant consideration in our about-to-be-presented meta-analysis. We therefore list several specific concerns and cautions that must be taken into account when interpreting our results.

We attempted to be as exhaustive as possible in identifying studies to be included in our analysis. To do this, we located (through various searches) studies published in professional journals, convention papers, and unpublished theses and technical reports. We ended up incorporating 150 "units" (to be described later) representing some 100 experiments from 87 separate documents (see the appendix at the end of the chapter). Yet, more than 50 "pictures-in-prose" studies that were located could not be included for one or more of the following reasons.

1. They did not provide the "sufficient statistics" that are required for a meta-analysis. That is, in the absence of presenting means and standard deviations, sample sizes (or degrees of freedom) and t or F statistics (or relevant portions of an analysis-of-variance table) are needed. In cases where no numerical data were reported, or where means were reported without accompanying variability measures or statistical tests, picture-facilitation effect sizes could not be computed and, hence, such studies could not be included in the meta-analysis.
2. Only studies that assessed students' ability to *remember* information presented in *prose passages* were included. This criterion served to eliminate both studies that assessed something other than learning (e.g., students' attitudes about or interest in the text, or their ability to follow procedural directions with the text present) and those whose "prose passages" consisted of single sentences rather than connected discourse.
3. Many studies were eliminated for not incorporating an appropriate control group. Because the major intent of the present analysis is to compare prose-only conditions with prose-plus-pictures conditions, the former type of condition had to be included in the study. A few studies compared pictures-only (pictures with no accompanying text) with prose-only conditions (e.g., Levin, 1973; Rohwer & Harris, 1975), and such comparisons also were excluded. In addition, so that modality confoundings would not occur, reading-plus-picture conditions had to be compared with reading-only conditions, and listening-plus-picture conditions with listening-only conditions.
4. Studies in which pictures consisted of only one component of multiple-component treatments were not included. For example, in some studies pictures were used to augment an adjunct aid such as an advance organizer or an analogy. If the adjunct-plus-picture condition was compared with a no-adjunct condition, the picture effect would be confounded with the effect of the adjunct per se; hence, such studies were excluded from the meta-analysis (e.g., Davidson, 1976; Mayer & Bromage, 1980). However, studies were included if prose plus a strictly pictorial adjunct aid was compared with prose alone (e.g., Arnold & Brooks, 1976; Bransford & Johnson, 1972, Experiment 1; Royer & Cable, 1976).
5. There is a growing body of literature that details the effects of pictures that *conflict* with text information, or so-called "mismatched" pictures (e.g., Peeck, Chapter 4, this volume; Pressley, Levin, Pigott, LeComte, & Hope, 1983; Willows, 1980). Mismatched pictures depict objects or events that are directly contradicted by ones mentioned in the text. Mismatched picture conditions were not included in the meta-analysis because they do not fit well with any of the present functional definitions. They clearly are not text-relevant pictures, but they are not text-irrelevant (neutral) pictures either. Although there are few textbook instances of mismatched pictures that can be identified, such pictures are nonetheless interesting from a theoretical perspective. Consequently, the creation of another functional category (along with its presumed inhibitory consequences) may be justified.

6. Studies in which the "pictures" consisted of graphs, tree diagrams, flow charts, "marginal gloss" (e.g., Otto, White, & Camperell, 1980), and the like were not included. Although such graphic aids have received some attention in the prose-learning literature, they fit neither the definition nor spirit of the present picture-function classification scheme.

Apart from the inclusion/exclusion issue, four others need to be mentioned. First, functional classifications could not always be determined unambiguously from the descriptions of prose and pictures provided in a document. More complete descriptions led to more certainly correct classifications (according to the respective definitions presented earlier), but even these have some uncertainty associated with them. As Levin (1981b) noted, because a particular picture may serve more than one function, the various categories cannot be regarded as being mutually exclusive. For example, both organizational and interpretational pictures generally include a representational component, inasmuch as they concretely represent the information provided in the text (albeit in a "better" form); see Figures 2.5–2.8. Similarly, organizational and interpretational pictures may be thought to share critical "coherence" features. With this said, then, based on authors' descriptions of the nature of their texts and accompanying pictures, we attempted to do the best we could at classifying pictures into one of the five categories defined here.

Second, and as has been pointed out previously (e.g., Levin & Lesgold, 1978), some special problems are associated with interpreting pictures-in-prose effects when the prose passages are presented in exclusively written form. When unskilled decoders (young children, dyslexics, or other students with poor word-decoding skills) comprise the target population, how is one to interpret the results if, say, no picture effect occurs? In cases where decoding inadequacy may preclude any meaningful prose processing, something other than prose *learning* is being measured, and so the effects of various prose-learning aids cannot be assessed unambiguously. This is why, in their review of the literature on pictures in *children's* prose learning, Levin and Lesgold opted for considering only studies where texts were presented *orally* (see also Pressley & Miller, Chapter 3, this volume). In the present meta-analysis, we include both reading and listening prose-learning studies in an attempt to be as comprehensive as possible. Results are reported both across the two processing modes and for each separately.

Another issue is that the "pictures" used in different studies differ considerably in substance, form, and detail. As was noted at the outset, one of our tasks was to identify the function served by the pictures of a particular study. Another task confronting us, however, was to ascertain both the degree to which pictures were actually *provided* and the extent to which they conveyed the critical text information. Some "pictures" can be identified clearly as illustrations, and others as experimenter instructions to form visual images of the text content. Yet, in some cases only *parts* of an illustration were included, and in others students were required to draw their own pictures or to construct them from supplied props.

How should such "pictures" be called? We discuss this later in more detail. Additional picture variations include their degree of realism (e.g., photograph vs. line drawing), color, format (on a page vs. on a slide), numerousness (one vs. several per passage), and specific relationship to the target information (along a direct/indirect continuum), among others.

Finally, clear interpretation of the effect sizes associated with the different picture functions is complicated by the occurrence of several natural confoundings. This is a problem inherent in any nonexperimental study, of which a meta-analytic synthesis is a perfect example. In the present context, prose-learning studies employing representational pictures often involve children listing to narrative texts, whereas those employing interpretational or organizational pictures generally involve adults reading expository texts. Any results attributed to functions, therefore, are potentially associated with subject-population, processing-mode, and/or text-type differences as well. Consequently, apparent between-function differences in effect sizes must be interpreted with these possibly contaminating concomitants in mind.

A Meta-Analysis of Picture Functions

Definition of "Units"

The 150 "units" that comprise the meta-analysis consist of one or more comparisons within a given experiment. In addition to classifying each unit by one of the five functions of interest, we also classified it by one of three picture types (illustrations, imagery, or other), by one of two processing modes (reading vs. listening), and by one of three subject populations (adult/high school, children, and students identified as educationally handicapped). Individual experiments within a multiexperiment study were considered to be independent entities, with data units defined in terms of separable components of the classifying factors. Thus, for example, if one experiment of a multiexperiment study included both reading and listening conditions (with and without pictures for each), then two effect sizes were calculated for that experiment. Similarly, if an experiment included both illustration and imagery conditions (along with a text-only condition), two effect sizes were computed using the same control condition for each.

However, in experiments where children's performance was reported separately by age/grade, gender, social class, achievement level (excluding educationally handicapped), and so on, only a single effect size was computed (averaged across levels of the reported factors). A similar averaging approach was adopted when multiple measures of performance were administered in a single experiment (e.g., more than one dependent variable, or both immediate and delayed tests). With respect to multiple dependent measures, only those tests (or items within tests) purporting to measure picture-relevant content were included—although decorational pictures constitute a notable exception that will be discussed. Finally, wherever deemed appropriate, two or more "conceptually similar" treatment (or control) conditions in a given experiment were averaged together in the effect-size calculations (e.g., the several different picture variations of Dwyer, 1967).

EFFECT-SIZE CALCULATIONS

The basic approach consisted of comparing a text-plus-picture condition (referred to hereafter as *picture*) with a text-only condition (*control*), either individually or averaged across conceptually similar conditions. When performance means for the constituent conditions were supplied (or could reasonably be estimated from graphs), these were used in conjunction with standard deviations (or standard-deviation estimates derived from other information provided). In other cases, comparisons were made on the basis of transformed t or F statistics. The specific effect-size measure calculated was the difference in means divided by the pooled within-group standard deviation. In cases where a choice could be made between pooling the standard deviations of just the groups being compared and pooling those based on all conditions included in the experiment, we chose the former. Thus, for example, an effect size of 0.00 indicates that the picture and control groups being compared have the same mean level of performance, whereas an effect size of +0.50 indicates that there is a mean difference representing one-half of a within-group standard-deviation unit in favor of the picture condition (e.g., see Cohen, 1977; Glass, 1976).

RESULTS

Throughout our discussion, we focus on the *descriptive* results of the analysis. We have elected not to conduct *inferential* tests and interpret their outcomes because of both (a) the partial *nonindependence* among the meta-analysis units and (b) the multiple confoundings associated with them (see above).

The first (and most general) analysis we report investigates differences in mean effect size *by function*, ignoring all other potentially relevant classifications (i.e., picture type, processing mode, and subject population). The total number of units associated with each of the five functions is as follows: decoration, $N = 8$; representation, $N = 79$; organization, $N = 21$; interpretation, $N = 24$; and transformation, $N = 18$. Thus, with the exception of the decoration function, all functions are based on a reasonable number of units (at least 18).

The findings are summarized in Figure 2.11. For purposes of reference, note that the eight units identified as serving a decoration function produce an average effect size near zero (-0.11). On the basis of even this limited evidence, one would have to conclude that pictures that are not related to the to-be-learned text content (e.g., Figures 2.1 and 2.2) do not produce prose-learning benefits. This certainly fits with Levin's (1981b) assertion that such pictures are associated with "little or no" prose-learning facilitation. Because decorational pictures do not display text-relevant content, they are not included in the subsequent analyses of picture effects—a procedure also adopted by Levie and Lentz (1982).

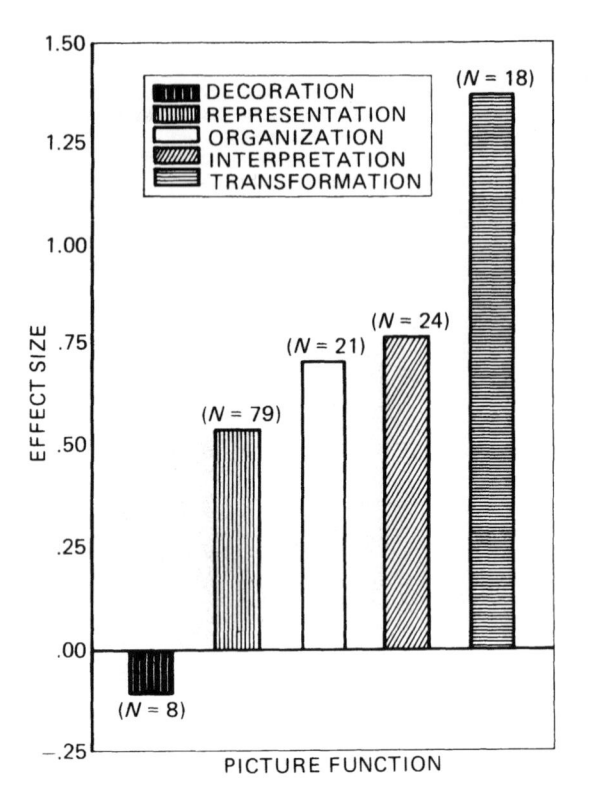

FIGURE 2.11. Average effect size by picture function, across all units.

Across the 142 text-relevant units, the average effect size produced was equal to 0.71, which is somewhat larger than the 0.55 value reported by Levie and Lentz. It should be noted, however, that the Levie and Lentz value was based on considerably fewer units ($N = 46$). As will be seen shortly, a major contributing factor to the larger present value is our inclusion of the 18 transformational picture units (not included by Levie and Lentz). Other differences associated with the Levie and Lentz meta-analysis are that their units were restricted to conditions that employed actual illustrations (rather than both illustrations and imagery) in pure reading (rather than both reading and listening) situations and that some of their units consisted of dependent variables that assessed something other than students' memory for prose content (the target variable here). Despite all these differences, however, the two independently conducted meta-analyses seem to yield reasonably consistent average effect-size estimates.

Function Effects

Concerning the effects of text-relevant pictures, we refer again to the summary data presented in Figure 2.11. As was anticipated from the much smaller set of empirical studies available at the time of Levin's (1981b) review, increasing effect sizes can be seen as one progresses from (a) representational pictures through (b) organizational and interpretational pictures to (c) transformational pictures. Levin posited these to be "moderate," "moderate to substantial," and "substantial," respectively. Given that an effect size of about 0.5 within-group standard-deviation units is regarded by some as "medium" and an effect size larger than 0.8 standard-deviation units is regarded as "large" (Cohen, 1977), Levin's previous speculations appear to be not too far from the empirical "truth." Interestingly, the between-unit variability in effect sizes is quite similar from one picture function to the next, with standard deviations ranging from 0.48 to 0.55.

Function Effects by Processing Mode and Subject Population

The same function profile is produced when the data are further broken down by processing mode (reading vs. listening). Although relative to reading the listening mode is associated with a slightly higher effect-size estimate for each function (ranging from 0.06 to 0.29 standard-deviation units), each processing mode's ordering of picture-function means is the same. With respect to subject populations, text-relevant pictures produce an average effect size of at least half a standard deviation, ranging from 0.50 ($N = 65$) for children given representational pictures to 1.43 ($N = 15$) for children given transformational pictures. The corresponding older-subject means for representational and transformational pictures are, respectively, 0.75 ($N = 9$) and 1.04 ($N = 3$). The children's data ($N = 99$) nicely reproduce the overall function profile, whereas the data from the much smaller ($N = 37$) older-subject sample do not. Attempting to account for these profile differences is a difficult task, however, as a result of potentially important differences in the kind of prose and pictures typically used in studies with older and younger subjects (see our previous caveats about natural confoundings).

Function Effects by Picture Type

The primary reason for more closely examining the effect sizes associated with the different functions was to assess the validity of Levin's (1981b) distinction between "pictures as illustrations" and "pictures as imagery." Focusing on representational pictures, he argued that even though experimenter-provided *illustrations* had been found repeatedly to produce positive prose-learning effects, subject-generated *visual imagery* had not. That is, the literature at the time suggested that in contrast to the consistently positive effects associated with prose-learning illustrations, representational-imagery instructions (instructions to subjects to visualize the characters and events of concrete, well-organized prose passages) often proved not to be beneficial.

Several explanations for this outcome could be offered, but the most parsimonious one was that internally generated representational images do not add much in the way of concreteness to an already concrete passage. Yet, if true, why then should representational illustrations be beneficial? By virtue of their being externalized (i.e., on the page), they are generally better structured, more concretely represented, and therefore more reliably processed than the analogous internal representations (in the head). As a result, representational illustrations should consistently facilitate students' prose learning, whereas representational images should not.

Such distinctly different levels of prose-learning facilitation might not be expected of the other picture types, however. With specific regard to transformational pictures, by virtue of their capitalizing on specially designed techniques for improving content-specific memory, transformational pictures should produce prose-learning facilitation that is "substantial" irrespective of whether the pictures are defined by experimenter-provided illustrations or subject-generated visual imagery. The across-study data available at the time of Levin's (1981b) review were consistent with that position. Moreover, the two empirical studies that have directly tested the "representational vs. transformational picture" distinction provide strong support for it (Peters, Levin, McGivern, & Pressley, 1985; Shriberg, Levin, McCormick, & Pressley, 1982, Experiment 3).

Our meta-analysis data bearing on picture-function by picture-type differences are presented in Figures 2.12 and 2.13. The present breakdown involves only exclusively experimenter-provided illustrations and exclusively subject-

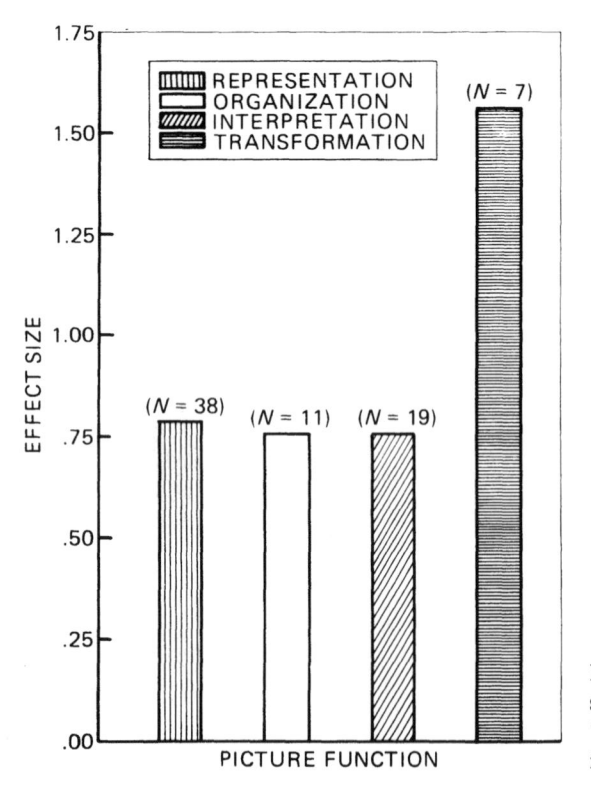

FIGURE 2.12. Average Effect size by picture function, for "pictures" defined by actual illustrations.

FIGURE 2.13. Average effect size by picture function, for "pictures" defined by visual imagery instructions.

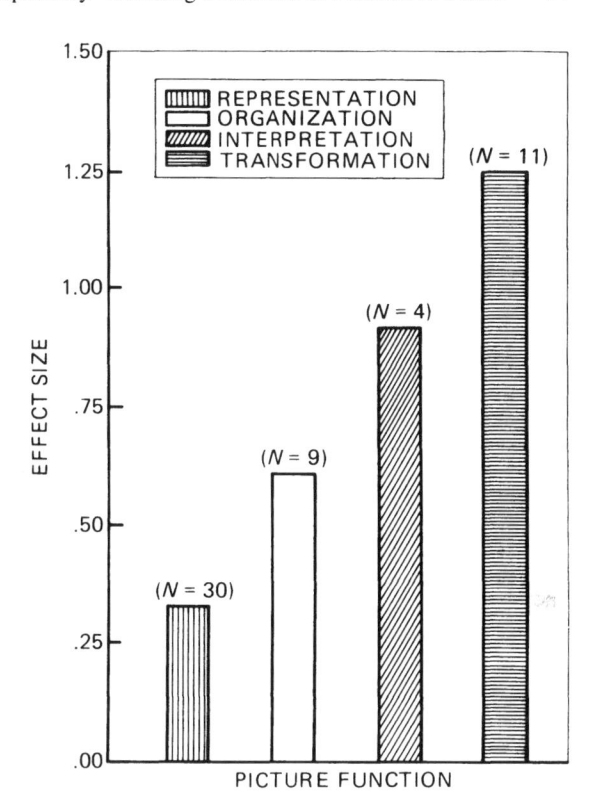

generated imagery. The 13 units encompassing features of both experimenter-provided and subject-generated pictures, such as those based on experimenter-provided "partial" pictures (e.g., Guttmann, Levin, & Pressley, 1977; Pressley & Miller, Chapter 3, this volume) and subject-generated drawings (e.g., Snowman & Cunningham, 1975) or constructions (e.g., Lesgold, Levin, Shimron, & Guttmann, 1975), are not included here.

For pictures as illustrations (Figure 2.12), all four functions exhibit at least moderate degrees of facilitation. The effect size associated with the transformational function (more than 1.50 standard-deviation units) is clearly substantial. Of particular interest to the present discussion, the effect size associated with representational illustrations is also reasonably large (amounting to more than 0.75 standard-deviation units)—as large, in fact, as that associated with the two other text-relevant picture functions (organization and interpretation). Thus, there is no denying that representational pictures *as illustrations* are effective prose-learning facilitators.

But what of representational pictures *as images*? The picture changes if one looks at Figure 2.13. Again we see substantial facilitation associated with transformational pictures (1.25 standard-deviation units) and at least moderate facilitation resulting from organizational and interpretational pictures (about 0.60 and 0.90 standard-deviation units, respectively). However, the facilitation produced by representational pictures is considerably diminished, amounting to a modest one-third of a standard-deviation unit. In terms of the present *functional* significance, even if the representational-imagery effect were associated with *statistical* significance it is too small to be of any *educational* significance. On the basis of such data, many people *would* deny that representational images are effective prose-learning facilitators. The same cannot be denied for organizational interpretational, and (especially) transformational images.

COMMENT

We conclude this section by making an important point about the picture-function profiles that were anticipated, and subsequently confirmed, in our meta-analysis. Some might be tempted to interpret the increasing amounts of picture facilitation in Figure 2.11 strictly in terms of increasing passage complexity. That is, more prose-learning facilitation was observed with picture functions that are associated with more complex text types.

We think that this is a mistake, for several reasons. First, concerning just the representation, organization, and interpretation functions, one must assume that their associated text complexities increase in that order. But who is to say that a science test presented to a college student is any more "complex" than a narrative passage presented to an educationally handicapped child? Given comparable mean levels and variability of performance in these two different samples, the *relative* complexities may well be the same. Second, one must remember that although most of the representational pictures accompanied narrative texts in studies with children, in studies with older subjects representational pictures often accompanied not-so-simple expository texts. Some of these texts were quite comparable to those accompanied by organizational or interpretational pictures. It was just that the *kinds* of picture presented differed for the different functions. Third, although the three just-mentioned picture functions exhibit an increasing average effect size in Figure 2.11, recall that the data there represent a composite of illustration and imagery studies. In Figure 2.12, where only the illustration studies are considered, the average effect sizes associated with the three functions are virtually identical. How can this be explained in terms of text complexity? Finally, how does one account for the superiority of the transformation function, for both illustrations (Figure 2.12) and imagery (Figure 2.13), relative to the three other functions? Does a series of town/attribute passages such as the one presented in Figure 2.9 seem more complex than the ecology passage of Figure 2.7? Unless "complexity" and "memorability" are being used interchangeably, we think not.

As can be seen in all these examples, if one wishes to propose text complexity as a rival explanation of function effects, one would have to do a very thorough job of defining exactly what is meant by "complexity."

An Analysis of the Meta-Analysis: Prescriptions and Proscriptions

Ten Commandments of Picture Facilitation

We knew something about the properties of effective prose-learning pictures before we conducted our functional meta-analysis. After having conducted it, we believe we know more. In this section, we summarize some of these beliefs in a set of "Ten Commandments" for maximizing one's chance of obtaining picture facilitation. Our commandments are heavily function-based and reflect the conditions under which pictures are and are not likely to facilitate students' learning of prose content. In differentiating between empirically documented "success" and "failure" conditions, the commandments focus on potential remedies that logically follow from the failures.

1. *Pictures shalt be judiciously applied to text, to remember it wholly.* This is the fundamental pictures-in-prose commandment, from which all others evolve. Note that it circumscribes the conditions defined "in the beginning," namely, that we are focusing here on pictures as facilitators of students' *learning of prose content*. To enlist pictures for different purposes, one would have to generate a different set of commandments.
2. *Pictures shalt honor the text.* As was stated at the outset, and as was empirically confirmed by a decorational-picture average effect size of -0.11, pictures that are not relevant to the text content will not facilitate one's learning of that content. "Relevance" in this context does not require either a one-to-one "correspondence" or a physical "resemblance." With respect to a correspondence, pictures capturing just the critical aspects of to-be-remembered facts and themes have been used effectively (e.g., Levin & Berry, 1980), as have partial pictures that leave something to the reader's imagination (see Pressley & Miller, Chapter 3, this volume). Regarding resemblance, transformational (mnemonic) pictures were found to be the most potent prose-learning facilitators of all (average effect size = 1.37), and they most certainly do *not* constitute veridical representations of the text content (see Figures 2.9 and 2.10). In contrast to decorational pictures, however, transformational pictures are *text relevant*. They contain recoded information that, when later decoded, provides the student with a direct link with the to-be-remembered text content.
3. *Pictures shalt not bear false fitness to the text.* Pictures that logically *conflict with* the text content (mismatched pictures) are extreme counterinstances of pictures that honor the text and might best be redressed in this corollary to Commandment 2. Although excluded from the present meta-analysis, in over a dozen experiments in which mismatched pictures have been subjected to scrutiny they have never been associated with prose-learning *facilitation*. At best, their effects have been null; at worst, they have depressed students'

prose-learning performance. Although potentially interesting from a theoretical standpoint (e.g., see Peeck, Chapter 4, this volume), from the perspective of our facilitation commandments such "depressing" pictures must be publicly castigated and exiled for at least 40 years.

4. *Pictures shalt not be used in the presence of "heavenly" bodies of prose.* When students read an unillustrated prose passage without having been given imagery-generation instructions, and they achieve extremely high levels of prose-learning performance, that particular passage should be deemed unsuitable for detecting picture facilitation. Of course, such a condition can be interpreted more technically as a "ceiling" effect being present in the no-picture control condition, which strongly precludes the possibility of obtaining a positive picture effect. The bottom line is simply that concrete, easy-to-follow, highly memorable prose passages do not require the addition of pictures to enhance their memorability. Yet, despite sounding simple enough, a review of the literature suggests that this commandment was apparently lost on a number of investigators who included ceiling-produced passages in their pictures-in-prose studies.

5. *Pictures shalt not be used with text cravin' for images.* This commandment is really a subcommandment of the fourth but is nonetheless accorded full commandment status because it pertains exclusively to "pictures as images" situations. When a prose passage is so concrete and image evoking that it is likely to elicit *spontaneous* visual imagery in its readers, then an experimenter's instructions to employ a visual-imagery strategy are superfluous and, in some cases, may even inhibit students' fluent prose processing (e.g., when unskilled readers need to allocate all their attention to the business of comprehending what they are reading). This, in part, accounts for the tiny positive effect associated with representational imagery in our meta-analysis (0.33).

6. *Pictures shalt not be prepared in vain.* While on the subject of students' skill-level differences, two additional commandments come to mind. Commandment 6 relates to the prerequisite capabilities of picture *users* (students provided with illustrations), whereas Commandment 7 addresses the prerequisite skills of picture *generators* (students constructing internal images). With respect to the former, students who are required to read a text passage must possess adequate word-decoding and word-recognition skills in order for illustrations to have a chance to "work." Undoubtedly, some of the negligible "illustration" effects appearing in the literature have resulted from the administration of reading passages to students deficient in basic reading skills (e.g., Harber, 1983; Rose & Robinson, 1984; Warner & Alley, 1981). As was noted earlier, prose-learning illustrations are intended as a supplement to processed text (making it more concrete, coherent, comprehensible, or memorable), rather than as a substitute for unprocessed text. Unless the illustrations provided are so self-contained that they permit a total text bypass, picture failures in the presence of word-reading failures should be neither disturbing nor surprising. Note that similar picture failures would

not be expected—and, in fact, have not materialized—when illustrations accompany *orally* presented prose passages (e.g., Levin & Lesgold, 1978).
7. *Pictures shalt be faithfully created from generation to generation.* With respect to Commandment 7, generating effective images while reading also requires that one must be able to read. This seemingly elementary precept was first demonstrated by Levin (1973) and then cleverly extended in a recent study by Evans and Kerst (1983). In the latter study, children deficient in both comprehension and word-reading skills did not benefit from instructions to apply an organizational visual-imagery strategy to a passage they were reading. However, when the vocabulary of the original passage was modified (viz., simplified to the point of producing adequate word decoding and word recognition in the children), benefits of the instructed visual-imagery strategy became quite apparent.

Other manifestations of Commandment 7 abuse include (a) assuming that all students are adept at generating images, when it is known that all students (and especially young children) are not (e.g., Levin, 1976; and Pressley, 1977), and (b) assuming that students are able to decide for themselves which text elements should and should not be included in their images. Given the now-extensive literature documenting that young children and other unskilled readers are not always able to differentiate between important and unimportant text information (e.g., Forrest-Pressley, MacKinnon, & Waller, 1985), this and other uncharted *metacognitive* aspects of prose-learning imagery deserve research attention.
8. *Pictures shalt not be adulterated.* Pictures differ not only in their relevance, but in other characteristics as well. For example, line drawings vary along such dimensions as artistic quality and abstractness. All pictures vary in their complexity. There is good reason to believe that effective prose-learning pictures are those that are clear and interpretable. Unfortunately, this belief cannot easily be validated on the basis of our meta-analysis. Authors typically do not provide complete picture sets and/or their terribly "sketchy" picture details are not sufficient. However, we have seen examples of pictures from studies associated with little or no prose-learning facilitation. When considering picture "quality," one would not be surprised by the negative outcomes of those studies. More objective suggestive evidence comes from research where it has been found that students' ability to interpret a visual illustration or diagram is critical to their benefiting from its inclusion (e.g., Guri, 1985; Higgins, 1980). Thus, we feel quite comfortable in recommending that pictures should be understood if they and their associated text content are to be remembered.
9. *Pictures shalt be appreciated for the art they art.* Our purview of "pictures" encompasses both photographs and true *pictorial* representations. It does not encompass *figural* representations, such as graphs and charts (Winn, Chapter 5, this volume). Making blanket generalizations from one "picture" class to the other is a serious mistake, in our view, and the literature bears this out. Much smaller effects are associated with the figural class of

provided adjuncts than with the pictorial class. In two recent studies, for example, we found that neither educationally handicapped nor nonhandicapped middle-school students benefited *at all* from the provision of a figural taxonomy designed to organize the names and associated attributes of minerals presented in the context of a science lesson (Levin, Morrison, McGivern, Mastropieri, & Scruggs, 1986; Scruggs, Mastropieri, McLoone, Levin, & Morrison, in press). In striking contrast, the provision of transformational illustrations *did* facilitate students' learning of that content. Relative to the text-relevant pictorial-illustration studies included in our meta-analysis, the excluded text-relevant figural-illustration studies were consistently less impressive in their ability to produce prose-learning benefits.

10. *Pictures shalt be made to perform their appropriate functions.* The final commandment summarizes the message of this chapter: The amount of prose-learning facilitation to be expected is a "function" of the pictures selected. In several studies that we encountered during our meta-analysis, researchers who claimed to be interested in increasing students' prose learning selected pictures and picture strategies that represented function mismatches. The most blatant mismatch, of course, was the use of text-irrelevant decorational pictures, but there were others as well. Sometimes pictures illustrated material that was only weakly connected to the text, or material that was never assessed in subsequently administered test items.

In other cases, simple representational or organizational pictures were selected to illustrate text content that was difficult to understand or remember (i.e., text that called for interpretational or transformational pictures). One example of this type of function mismatch is given by the Levin et al. (1986) and Scruggs et al. (in press) figural taxonomies mentioned in Commandment 9. Although providing a hierarchical organization of the text content, taxonomic figures did not help students remember that content. Another example is provided by Levin et al. (1983) in their study based on a series of town/attribute passages (see Figure 2.9). In an organizational-picture condition, students viewed an illustration that provided a coherent organization for the attributes of each town. For the *Fostoria* passage, for instance, the organizational illustration was identical to the transformational illustration of Figure 2.9, with the single exception that the frost/snow theme was not incorporated. Consistent with the assumption that the mnemonic theme is critical when several sets of attributes and towns must be associated, organizational pictures generally did not help students remember which towns went with which attributes. This was true even though such pictures *did* help the students remember which attributes went together (because the pictures integrated each set of attributes in a meaningful scene). Thus, in these two examples something more than a figural taxonomy or an integrated pictorial scene was necessary to elevate students' recall of prose-embedded facts.

An important point that is subsumed by this final commandment is that a particular function is not always what meets the eye. Consider, for example, representational pictures in narrative passages. Although these may be characterized as pictorial "redundancies" of a text for skilled readers, for less-skilled readers they are likely something else. In the case of a student with poor decoding skills, such pictures are better characterized as "replacements" than as redundancies. More interestingly, for present purposes, for students who can decode and identify the individual words within a passage but who lack the ability to organize the separate pieces into a coherent whole, representational pictures may well function the same way that organizational pictures do for skilled readers processing poorly organized text (e.g., Levin, 1973). In this case, then, one student's representational picture becomes another's organizational picture. An analogous argument can be made with respect to the interpretational function, where novices in a particular domain (i.e., those who are not fluent with the domain's technical terms and concepts) are likely to receive more interpretation than representation from an illustration such as Figure 2.7, whereas the reverse might be true for nonnovices.

... And a Postscription

Humorous (hopefully!) commandments aside, the moral of this exercise is simply that prose-learning pictures must be developed with both specific picture functions and picture recipients in mind. Otherwise, both will fall short of performance expectations. On the basis of the present functional analysis, we can safely assume that all types of text-relevant picture facilitate students' prose learning to some degree, ranging from an effect size of about 0.5 standard deviations for representational pictures to over 1.33 standard deviations for transformational pictures (see Figure 2.11).

These data also indicate that even though pictures serving "conventional" functions (representation, organization, and interpretation) are facilitative, pictures serving an "unconventional" function (transformation) can be even more facilitative. Of course, we are not so foolish as to offer a universal endorsement of transformational pictures in all prose-learning contexts, for they are optimally suited to the efficient storage and retrieval of text-embedded *factual information*. At the same time, we hope that others are not so foolish as to endorse their universal exclusion either, especially when enhancing students' processing of factual information is one's stated objective. Although some might question that objective, they cannot ignore the empirical evidence bearing on transformational-picture efficacy.

Acknowledgments. The first author's contribution was supported in part by a grant from the National Institute of Education, through the Wisconsin Center for Education Research, and by a Romnes Faculty Fellowship from the Graduate School of the University of Wisconsin. We are grateful to Beverly Dretzke and Michele Stewart for their assistance with the meta-analysis and to Lynn Sowle for typing the manuscript.

References

Alesandrini, K. L., & Rigney, J. W. (1981). Pictorial presentation and review strategies in science learning. *Journal of Research in Science Teaching, 18,* 465-474.

Anglin, G. J. (in press). Prose-relevant pictures and older learners' recall of written prose. *Educational Communication and Technology Journal.*

Arnold, D. J., & Brooks, P. H. (1976). Influence of contextual organizing material on children's listening comprehension. *Journal of Educational Psychology, 68,* 711-716.

Ausubel, D. P. (1963). *The psychology of meaningful verbal learning.* New York: Grune & Stratton.

Bellezza, F. S. (1981). Mnemonic devices: Classification, characteristics, and criteria. *Review of Educational Research, 51,* 247-275.

Bender, B. G., & Levin, J. R. (1978). Pictures, imagery, and retarded children's prose learning. *Journal of Educational Psychology, 70,* 583-588.

Bransford, J. D., & Johnson, M. K. (1972). Contextual prerequisites for understanding: Some investigations of comprehension and recall. *Journal of Verbal Learning and Verbal Behavior, 11,* 717-726.

Cohen, J. (1977). *Statistical power analysis for the behavioral sciences* (2nd ed.). New York: Academic Press.

Davidson, R. E. (1976). The role of metaphor and analogy in learning. In J. R. Levin & V. L. Allen (Eds.), *Cognitive learning in children: Theories and strategies* (pp. 135-162). New York: Academic Press.

Dean, R. S., & Kulhavy, R. W. (1981). The influence of spatial organization in prose learning. *Journal of Educational Psychology, 73,* 57-64.

Duchastel, P., & Waller, R. (1979). Pictorial illustration in instructional texts. *Educational Technology, 19,* 20-25.

Dwyer, F. M., Jr. (1967). The relative effectiveness of varied visual illustrations in complementing programmed instruction. *Journal of Experimental Education, 36,* 34-42.

Evans, R. A., & Kerst, S. M. (1983, April). *The effects of induced imagery and imposed synonyms upon prose comprehension.* Paper presented at the annual meeting of the American Educational Research Association, Montreal.

Forrest-Pressley, D. L., MacKinnon, G. E., & Waller, T. G. (Eds.). (1985). *Metacognition, cognition, and human performance* (Vol. 1). New York: Academic Press.

Glass, G. V. (1976). Primary, secondary, and meta-analysis of research. *Educational Researcher, 5,* 3-8.

Guri, S. (1985, March-April). *The function of diagrams in learning from social science self-study texts.* Paper presented at the annual meeting of the American Educational Research Association, Chicago.

Guttmann, J., Levin, J. R., & Pressley, M. (1977). Pictures, partial pictures, and young children's oral prose learning. *Journal of Educational Psychology, 69,* 473-480.

Harber, J. R. (1983). The effects of illustrations on the reading performance of learning disabled and normal children. *Learning Disability Quarterly, 6,* 55-60.

Haring, M. J., & Fry, M. A. (1979). Effect of pictures on children's comprehension of written text. *Educational Communication and Technology, 27,* 185-190.

Higgins, L. C. (1980). Literalism in the young child's interpretation of pictures. *Educational Communication and Technology, 28,* 99-119.

Lesgold, A. M., Levin, J. R., Shimron, J., & Guttmann, J. (1975). Pictures and young children's learning from oral prose. *Journal of Educational Psychology, 67,* 636-642.

Levie, W. H., & Lentz, R. (1982). Effects of text illustrations: A review of research. *Educational Communication and Technology Journal, 30,* 195-232.
Levin, J. R. (1972). Comprehending what we read: An outsider looks in. *Journal of Reading Behavior, 4,* 18-28.
Levin, J. R. (1973). Inducing comprehension in poor readers: A test of a recent model. *Journal of Educational Psychology, 65,* 19-24.
Levin, J. R. (1976). What have we learned about maximizing what children learn? In J. R. Levin & V. L. Allen (Eds.), *Cognitive learning in children: Theories and strategies* (pp. 105-134). New York: Academic Press.
Levin, J. R. (1981). The mnemonic '80s: Keywords in the classroom. *Educational Psychologist, 16,* 65-82. (a)
Levin, J. R. (1981). On the functions of pictures in prose. In F. J. Pirozzolo & M. C. Wittrock (Eds.), *Neuropsychological and cognitive processes in reading* (pp. 203-228). New York: Academic Press. (b)
Levin, J. R. (1982). Pictures as prose-learning devices. In A. Flammer & W. Kinstch (Eds.), *Discourse processing* (pp. 412-444). Amsterdam: North-Holland.
Levin, J. R. (1983). Pictorial strategies for school learning: Practical illustrations. In M. Pressley & J. R. Levin (Eds.), *Cognitive strategy research: Educational applications* (pp. 213-237). New York: Springer-Verlag.
Levin, J. R. (1985). Educational applications of mnemonic pictures: Possibilities beyond your wildest imagination. In A. A. Sheikh (Ed.), *Imagery in education: Imagery in the educational process* (pp. 68-87). Farmingdale, NH: Baywood.
Levin, J. R., & Berry, J. K. (1980). Children's learning of all the news that's fit to picture. *Educational Communication and Technology Journal, 28,* 177-185.
Levin, J. R., & Lesgold, A. M. (1978). On pictures in prose. *Educational Communication and Technology Journal, 26,* 233-243.
Levin, J. R., Morrison, C. R., McGivern, J. E., Mastropieri, M. A., & Scruggs, T. E. (1986). Mnemonic facilitation of text-embedded science facts. *American Educational Research Journal, 23,* 489-506.
Levin, J. R., & Pressley, M. (1981). Improving children's prose comprehension: Selected strategies that seem to succeed. In C. M. Santa & B. L. Hayes (Eds.), *Children's prose comprehension: Research and practice* (pp. 44-71). Newark, DE: International Reading Association.
Levin, , J. R., Shriberg, L. K., & Berry, J. K. (1983). A concrete strategy for remembering abstract prose. *American Educational Research Journal, 20,* 277-290.
Mayer, R. E., & Bromage, B. K. (1980). Different recall protocols for technical texts due to advance organizers. *Journal of Educational Psychology, 72,* 209-225.
Otto, W., White, S., & Camperell, K. (1980, October). *Text comprehension research to classroom application: A progress report* (Theoretical Paper No. 87). Madison: University of Wisconsin, Wisconsin Research and Development Center for Individualized Schooling.
Peters, E. E., & Levin, J. R. (1986). Effects of a mnemonic imagery strategy on good and poor readers' prose recall. *Reading Research Quarterly, 21,* 179-192.
Peters, E. E., Levin, J. R., McGivern, J. E., & Pressley, M. (1985). Further comparison of representational and transformational prose-learning imagery. *Journal of Educational Psychology, 77,* 129-136.
Pressley, M. (1977). Imagery and children's learning: Putting the picture in developmental perspective. *Review of Educational Research, 47,* 585-622.
Pressley, M., Levin, J. R., & Delaney, H. D. (1982). The mnemonic keyword method. *Review of Educational Research, 52,* 61-91.

Pressley, M., Levin, J. R., Pigott, S., LeComte, M., & Hope, D. J. (1983). Mismatched pictures and children's prose learning. *Educational Communication and Technology Journal, 31*, 131–143.

Rasco, R. W., Tennyson, R. D., & Boutwell, R. C. (1975). Imagery instructions and drawings in learning prose. *Journal of Educational Psychology, 67*, 188–192.

Readence, J. E., & Moore, D. W. (1981). A meta-analytic review of the effect of adjunct pictures on reading comprehension. *Psychology in the Schools, 18*, 218–224.

Rohwer, W. D., Jr., & Harris, W. J. (1975). Media effects on prose learning in two populations of children. *Journal of Educational Psychology, 67*, 651–657.

Rose, T. L., & Robinson, H. H. (1984). Effects of illustrations on learning disabled students' reading performance. *Learning Disability Quarterly, 7*, 165–171.

Royer, J. M., & Cable, G. W. (1976). Illustrations, analogies, and facilitative transfer in prose learning. *Journal of Educational Psychology, 68*, 205–209.

Rusted, J., & Coltheart, M. (1979). Facilitation of children's prose recall by the presence of pictures. *Memory and Cognition, 7*, 354–359.

Samuels, S. J. (1970). Effects of pictures on learning to read, comprehension and attitudes. *Review of Educational Research, 40*, 397–407.

Schallert, D. L. (1980). The role of illustrations in reading comprehension. In R. J. Spiro, B. C. Bruce, & W. F. Brewer (Eds.), *Theoretical issues in reading comprehension: Perspectives from cognitive psychology, linguistics, artificial intelligence, and education* (pp. 503–524). Hillsdale, NJ: Erlbaum.

Scruggs, T. E., Mastropieri, M. A., McLoone, B., Levin, J. R., & Morrison, C. R. (in press). Mnemonic facilitation of learning-disabled students' memory for expository prose. *Journal of Educational Psychology*.

Shriberg, L. K., Levin, J. R., McCormick, C. B., & Pressley, M. (1982). Learning about "famous" people via the keyword method. *Journal of Educational Psychology, 74*, 238–247.

Snowman, J., & Cunningham, D. J. (1975). A comparison of pictorial and written adjunct aids in learning from text. *Journal of Educational Psychology, 67*, 307–311.

Stone, D. E., & Glock, M. D. (1981). How do young adults read directions with and without pictures? *Journal of Educational Psychology, 73*, 419–426.

Warner, M. M., & Alley, G. R. (1981). *Teaching learning disabled junior high students to use visual imagery as a strategy for facilitating recall of reading passages* (Research Rep. No. 49). Lawrence, KS: The University of Kansas, Institute for Research in Learning Disabilities.

Willows, D. M. (1978). A picture is not always worth a thousand words: Pictures as distractors in reading. *Journal of Educational Psychology, 70*, 255–262.

Willows, D. M. (1979). *A distorted picture of "The effects of pictures on rate of learning sight words."* Unpublished manuscript, University of Waterloo, Department of Psychology, Waterloo, Ontario.

Willows, D. M. (1980, April). *Effects of picture salience on reading comprehension of illustrated and non-illustrated aspects of text*. Paper presented at the annual meeting of the American Educational Research Association, Boston.

Appendix: Studies Included in the Meta-Analysis

Alesandrini, K. L. (1981). Pictorial-verbal and analytic-holistic learning strategies in science learning. *Journal of Educational Psychology, 73*, 358–368.

Alesandrini, K. L., & Rigney, J. W. (1981). Pictorial presentation and review strategies in science learning. *Journal of Research in Science Teaching, 18*, 465-474.

Anderson, R. C., & Kulhavy, R. W. (1972). Imagery and prose learning. *Journal of Educational Psychology, 63*, 242-243.

Anglin, G. J. (in press). Prose-relevant pictures and older learners' recall of written prose. *Educational Communication and Technology Journal*.

Arnold, D. J., & Brooks, P. H. (1976). Influence of contextual organizing material on children's listening comprehension. *Journal of Educational Psychology, 68*, 711-716.

Bender, B. G., & Levin, J. R. (1978). Pictures, imagery, and retarded children's prose learning. *Journal of Educational Psychology, 70*, 583-588.

Bernard, R. M., Petersen, C. H., & Ally, M. (1981). Can images provide contextual support for prose? *Educational Communication and Technology Journal, 29*, 101-108.

Borges, M. A., & Robins, S. L. (1980). Contextual and motivational cue effects on the comprehension and recall of prose. *Psychological Reports, 47*, 263-268.

Boutwell, R. C., Low, W. C., & Hughes, J. (1973). *Imagery directions and relevant drawings in a prose learning task.* Unpublished manuscript, Bucknell University, Lewisburg, PA.

Bransford, J. D., & Johnson, M. K. (1972). Contextual prerequisites for understanding: Some investigations of comprehension and recall. *Journal of Verbal Learning and Verbal Behavior, 11*, 717-726.

Cunningham, D. J., Snowman, J., Miller, R. B., & Perry, F. L. (1982). Verbal and nonverbal adjunct aids to concrete and abstract prose learning. *Journal of Experimental Education, 51*, 8-13.

Dean, R. S., & Kulhavy, R. W. (1981). The influence of spatial organization in prose learning. *Journal of Educational Psychology, 73*, 57-64.

DeRose, T. M. (1976). *The effects of verbally and pictorially induced and imposed strategies on children's reading comprehension.* Unpublished doctoral dissertation, University of Wisconsin, Madison.

Digdon, N., Pressley, M., & Levin, J. R. (1985). Preschoolers' learning when pictures do not tell the whole story. *Educational Communication and Technology Journal, 33*, 139-145.

Dillingofski, M. S. (1980). *The effects of imposed and induced visual imagery strategies on ninth grade difference-poor readers' literal comprehension of concrete and abstract prose.* Unpublished doctoral dissertation, University of Wisconsin, Department of Curriculum and Instruction, Madison.

Donald, D. R. (1983). The use and value of illustrations as contextual information for readers at different progress and developmental levels. *British Journal of Educational Psychology, 53*, 175-185.

Duchastel, P. C. (1980). *Research on illustrations in instructional texts* (Occasional Paper 3). Bryn Mawr, PA: The American College.

Dunham, T., & Levin, J. R. (1979). Imagery instructions and young children's prose learning: No evidence of "support." *Contemporary Educational Psychology, 4*, 107-113.

Dwyer, F. M., Jr. (1967). Adapting visual illustrations for effective learning. *Harvard Educational Review, 37*, 250-263. (a)

Dwyer, F. M., Jr. (1967). The relative effectiveness of varied visual illustrations in complementing programed instruction. *Journal of Experimental Education, 36*, 34-42. (b)

Dwyer, F. M., Jr. (1969). The effect of varying the amount of realistic detail in visual illustrations designed to complement programmed instruction. *Programmed Learning, 6*, 147-153.

Evans, R. A., & Kerst, S. M. (1983, April). *The effects of induced imagery and imposed synonyms upon prose comprehension.* Paper presented at the annual meeting of the American Educational Research Association, Montreal.

Gambrell, L. B. (1981). *Induced mental imagery and the text prediction performance of first and third graders.* Paper presented at the annual National Reading Conference, Dallas.

Gambrell, L. B., & Koskinen, P. S. (1982, March). *Mental imagery and the reading comprehension of below average readers: Situational variables and sex differences.* Paper presented at the annual meeting of the American Educational Research Association, New York.

Goldberg, F. (1974). Effects of imagery on learning incidental material in the classroom. *Journal of Educational Psychology, 66,* 233–237.

Goldston, D. B., & Richman, C. L. (1985). The effect of partial pictures and imagery instructions on the recall of young children. *Journal of Experimental Child Psychology, 40,* 395–405.

Guttmann, J., Levin, J. R., & Pressley, M. (1977). Pictures, partial pictures, and young children's oral prose learning. *Journal of Educational Psychology, 69,* 473–480.

Haring, M. J., & Fry, M. A. (1979). Effect of pictures on children's comprehension of written text. *Educational Communication and Technology Journal, 27,* 185–190.

Hayes, D. A., & Readence, J. E. (1982, March). *Transfer of learning from illustration dependent text.* Paper presented at the annual meeting of the American Educational Research Association, New York.

Heckler, J. H. (1975). *Some factors in the comprehension of prose materials.* Unpublished doctoral dissertation, University of Wisconsin, Madison.

Hempstead, J. O. (1973). *Media and the learner: The influence of media-message components on students' recall and attitudes toward the learning experience.* Unpublished doctoral dissertation, University of Wisconsin, Madison.

Holliday, W. G. (1975). The effects of verbal and adjunct pictorial–verbal information in science instruction. *Journal of Research in Science Teaching, 12,* 77–83.

Holliday, W. G., & Harvey, D. A. (1976). Adjunct labeled drawings in teaching physics to junior high school students. *Journal of Research in Science Teaching, 13,* 37–43.

Jahoda, G., Cheyne, W. M., Deregowski, J. B., Sinha, D., & Collingbourne, R. (1976). Utilization of pictorial information in classroom learning: A cross-cultural study. *AV Communication Review, 24,* 295–315.

Johnson, H. E. (1975). *A developmental study of imagery and oral prose comprehension.* Unpublished honors thesis, Department of Psychology, University of Minnesota.

Koskinen, P. S., & Gambrell, L. B. (1979, November). *The effects of induced visual imagery upon the reading comprehension of below average readers.* Paper presented at the National Reading Conference, San Antonio.

Kulhavy, R. W., & Swenson, I. (1975). Imagery instructions and the comprehension of text. *British Journal of Educational Psychology, 45,* 47–51.

Lesgold, A. M., DeGood, H., & Levin, J. R. (1977). Pictures and young children's prose learning: A supplementary report. *Journal of Reading Behavior, 9,* 353–360.

Lesgold, A. M., Levin, J. R., Shimron, J., & Guttmann, J. (1975). Pictures and young children's learning from oral prose. *Journal of Educational Psychology, 67,* 636–642.

Lesgold, A. M., McCormick, C., & Golinkoff, R. M. (1975). Imagery training and children's prose learning. *Journal of Educational Psychology, 67,* 663–667.

Levin, J. R. (1973). Inducing comprehension in poor readers: A test of a recent model. *Journal of Educational Psychology, 65,* 19–24.

Levin, J. R., Bender, B. G., & Lesgold, A. M. (1976). Pictures, repetition, and young children's oral prose learning. *AV Communication Review, 24*, 367-380.

Levin, J. R., & Berry, J. K. (1980). Children's learning of all the news that's fit to picture. *Educational Communication and Technology Journal, 28*, 177-185.

Levin, J. R., & Divine-Hawkins, P. (1974). Visual imagery as a prose-learning process. *Journal of Reading Behavior, 6*, 23-30.

Levin, J. R., Divine-Hawkins, P., Kerst, S., & Guttmann, J. (1974). Individual differences in learning from pictures and words: The development and application of an instrument. *Journal of Educational Psychology, 66*, 296-303.

Levin, J. R., Morrison, C. R., McGivern, J. E., Mastropieri, M. A., & Scruggs, T. E. (1986). Mnemonic facilitation of text-embedded science facts. *American Educational Research Journal, 23*, 489-506.

Levin, J. R., Shriberg, L. K., & Berry, J. K. (1983). A concrete strategy for remembering abstract prose. *American Educational Research Journal, 20*, 277-290.

Maher, J. H., Jr., & Sullivan, H. (1982). Effects of mental imagery and oral and print stimuli on prose learning of intermediate grade children. *Educational Communication and Technology Journal, 30*, 175-183.

Main, R. E., & Griffiths, B. (1977). Evaluation of audio and pictorial instructional supplements. *AV Communication Review, 25*, 167-179.

McCormick, C. B., & Levin, J. R. (1984). A comparison of different prose-learning variations of the mnemonic keyword method. *American Educational Research Journal, 21*, 379-398.

McCormick, C. B., Levin, J. R., Cykowski, F., & Danilovics, P. (1984). Mnemonic-strategy reduction of prose-learning interference. *Educational Communication and Technology Journal, 32*, 145-152.

Miccinati, J. L. (1982). The influence of a six-week imagery training program on children's reading comprehension. *Journal of Reading Behavior, 14*, 197-203.

Nugent, G. C. (1982). Pictures, audio, and print: Symbolic representation and effect on learning. *Educational Communication and Technology Journal, 30*, 163-174.

Peeck, J. (1974). Retention of pictorial and verbal content of text with illustrations. *Journal of Educational Psychology, 66*, 880-888.

Peng, C.-Y., & Levin, J. R. (1979). Pictures and children's story recall: Some questions of durability. *Educational Communication and Technology Journal, 27*, 39-44.

Peters, E. E., & Levin, J. R. (1986). Effects of a mnemonic imagery strategy on good and poor readers' prose recall. *Reading Research Quarterly, 21*, 179-192.

Peters, E. E., Levin, J. R., McGivern, J. E., & Pressley, M. (1985). Further comparison of representational and transformational prose-learning imagery. *Journal of Educational Psychology, 77*, 129-136.

Petros, T., & Levin, S. R. (1980, April). *Influence of imagery instructions on prose comprehension in good and poor readers.* Paper presented at the annual meeting of the American Educational Research Association, Boston.

Pressley, G. M. (1976). Mental imagery helps eight-year-olds remember what they read. *Journal of Educational Psychology, 68*, 355-359.

Rasco, R. W., Tennyson, R. D., & Boutwell, R. C. (1975). Imagery instructions and drawings in learning prose. *Journal of Educational Psychology, 67*, 188-192.

Reid, D. J., Briggs, N., & Beveridge, M. (1983). The effect of picture upon the readability of a school science topic. *British Journal of Educational Psychology, 53*, 327-335.

Rice, D. R., Doan, R. L., & Brown, S. J. (1981). The effects of pictures on reading comprehension, speed and interest of second grade students. *Reading Improvement, 18*, 308-312.

Riding, R. J., & Shore, J. M. (1974). A comparison of two methods of improving prose comprehension in educationally subnormal children. *British Journal of Educational Psychology, 44,* 300-303.

Rigney, J. W., & Lutz, K. A. (1976). Effect of graphic analogies of concepts in chemistry on learning and attitude. *Journal of Educational Psychology, 68,* 305-311.

Rohwer, W. D., Jr., & Harris, W. J. (1975). Media effects on prose learning in two populations of children. *Journal of Educational Psychology, 67,* 651-657.

Rohwer, W. D., & Matz, R. D. (1975). Improving aural comprehension in white and black children. *Journal of Experimental Child Psychology, 19,* 23-36.

Rose, M. C., Cundick, B. P., & Higbee, K. L. (1983). Verbal rehearsal and visual imagery: Mnemonic aids for learning-disabled children. *Journal of Learning Disabilities, 16,* 352-354.

Royer, J. M., & Cable, G. W. (1976). Illustrations, analogies, and facilitative transfer in prose learning. *Journal of Educational Psychology, 68,* 205-209.

Ruch, M. D., & Levin, J. R. (1977). Pictorial organization versus verbal repetition of children's prose: Evidence for processing differences. *AV Communication Review, 25,* 269-280.

Ruch, M. D., & Levin, J. R. (1979). Partial pictures as imagery-retrieval cues in young children's prose recall. *Journal of Experimental Child Psychology, 28,* 268-279.

Rusted, J., & Coltheart, V. (1979). The effect of pictures on the retention of novel words and prose passages. *Journal of Experimental Child Psychology, 28,* 516-524. (a)

Rusted, J., & Coltheart, M. (1979). Facilitation of children's prose recall by the presence of pictures. *Memory & Cognition, 7,* 354-359. (b)

Schwartz, N. H., & Kulhavy, R. W. (1981). Map features and the recall of discourse. *Contemporary Educational Psychology, 6,* 151-158.

Sewell, E. H., & Moore, R. L. (1980). Cartoon embellishments in informative presentations. *Educational Communication and Technology Journal, 28,* 39-46.

Sherman, J. L. (1976). Contextual information and prose comprehension. *Journal of Reading Behavior, 8,* 369-379.

Shimron, J. (1974). *Imagery and the comprehension of prose by elementary school children.* Unpublished doctoral dissertation, University of Pittsburgh.

Shriberg, L. (1982). *Comparison of two mnemonic encoding strategies on children's recognition and recall of abstract prose information.* Unpublished doctoral dissertation, University of Wisconsin, Madison.

Shriberg, L. K., Levin, J. R., McCormick, C. B., & Pressley, M. (1982). Learning about "famous" people via the keyword method. *Journal of Educational Psychology, 74,* 238-247.

Silvern, S. B. (1980). Play, pictures, and repetition: Mediators in aural prose learning. *Educational Communication and Technology Journal, 28,* 134-139.

Small, M. Y., Dowling, S. B., & Lovett, S. B. (1981, April). *Semantic elaboration and children's recall of pictures and prose information.* Paper presented at the annual meeting of the American Educational Research Association, Los Angeles.

Snowman, J., & Cunningham, D. J. (1975). A comparison of pictorial and written adjunct aids in learning from text. *Journal of Educational Psychology, 67,* 307-311.

Snowman, J., Krebs, E. W., & Lockhart, L. (1980). Improving recall of information from prose in high-risk students through learning strategy training. *Journal of Instructional Psychology, 7,* 35-40.

Steingart, S. K., & Glock, M. D. (1979). Imagery and the recall of connected discourse. *Reading Research Quarterly, 15,* 66-83.

Thomas, J. L. (1978). The influence of pictorial illustrations with written text and previous achievement on the reading comprehension of fourth grade science students. *Journal of Research in Science Teaching, 15*, 401–405.

Triplett, D. (1980). *A test of two prose learning strategies: Imagery and paraphrase.* Unpublished doctoral dissertation, University of Wisconsin, Madison.

Warner, M. M., & Alley, G. R. (1981). *Teaching learning disabled junior high students to use visual imagery as a strategy for facilitating recall of reading passages* (Research Rep. No. 49). Lawrence, KS: The University of Kansas, Institute for Research in Learning Disabilities.

Willows, D. M. (1979, April). *Reading comprehension of illustrated and non-illustrated aspects of text.* Paper presented at the annual meeting of the American Educational Research Association, San Francisco.

3
Effects of Illustrations on Children's Listening Comprehension and Oral Prose Memory

MICHAEL PRESSLEY AND GLORIA E. MILLER

Introduction

It is important for children to acquire extensive knowledge about the world, because this knowledge base mediates a panorama of thinking and problem-solving encounters (Glaser, 1984). Thus, there have developed research programs in the area of children's learning that are aimed at developing ways to increase what children acquire from academic encounters (e.g., Brainerd, 1978; Levin, 1976). This chapter documents one approach that has been hypothesized to improve children's learning and memory—the illustration of meaningfully connected oral prose materials.

The main concerns in this chapter are a few very basic questions regarding the effects produced by representational pictures on children's prose learning. By representational pictures we mean ones that are redundant with at least part of the text (i.e., they visually represent the meaning of the text). Do such pictures assist learning of meaningful, connected materials? Are some types of representative illustration more potent than others? How do pictures enhance learning?

There is no doubt that the cognitive operations investigated in listening studies approximate an important situation in the world of children. Preschoolers hear stories while looking at pictures before they can read texts. In fact, many picture books are intended more for children to hear than for them to read! In addition, these studies of listening comprehension are purer tests of picture effects than are reading experiments which are covered in other chapters of this volume. From an experimental control point of view, studies of listening permit assessment of pictures effects on prose memory with children's reading/decoding skills removed as an influence. This is important because there are pronounced individual differences in decoding both between and within age levels during childhood. Before turning to the review of research, however, some background information will make more obvious why research resources should be diverted to the study of illustration effects on children's meaningful learning.

Motivation for Studying Picture Effects
Theoretical Concern

The most important motivation for conducting the research reviewed here was its relevance to theory, particularly Paivio's dual-coding approach to memory. Because of some persistent misperceptions about the theory and because of recent revisions in the framework itself, we briefly review the most current version of Paivio's (1986) position. We choose for emphasis those aspects of the theory that are most relevant to research on text illustration.

There are two functionally distinguishable symbolic systems according to Paivio—one verbal and the other nonverbal. The nonverbal system consists of visual, auditory, and haptic subsystems. The lowest-level units in the verbal system are termed *logogens* (roughly equivalent to Morton's [1969] use of the term). The basic unit in the nonverbal system is the *imagen* (again, following Morton). Generally, the verbal and nonverbal systems are activated at the unit level. For instance, particular visual stimuli activate particular logogens initially, with the possibility of spreading activation both within the verbal system and across to the nonverbal system. Thus, hearing the word *cat* can result both in associative activation of *dog* and in a mental image of a particular cat.

Important points to emphasize are that the two systems can be activated independently and that there are interconnections between the systems that permit parallel operation. Parallel representations are dual codes, and a main tenet of the theory is that two codes are better than one. Particularly relevant to the discussion here, memory is expected to be greater when two codes are activated rather than one, a claim supported by a substantial volume of research (Paivio, 1986, especially Chapter 8). Of the two codes, the nonverbal one has a greater effect on memory.

The additive effects of verbal and nonverbal coding on children's learning were apparent by the mid-1980s, particularly with respect to the potency of pictures on children's learning. So much so that after reviewing picture effects on children's learning in basic tasks such as free recall and recognition of list items, Pressley (1977) concluded, "No more experiments are required to substantiate the positive effect of pictures on children's learning" (p. 613). Levin and Lesgold (1978) reviewed the effects of pictures that reiterate a story on children's memory of story elements. Their conclusion was much the same as Pressley's, that providing reiterative pictures (i.e., pictures that duplicated the verbal content) increased children's memory of story content.

Paivio (1986) argues persuasively that pictorial representation is only one approach to activation of the nonverbal symbolic system. The most common alternative is to instruct people to construct a second nonverbal code for themselves, for instance, directions to construct referential images of verbal input (e.g., Pressley, 1976). Unfortunately, a simple direction to code using imagery often does not facilitate young children's verbal learning (e.g., Pressley & Levin, 1977, 1978) and particularly does not facilitate learning of prose (e.g.,

Guttmann, Levin, & Pressley, 1977). The exact mechanisms mediating young children's difficulties in carrying out imagery instructions have yet to be well worked out, although one likely contributing problem is that imagery construction given a verbal stimulus may overtax children's functional working memory limitations (Pressley & Levin, 1978) for all but the simplest verbal input (Ghatala & Levin, 1976). This failure of children to benefit from simple imagery generation instructions motivated much of the research reported here that was aimed at engineering materials so that children could produce more complete imaginal representations. The most frequently used prompts in such studies have been partial pictures that do not completely tell the story, requiring children to imagine missing details in order to construct complete dual-coded representations. The most important result in these investigations was that less-than-complete pictures sometimes produced enhanced learning, but not always. It should be apparent by the conclusion of this chapter that a picture is not a picture is not a picture as far as promoting children's encoding of stories is concerned.

In addition to addressing issues of encoding, Paivio's (1986) theory also provides guidance as to how to maximize retrieval of specific content that has been learned. In general, effective retrieval cues activate the representations created at encoding. Thus, if a story was presented both verbally and pictorially, the more a retrieval cue suggested part of the exact coding of the presentation, the more likely that correct recall would occur, an explanation similar to Tulving's (1983, Chapter 11) encoding specificity theory of retrieval. The most unique aspect of Paivio's position is that imaginally based retrieval cues are especially effective when content is dual coded in memory and that such cues more certainly lead to recall of the original stimulus than do verbal cues. Thus, presentation at testing of both verbal prompts and part of a picture that was used to code content at study should be more effective than verbal cues alone. Given many demonstrations of retrieval failure in children (e.g., Kobasigawa, 1974; Pressley & Levin, 1980; Pressley & MacFadyen, 1983), the possibility of stimulating retrieval of prose by picture-cue manipulations at testing has been studied several times. Evidence consistent with Paivio's theory of retrieval will be reviewed here. This work suggests that there is a time in development when young children can code prose materials imaginally, although they often fail to retrieve and use imaginal mediators at testing without explicit prompting to do so.

Throughout the chapter, discussion will return to dual-coding interpretations of cognition. The evidence presented here converges on the conclusion (a) that pictorial-imaginal mediation is possible with young children, but (b) that for such mediation to occur, more explicit prompting is required than with older children (Pressley, 1982; Rohwer, 1973; Waters & Andreassen, 1983). There can be little doubt from the available data, however, that if picture and verbal codes can be activated, they promote children's learning of stories relative to verbal codes alone.

Pragmatic Concerns

Illustration is an ancient human endeavor. The cave paintings at Lascaux are some 20,000 years old. Illustrations in "books" have been around for a long time as well. The oldest surviving text is an Egyptian papyrus dating from about 1980 B.C. (Bland, 1969). The Egyptian *Book of the Dead* (1300 B.C.) contained drawings, as did the earliest versions of the *Aeneid* and the *Iliad* (Bland, 1962; 1969). More pertinent to this chapter, there have been illustrated books for children for over 500 years, although Bishop Comenius' *Orbis sensualium pictus*, which was published in 1658, is often credited as the first such contribution (Norton, 1983; Pitz, 1963). Perhaps Comenius' work commands so much attention because he so forcefully presented the case for putting illustrations in texts intended for children. One of his most famous and frequently quoted statements is that, "Pictures are the most intelligible books that children can look upon." Nonetheless, the first illustrated children's book that was printed with movable type was a collection of fables written by one Ulrich Boner, entitled *Der Edelstein* (The gem), and printed by Albrecht Pfister in 1461 (Muir, 1971). Other early books included *Der Ritter von Turm* (The knight of the tower) produced in Switzerland in 1493 and Caxton's *Aesop* published in England in 1484. Bland (1962, 1969), Muir (1971), and Pitz (1963) provide reviews of many of these early books, as well as some sample illustrations.

Illustrated books in English were common by 1840 (Slythe, 1970), enough so that British artists like Thomas Bewick and George Cruickshank could make most of their living by producing pictures for books (Muir, 1971). There was an enormous increase in the popularity of picture books in the mid- to late nineteenth century when they became truly artistic (Feaver, 1977; Meyer, 1983; Peppin, 1975). Indeed, many children's books from the mid-nineteenth to early twentieth centuries are illustrated so elaborately and beautifully that they are recognized as easily by their pictures as by their story lines. Some of these famous and memorable illustrations are now widely known. Who does not have an image of Winnie-the-Pooh (drawn by E. H. Shepard) stored in long-term memory? John Tenniel's drawings of Alice, Mad Hatter, March Hare, and the Cheshire Cat are familiar to millions. Then there are Beatrix Potter's portraits of Peter Rabbit and his associates, as well as Howard Pyle's definitive portraits of Robin Hood. W. W. Denslow brought the characters in Oz to life almost 40 years before they appeared in the famous film starring Judy Garland, with Denslow's line drawings well known to four generations of children and their parents.

In addition to the very famous examples, there are tens of thousands of other illustrated books for children. In fact, it is almost impossible to find a volume that is intended for children under 8 years of age that is not illustrated. This generalization holds across a variety of cultures. See, for examples, the July 1975 issue of *Graphis*, Vol. 177, that presented a selection of children's book illustrations from around the world. Cimino (1947) reviewed many foreign picture books produced since 1900.

In addition to serving as accompaniments to fiction, picture books also are used in our culture to introduce children to the alphabet and to numbers, as well as to society's shared body of knowledge and to values about family and social relations, history, and science (Ciancolo, 1973). Picture books have served all these functions for over two centuries. Whalley's (1974) impressive overview of nursery and school picture books includes reference to many ABC and counting books, as well as to volumes aimed at conveying religious instruction (e.g., illustrated new testaments for children), moral instruction (e.g., John Newberry's *Little stories for little folks of all denominations*, published in 1795), history (e.g., John Davis' *Captain Smith and Princess Pocahontas*), geography (e.g., *Peter Parley's tales about China*), occupations, natural history, science, grammar, music, and language (e.g., *Pretty lessons in verse for good children, with some lessons in Latin in easy rhyme* by Sara Coleridge).

In short, one major motivation for studying picture effects is that the illustrated book has been and continues to be the most important literary form presented to young children. In addition, picture books have been and continue to be prominent tools for teaching children important social and intellectual content. Creators of picture books expect their illustrations to aid comprehension, learning, and retention substantially. As Norton (1983) summarized:

The illustrations should help the reader *anticipate actions* . . . the artist used visual elements to create composition to be seen and *convey meaning* . . . outstanding picture book artists . . . create *memorable* illustrations that integrate story and pictures. (p. 129, emphasis ours)

Methodological Issues in Studying Picture Effects

Before embarking on a description of recent experiments, a few general points should be made about the methods that are used to study picture effects on prose learning. First, analytical research on picture attributes requires substantial investment. Two-group experiments in which one group of children gets pictures while they listen to a story, and the other group does not, are minimally revealing. If there is a positive effect produced by a picture intervention in such an experiment, it could be due to any of the picture's attributes. If the treatment fails, it is often difficult to surmise what was wrong with the illustration and impossible to know what was wrong for certain without additional experimentation. This point is emphasized because the most common design in picture research is the two-group experiment. See, for instance, the many studies reviewed by Levie and Lentz (1982). Because of the limited informativeness of such two-group studies, few of them are taken up in the discussion presented here.

A second point is that most research about picture effects on children's prose learning has been conducted using between-subject designs. Picture types within prose have not been manipulated within subjects because of the possibility of carryover effects. For instance, seeing complete pictures for some text segments might result in greater imagery being generated for less completely illustrated sections. Although carryover warrants formal evaluation as one mechanism short of direct instruction for increasing children's processing of pictures (i.e., there are only a few relevant, inconclusive examinations in the literature; Digdon, 1982; Dunham & Levin, 1979), the identification of simple effects produced by different types of pictures has been easier to accomplish with carryover effects eliminated (and thus the additional expense of between-subject designs).

Third, one of the greatest shortcomings in the research thus far involves the breadth of materials studied. Most of the analytically revealing studies have been conducted with simple, connected text. Sometimes the "stories" have been as short as one sentence. Even the longer presentations in these studies were not more than a couple of hundred words long. In addition, in most of these investigations the prose was either simple fiction or simple nonfiction. There is a clear need for studies of depiction effects on comprehension and memory for such linguistic forms as expository materials, ABC books, and intentionally persuasive communications, such as advertisements (Harris, 1983).

Finally, past investigations of picture effects on young children's learning of connected discourse have been restricted primarily to pictures that are considered to be completely redundant with text content (Levie & Lentz, 1982; Levin & Lesgold, 1978; Schallert, 1980). The effects of less-than-complete or mismatched illustrations have been studied only recently, despite the fact that pictures in children's books often do not overlap prose content completely or perfectly (Levin, 1981; Shriberg & Shriberg, 1974). The importance of specifying the type of illustration being investigated is underscored by the fact that occasionally there are reports suggesting that complete pictures do not aid children's learning of prose. An example is Silvern (1980) who read single sentences to kindergarten children. In the two relevant conditions of the study, children either saw an illustration of the sentence content as they listened, or they did not. There were only nonsignificant trends in favor of the picture group. One problem was that some of Silvern's pictures were less-than-complete (i.e., partial) pictures, a point that he acknowledged only in his discussion section. As we review later in this chapter, partial pictures often fail to improve the learning of very young children. It seems obvious from examples like Silvern (1980) that researchers must be maximally explicit about the characteristics of the illustrations that they are investigating. Without information about the relationship of illustrations to the text that they accompany, it is difficult, if not impossible, to evaluate the contribution that an experiment makes to the picture facilitation literature. Any study that failed to provide such detailed information was not included in this chapter.

Despite these caveats, there is a strong case that substantial progress has been made in understanding when illustrations facilitate children's prose learning and when they do not. We review here studies that examined the parameters associated with matched illustration facilitation, as well as studies of less-than-complete illustrations. After reviewing the research, we take up some of the many additional questions suggested by the research conducted to date.

Recent Studies of Illustration Effects on Children's Prose Learning

Effects Produced by Illustrations that Completely Match Prose

By the mid-1970s it was well established that children's immediate, factual recall of simple fiction was improved when picture content was completely redundant with story content (Levin & Lesgold, 1978). More recent reviews (Levie & Lentz, 1982; Schallert, 1980) substantiate the Levin and Lesgold conclusions. That is not to suggest that by 1978 there were no important issues remaining to be resolved about the effects of matched pictures on prose learning. More recent data substantiate that matched picture facilitation extends beyond (a) simple, concrete fictional prose, (b) occasions when testing occurs very soon after presentation of prose, (c) normal children, and (d) tests that tap only the most central aspects of prose. We discuss evidence relevant to each of these points.

One of the most convincing demonstrations that matched illustrations work for more than simple fictional prose was provided by Levin and Berry (1980). Those investigators presented to fourth-grade children five human-interest stories adapted from newspaper articles. Subjects in the matched-picture condition saw an illustration for each article that depicted all the main ideas of the passage. For example, subjects heard, "The Dying Honey Bees" as they viewed Figure 3.1:

The honey bee, Wisconsin's official state insect, is dying. It is dying from a poisonous spray that farmers use to destroy bugs on their crops. The farmers don't mean to kill the bees, but some spray they use gets carried through the air to the hives of neighboring beekeepers. These beekeepers want the farmers to stop spraying their crops so the bees won't die. If the farmers won't stop spraying, the beekeepers want the farmers to tell them when and where they will be spraying so the beekeepers can move their bees away from the sprayed crops. (p. 178)

Control subjects only heard the passage. Subsequent to the presentations, subjects answered short-answer questions about the passages. The usual matched-

FIGURE 3.1. Fully matched picture. From "Children's Learning of All the News that's Fit to Print" by J. Levin and J. K. Berry, 1980, *Educational Communication and Technology*, 26, p. 179. Copyright 1980 by Association for Educational Communication and Technology. Reprinted by permission.

picture effect was observed. Levin and Berry (1980) also replicated the matched-picture effect relative to a control condition in which subjects received additional verbal input in the form of summaries emphasizing the main ideas of the passage that were later questioned on the test. In a followup experiment, Levin and Berry (1980) showed that an alternative picture condition with one illustration per sentence was also effective in promoting memory of factual prose. Other data relevant to the materials generalization issue includes Hannafin's (1983) demonstration of matched-picture facilitation of abstract prose.

Are matched-picture effects limited to occasions when recall occurs immediately after presentation of the materials? Levin and Berry (1980) examined this question directly in their study of expository recall. When testing was delayed until 3 days after presentation of text, matched-picture subjects recalled more of the illustrated materials than no-picture control learners. Purkel and Bornstein (1980) demonstrated the same effect for 1-day delayed recall of short, fictional stories; Peng and Levin (1979) reported positive effects of matched pictures on learning of fiction when testing was delayed by 3 days. Hannafin (1983) obtained matched-picture facilitation both on an immediate test and a 2-week delayed test.

The preponderance of pictures and prose research has been conducted with normal children. The small amount of comparative research with advantaged and disadvantaged children of normal intelligence, however, suggests that if anything, matched-picture effects are even stronger for children from economically depressed environments than they are for middle-class samples (e.g., Rohwer & Harris, 1975). That matched-picture effects are not limited to middle-class, normal IQ groups was especially apparent in a study reported by Bender and Levin (1978). They presented a multiepisode concrete story to educable mentally retarded children. Short-answer questions followed presentation of the story. Control subjects simply heard the story. Imagery subjects were told to construct mental images representing the contents of the sentences just presented. Matched-picture subjects saw pictures, each presented as the corresponding text was heard. Learning was increased substantially by the matched pictures, with no effects produced by the imagery instruction. In fact, matched-picture retarded subjects remembered the story about as well as same-chronologically-aged children who only heard the story!

Levin, Bender, and Pressley (1979) addressed directly the issue of whether matched-picture effects are limited to recall of central content. Second- and fifth-grade subjects were presented 10 sentences to learn. Each sentence contained an animate and an inanimate object in a central interaction. Each animate object had a randomly determined facial expression; each inanimate object had a randomly determined color. The facial expression and colors were incidental features. Thus, the children heard sentences like, "The happy rabbit chewed on the blue pencil," and, "The black car zoomed by the surprised duck." The experiment included a sentence-only condition and a matched-picture condition. Matched-picture subjects saw the pictures in Figures 3.2a and 3.2b corresponding to the sample sentences presented above. The most important result was that at both age levels, matched pictures produced superior recall of both central and incidental

FIGURE 3.2. Matched pictures. From "Pictures, Imagery, and Children's Recall of Central Versus Peripheral Sentence Information" by J. Levin, B. G. Bender, and M. Pressley, 1979, *Educational Communication and Technology*, 27, p. 90. Copyright 1979 by Association for Educational Communication and Technology. Reprinted by permission.

content compared to the sentence-only condition. There was nothing in this careful examination of central and incidental recall to suggest that matched-picture effects are confined only to recall of main ideas.

Summary and Discussion

A number of studies produced in the last decade have helped to substantiate that matched-picture effects are durable and pervasive. In addition to demonstrations of simple strength, however, there was at least one major theoretical clarification. Levin, Bender, and Lesgold (1976) produced data consistent with dual-coding theory demonstrating that adding pictures to a prose presentation was not tantamount to simply one more repetition of the material. In their most telling experiment on the problem, Grade 1 subjects heard two 10-sentence, concrete stories. The experiment included a no-strategy, single-exposure-to-the-story condition; a condition where subjects repeated each sentence after they heard it; a condition where subjects heard each of the story sentences twice; and a matched-picture condition. The matched-picture condition produced significantly better recall than occurred in any other condition, with recall in both of the repetition conditions higher than recall in the control condition. Combined verbal and pictorial presentation was superior to two verbalizations of the material. Redundant verbal and pictorial presentations have surpassed all alternatives studied to date!

Effects Produced by Illustrations that Do Not Completely Match Prose

LESS-THAN-COMPLETE CONSISTENT PICTURES AND ENCODING

Pictures in children's books often do not overlap prose content completely (Shriberg & Shriberg, 1974), for reiterative coding is not necessary to fulfill many of the functions that pictures serve in text (Duchastel, 1980; Levin, 1981; Levin, Anglin, & Carney, Chapter 2, this volume). These include decoration, making text more interesting, as well as guiding interpretation of prose (e.g., accentuating the moods). Given their frequency of occurrence, it is important to determine if less-than-complete pictures increase children's learning.

Since 1977, most of the important studies about the effects of partially reiterative illustrations on text learning were stimulated in part by the results of a single series of experiments conducted at the University of Wisconsin by Guttmann, Levin, and Pressley (1977). When Guttmann was designing his doctoral thesis study in 1975, it was already apparent that children younger than 7–8 years old could not generate representational images of prose or could do so only with great difficulty (Shimron, 1975). Guttmann proposed that less-than-complete illustrations, however, might prompt imaginal representations of connected materials that would not occur without external support and, thus, improve children's learning of these more complex materials. To test this hypothesis, Guttmann created what he termed "partial pictures" (Guttmann, Levin, & Pressley, 1977, Experiment 1) to accompany short stories presented to children.

In his partial-picture condition, the sentence, "One evening Sue's family sat down to eat a big turkey for dinner," was accompanied by the partial picture in Figure 3.3 (fully colored in the actual presentation) and an instruction to create an internal imaginal representation of the complete-prose content. The partial pictures completely reiterated the texts they accompanied except for one object that was either occluded by another object in the picture or outside the frame of the illustration. Guttmann's experiment included three other conditions, one of which was a complete-picture condition. These complete-picture subjects saw an illustration identical to the partial picture in Figure 3.3 except that the turkey was in full view on the table, not obscured by the mother's head. Subjects in an imagery instructional condition were shown no pictures as they heard the stories but were instructed to create representational images. Control subjects only heard the story.

After the story was presented to the kindergarten, second-, and third-grade subjects, they were given a test, one objective question per story sentence with each question requiring recall of the part of the sentence not depicted in the partial picture (e.g., Figure 3.3 accompanied, "What did Sue's family eat for dinner one evening?"). The most important result of this first experiment was that there

FIGURE 3.3. Partial picture. From "Pictures, Partial Pictures, and Young Children's Oral Prose Learning" by J. Guttmann, J. R. Levin, and M. Pressley, 1977 (Experiment 1), *Journal of Educational Psychology,* 69, p. 474. Copyright 1977 by American Psychological Association. Reprinted by permission of the publisher.

was an important developmental shift. At the kindergarten level the performance of control, imagery, and partial-picture conditions were statistically indistinguishable and well below performance in the complete-picture condition. At the third-grade level, imagery, partial-picture, and complete-picture subjects remembered more than control subjects. Although the differences in the three more potent conditions did not differ significantly, there was a trend favoring complete pictures over partial pictures and a very strong trend favoring complete pictures relative to the imagery condition. Most surprising, however, although partial-picture recall was slightly better than imagery recall at all three grade levels, there was never a significant difference between these conditions. In short, there was no compelling support for the important partial-picture effects that Guttmann had hypothesized.

Guttmann, Levin, and Pressley (1977, Experiment 2) reasoned that Guttmann's thesis study might not have been more successful because the long story posed too great a processing load for the young children. Thus, their followup experiment involved learning of single sentences, with two different partial picture types investigated. Dynamic partial-picture subjects were instructed to create images representing sentences as they viewed illustrations of the actors in the sentences doing the action, but with the direct object of the sentence occluded in some fashion. For the sentence, "The clown threw his hat in the air," dynamic partial-picture subjects saw the picture in Figure 3.4a. In contrast, subjects in the static partial-picture condition saw Figure 3.4b, and complete-picture subjects saw Figure 3.4c with the hat visible rather than outside the frame of the picture. Imagery-only subjects were never shown pictures but were instructed to construct internal, representative images. The kindergarten participants were comparable in age and other characteristics to the youngest subjects in Guttmann's thesis.

The posttest consisted of two types of questions, ones with the object mentioned (e.g., Who threw the hat in the air?) and ones with no mention of the object (e.g., What did the clown throw in the air?). As in Guttmann's dissertation, the performances ordered imagery lowest, partial pictures second, and complete

FIGURE 3.4. (a) Dynamic partial picture, (b) static partial picture, and (c) complete picture. From "Pictures, Partial Pictures, and Young Children's Oral Prose Learning" by J. Guttmann, J. R. Levin, and M. Pressley, 1977 (Experiment 2), *Journal of Educational Psychology, 69*, p. 478. Copyright 1977 by American Psychological Association. Reprinted by permission of the publisher.

pictures highest. This time, however, partial pictures produced significantly better recall for the kindergarten students than imagery instructions alone. The two types of partial picture produced equivalent recall, with recall in both of these conditions not differing significantly from recall in the complete-picture condition. There was no difference in the pattern of results as a function of type of question. In short, Guttmann, Levin, and Pressley (1977, Experiment 2) provided the first evidence that less-than-complete pictures could produce dual-coding advantages in young children, almost as great as the gains produced by complete pictures.

In a third experiment, Guttmann, Levin, and Pressley (1977) demonstrated that there was a qualitative difference in the encoding produced by static and dynamic pictures. In particular, dynamic pictures lead to stronger encoding of the action of the verb, as was expected, since the action was fully depicted in the dynamic partial picture.

Additional evidence was provided by Purkel and Bornstein (1980) that partial pictures as defined by Guttmann et al. (1977) facilitate the prose learning of children given an imagery instruction. In that experiment, 7–8-year-olds heard 10 one-sentence stories. Control subjects only heard the sentences. Sentences were accompanied by full illustration in the complete-picture condition and by partial pictures and imagery instruction in the partial-picture condition. Complete-picture and partial-picture subjects recalled more about the stories than no-picture subjects, both immediately following presentation and 1 day after study, with nonsignificant trends in favor of complete pictures over partial pictures at both testing intervals. Consistent with Guttmann et al. (1977), Goldston and Richman (in press) observed only a trend in favor of a partial-pictures-plus-imagery-instructions condition over a simple imagery condition when kindergarten and Grade 1 children learned more complex 10-sentence stories.

One of the more informative demonstrations of partial-picture effects was produced by Ruch and Levin (1977) who contrasted a partial-picture condition with an especially challenging control condition. Grade 3 children heard the 10-sentence stories used in Guttmann's dissertation. The conditions of the Ruch–Levin experiment that are relevant to the current discussion were a partial-picture condition, a repetition condition where each sentence was heard twice, and a no-strategy control condition. For each story, the posttest consisted of five verbatim questions (i.e., a question transformation applied to one of the sentences in the story exactly as presented) and five paraphrased questions (i.e., ones containing synonyms for the nouns, adjective, and verbs of the original sentences). Paraphrased questions appear to tap "understanding" better than do verbatim questions (Anderson, 1972).

Partial-picture and repetition subjects performed at approximately the same level and better than controls on verbatim questions; partial-picture subjects answered more paraphrased questions than repetition subjects who performed only nonsignificantly better than controls. Thus, unlike matched pictures that produce superior performance on verbatim questions compared to the two verbal repetition conditions (Levin et al., 1976), partial-picture subjects do not perform better than repetition participants when questions contain the exact same verbal cues that were available at study. In contrast, when the exact verbal cues are eliminated, and thus the child must rely on memory of meaning to answer the questions, the partial-picture intervention is better than the repetition alternative, at least with 8-year-old subjects.

The success of the partial pictures with kindergarten and older grade-school children prompted the hypothesis that such less-than-complete pictures could enhance the learning of even younger children. Pressley, Pigott, and Bryant (1982, Experiment 1) examined this question explicitly by presenting 3- and 4-year-olds with the types of simple sentence used by Guttmann et al. (1977, Experiments 2 and 3). Pressley et al. (1982, Experiment 1) included a completely-matched-picture condition, a static partial-picture condition, and a dynamic partial-picture condition. In addition, a third partial-picture condition included depictions of the direct objects of the sentences but nothing else. There was an important difference between these conditions and the ones discussed previously. Subjects were not explicitly instructed to generate images in these studies so that the effects of the pictures per se could be isolated. Control subjects only heard the sentences.

The results were disappointing. Provision of partial pictures did not significantly increase the number of short-answer questions responded to correctly by the 3- and 4-year-olds over the number answered by sentence-only subjects. Also, complete pictures produced greater recall than occurred in any other condition of the study. The Pressley et al. (1982, Experiment 1) data suggested that the types of partial picture that worked with kindergarten children would not work with preschoolers. Thus, Pressley et al. (1982, Experiment 2) explored a new type of partial-picture intervention, again with 3–4-year-old children and without instructions to generate images. Partial-picture subjects were presented two separate pictures, one of the sentence subject and one of the sentence direct object. Two such conditions were studied, one with dynamic pictures of the sentence subjects and one with static illustrations of the sentence subjects. These 2 two-picture conditions were contrasted with a sentence-only condition and a completely-matched-picture treatment.

Both two-picture conditions significantly improved performance relative to the sentence-only condition. Although there were trends toward better performance in the completely-matched-picture condition compared to the two-picture conditions, the differences were not significant. The performance difference between the 2 two-picture conditions was very small. Thus, young children were able to integrate simple text information presented across two separate partial pictures without explicit imagery instructions. What was not clarified in this study was whether two partial pictures were superior to the single-partial-picture conditions tested in earlier studies.

Digdon, Pressley, and Levin (1985) did explore the potential of the two-picture intervention relative to the single-partial-picture condition. They once again turned attention to the learning of longer, connected stories versus isolated sentences. The preschool children in the study heard 10-sentence stories very similar to the ones used in Guttmann's dissertation. The sentences of the stories were accompanied either by a dynamic partial picture alone (with the direct object of the sentence missing), a picture of only the direct object, separate pictures of both the subject (the dynamic partial picture) and the direct object in the two-picture condition, or no pictures. Digdon et al. (1985) also reexamined the imagery-instructional variable, with an imagery-instructional version of each of the four picture conditions contrasted with a no-imagery version of the condition. Digdon et al. (1985) reasoned that the two-picture conditions would be sensitive to imagery-instructional effects if any partial-picture variations would. All a subject had to do with a two-picture version was imaginally "move" the direct object into the partial picture of the sentence's subject.

The Digdon et al. (1985) results were clear and completely consistent with those reported by Pressley et al. (1982). The most striking aspect of the data was the superiority of the two-picture performance over the other conditions under both imagery and no-imagery instructions. Single partial pictures (of subjects) and single object pictures produced nonsignificant improvement relative to the control condition, and imagery instructions had no impact whatsoever.

Summary

The experiments reviewed in this section produced very consistent results. Collapsing across all studies suggests the following ordering of conditions with respect to their potency for affecting children's learning of prose: sentences only < sentences + single incomplete pictures < sentences + two incomplete pictures < sentences + complete pictures. Whether providing single incomplete pictures (i.e., partial pictures) produces statistically significant learning gains relative to a sentence-only condition seems to vary with development and complexity of the to-be-learned stories. With semantically independent sentences, there were significant partial-picture effects at the kindergarten level but not among nursery-school-age children. Single-partial-picture effects are not obtained when 5-6-year-olds learn more complex stories. That complete pictures were always at least a little bit better than the incomplete-picture conditions in these studies provides additional confirmation that complete illustrations can reliably facilitate learning of prose. Guttmann et al. (1977), as well as others, certainly tried to produce better performance with less-than-complete pictures than occurs with complete pictures, but try as they might, they never succeeded.

LESS-THAN-COMPLETE PICTURES AS RETRIEVAL CUES

The studies discussed up until this point established that provision of partial pictures and imagery instructions at study produces better learning by young grade schoolers than do imagery instructions alone. There is a point in development, however, when less-than-complete pictures need to be present both at studying and testing. The presence of partial pictures at study does facilitate encoding for these children, but retrieval of the mediating image fails to occur without a fairly strong prompt (i.e., the partial illustration).

Ruch and Levin (1979, Experiment 1) were the first to report this retrieval deficiency. In that experiment, first-grade children were presented two 10-sentence short-story passages. In one condition, partial pictures and imagery instructions occurred at study with partial pictures reinstated at testing. In a second condition, partial pictures and imagery instructions occurred at study only. The third condition included only the imagery instruction. Mean recall levels were 64.8%, 49.0%, and 49.7%, respectively, in these three conditions, consistent with a retrieval deficiency interpretation.

In a second experiment, Ruch and Levin (1979) replicated the superiority of the condition in which partial pictures were provided at both study and testing relative to the condition in which partial pictures occurred at study only, again with Grade 1 children as subjects. This same type of retrieval deficiency was obtained by Goldston and Richman (in press) with kindergarten and Grade 1 children and by Wooldridge et al. (1982) with 6-year-old subjects.

Summary

There is a point in development (roughly between 5 and 7 years of age) when children can imaginally encode given partial pictures but seem not to retrieve imaginal mediators. Much more research is necessary to determine the generality of this retrieval deficiency, since all demonstrations of the retrieval effect reported thus far have been when children are learning highly concrete short stories about 75–100 words in length.

LESS-THAN-COMPLETE PICTURES AS INFERENTIAL PROMPTS

So far the discussion has focused on learning of content explicitly stated in text. A new direction is investigation of the effects of less-than-complete versus complete pictures on learning of material that must be inferred. Researchers have hypothesized that pictures may increase the probability that appropriate inferences are made at both encoding and retrieval.

Similar to earlier hypotheses regarding the influence of less-than-complete pictures on young children's memory of prose information, Miller, Pressley, Caldwell, and Hackling (1985) hypothesized that partial-picture prompts might promote inferential representations during encoding. Four- to five-year-olds and seven- to eight-year-olds heard 10 sentences, each about a particular type of person carrying out an action. In one condition (explicit sentence only) the tool that

FIGURE 3.5. (a) Complete picture and (b) partial picture. From *Developmental Differences in Children's Memory for Prose When Part of the Picture is Missing* by G. E. Miller, M. Pressley, C. Caldwell, and M. Hackling, 1985, April. Paper presented at the annual meeting of the American Educational Research Association, Chicago.

the person used was explicitly stated (e.g., "The workman dug a hole in the ground with the shovel"). In three other conditions the tool had to be inferred (e.g., "The workman dug a hole in the ground"). Pictures accompanied sentences in two of these three implicit-sentence conditions. Complete-picture/implicit-sentence subjects saw a picture of the particular type of person specified in the sentence carrying out the action with the appropriate instrument (e.g., a man digging with a shovel as in Figure 3.5a). Partial-picture/implicit-sentence subjects saw identical pictures with the instruments deleted (e.g., Figure 3.5b). At testing, subjects were told the instrument as a cue and were required to recall the entire sentence, following Paris and Lindauer (1976).

There were clear developmental differences in performance. At the preschool level, only subjects in the explicit-sentence condition recalled significantly more sentences (43.1%) than subjects in the implicit-sentence condition (20.6%). In short, there was very little suggestion that either the partial pictures (31.25%) or even the complete pictures (30.00%) resulted in sentence representations that included the instruments. The effects produced by the pictures were more striking at the older age level, however. The explicit-sentence-only (46.9%), the complete-picture/implicit-sentence (52.5%), and the partial-picture/implicit-sentence (44.4%) conditions all produced significantly better memory than the implicit-sentence-only condition (21.9%). Miller et al. (1985) interpreted the older children's data to mean that partial pictures prompted inference of instruments at encoding.

Issues that follow from this experiment included the following: (a) How much must the partial picture "suggest" the missing objects in order for inferential learning gains to occur? (b) Can objects besides instruments be inferred? (c) The developmental trend in Miller et al. (1985) raises the question of the lower developmental boundary for production of inferences in response to picture cues. The trend observed in Miller et al. (1985) is consistent with outcomes reported when children are presented pictures only. Higgins (1980) presented illustrations where parts of objects were obscured (e.g., a dog's head was occluded by another dog). The 4–5-year-olds in that study often responded as if the occluded part did not exist, with some developmental improvements in making inferences that hidden parts of pictures really do exist. (d) Perhaps the young children in the Miller et al. (1985) study would have been aided by the pictures if they were provided with some additional instruction about how to construct inferences? For instance, Higgins (1979) trained slightly older children to make inferences about pictures. Instruction in that study extended over 16 lessons aimed at teaching students to make inferences by considering the natures of characters in pictures, the antecedents and implications of actions in pictures, and attributes of the physical setting in which the action took place. Extended practice was provided until these skills were internalized. (e) Alternatively, the requirement to recall an entire sentence, given only a single inferred cue, may have been too demanding in the Miller et al. (1985) study. Inferences might be more obvious given greater cuing at testing. As in the Ruch and Levin (1979) study discussed previously, young children may benefit from partial pictures only if the illustrations are reinstated at testing. These questions and others are currently being explored by Miller and her associates.

An alternative approach to the study of picture effects on children's inferences was taken by Wood, Pressley, Turnure, and Walton (1985). These researchers presented four picture dictionary definitions to 3-5-year-old children to learn. Research on these types of definition was motivated by concerns for ecological validity, since preschoolers frequently are exposed to such definitions (e.g., Hayward, 1980). Wood et al. (1985) first presented the definitions as a series of declarative sentences, followed either by reiteration as declarative sentences or as questions the child had to answer. The criterion task was recall of the definitions. Because the children were already somewhat familiar with the four concepts that were defined for them, the task was to add to and fine tune the concepts (Norman, 1982), a situation mirroring much of lexical development.

The manipulations in Wood et al. (1985) can be made obvious by considering how one of the words was presented to subjects. "Needle" was first defined for all subjects as follows:

A needle is a long, thin tool used for sewing with thread. A needle has a small hole at one end and a sharp point at the other. (p. 27)

Half of the subjects then heard the definition reiterated in four short sentences:

A needle has a small hole at one end. A needle has a short point at the other end. You use a needle for sewing. A needle is a long, thin tool. (p. 27)

The other half of the subjects answered four questions:

Why does a needle have a small hole at the end? Why does a needle have a sharp point at the other end? Why should you use a needle for sewing? Why is a needle a long, thin tool?

Most relevant to the concerns in this chapter, as subjects heard the definitions, half of the restatement subjects and half of the questioned subjects saw pictures detailing most or all of the attributes mentioned in the definitions (elaborated pictures). The remaining subjects viewed much less complete illustrations of the defined concepts (simple pictures). See Figures 3.6a and 3.6b for the elaborated and simple pictures accompanying needle. Like partial pictures in other studies, the simple pictures in Wood et al. (1985) did not include all the elements mentioned in the prose.

After presentation of all four definitions, subjects were asked to recall the meanings of each one with four probes employed to maximize the likelihood that subjects would report all that they knew: (1) What is a _____? (2) What do you do with a _____? (3) What did I tell you about _____? (4) Tell me everything you know about a _____.

The most important results were that more complete pictures produced better recall of attributes exactly as they were stated in the definition. Questioning had almost no effect on exact recall. In addition, presentation of elaborated pictures resulted in recall of more inferential information, that is, content congruent with

FIGURE 3.6. (a) Elaborated and (b) simple pictures accompanying "needle." From *Enriching Children's Recall of Picture-Dictionary Definitions with Interrogation and Elaborated Pictures* by E. Wood, M. Pressley, J. E. Turnure, and R. Walton, 1986, April. Paper presented at the annual meeting of the American Educational Research Association, San Francisco.

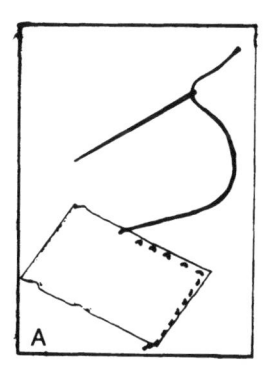

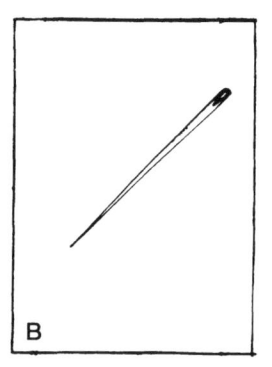

but not actually stated in the definitions or depicted in the pictures. There was only a nonsignificant trend toward more inferential recall due to questioning.

Wood et al. (1985) interpreted the significant increase in inferencing when more complex pictures were provided as evidence that elaborated pictures produce deeper processing than do nonelaborated illustrations. Very importantly, they were able to discount two alternative explanations for pictures producing better recall of congruent information. Greater congruent recall could have been a by-product of greater encoding and recall of definitions as stated in the elaborated-picture conditions. Better learning of the text as stated in these conditions would have provided more grist for inferential processing during storage and retrieval. This alternative explanation loses creditability, however, because there were low correlations between exact recall and recall of congruent information. High correlations would have been expected if congruent recall were due only to better encoding of the definitions as stated. Next, increased congruent recall in the elaborated-picture conditions could have been due simply to children saying more during testing in those conditions. If that were the case, recall of incongruous information should have been higher in the elaborated-picture condition than in the nonelaborated-picture condition. In fact, incongruous recall was low in all conditions. With these alternative explanations ruled out, the argument gains strength that the increased congruent recall in the elaborated-picture conditions occurred because the more detailed pictures led preschoolers to go "beyond the information given" more certainly than did the less detailed pictures.

Summary and Discussion

The experiments reviewed in this section further our understanding of the differential effects of variations in illustrations.

Facilitative effects of less-than-complete pictures on inferential encoding varied with the developmental level of the child in the Miller et al. (1985) study. Children below the ages of six may need more elaborate picture cues to enhance inferencing. Alternatively, young children may need more explicit instruction on how to employ picture aids during learning in order to make inferences, or they may need a picture reinstated at retrieval for positive picture effects on inferencing to be manifested on a test. Thus, future studies may reveal even richer, more extensive effects of illustration on inferencing. We foresee two profitable routes in this regard, one being the examination of more subtle indicators of processing and inference. The other is comparison of picture effects to benefits produced by other media.

Meringoff (1980) offered a start on both of these fronts. Seven- to ten-year-olds either heard a story read from an illustrated book or saw the story on a televised film. Meringoff scored inferences as to whether they were based on visual-only or text-only information. Inferences also were examined to determine if they were logical inferences following from the premises of the story, general knowledge of the world that was compatible with the story, or personal associations to story content. TV subjects made more visual inferences, with text subjects making more use of nonillustrated text and world knowledge. In addition, Meringoff (1980) found some pronounced differences in some very specific inferences. Children viewing the TV version inferred that events in the story took less time and transversed shorter distances than did the picture-book subjects.

We expect many additional investigations of inferencing in response to pictures, given great motivation for this work. There are a growing variety of ways that information can be presented to children, with concomitant increased interest among researchers to evaluate the media alternatives (e.g., Baggett, 1984; Baggett & Ehrenfeucht, 1983; Beagles-Ross & Gat, 1983; Pezdek & Stevens, 1984). Theories that posit specific media effects are becoming more explicit. For instance, joint picture-book reading is a method of presentation consistent with suggestions following from Vygotsky's (1978) theory of cognitive development. When interacting with children, adults are presumed to embellish materials to match the child's cognitive level, simultaneously modeling for the child thought processes including inferencing that are internalized eventually by the youngster. If this is so, an association between the amount of children's exposure to such interactions and their inferencing skills would be expected.

LESS-THAN-COMPLETE MISMATCHED PICTURES

Several studies have specifically addressed the question of whether pictures that were out of synchrony with the contents of prose might actually interfere with learning. We believe that this is an important problem because of the large number of such mismatches that we have detected during informal surveys of illustrated books that are intended for young children. (More formal reports on this problem will be forthcoming.)

Pressley et al. (1982) examined two forms of mismatched pictures to evaluate the possibility of interference for preschoolers listening to simple prose. In one condition, subjects saw a complete picture, correct except that the object of the sentence was deleted and replaced by another object. In the other mismatched-picture condition, subjects viewed illustrations of incorrect objects only. The most striking finding produced by these manipulations was that *only* the mismatched-object-alone condition produced recall lower than the sentence-only condition. Thus, there was some evidence that preschoolers could resist a mismatched picture, at least if only part of the picture were inconsistent with the sentence. It was somewhat surprising to Pressley et al. (1982) that the presence of mismatched pictures did not consistently devastate the performance of 3–5-year-olds. This counterintuitive outcome motivated additional study.

Pressley, Levin, Pigott, LeComte, and Hope (1983) reexamined the effects of mismatched pictures on children's oral prose learning, this time with young grade-school children. Their first experiment involved second- and third-grade children who heard 33 concrete sentences (e.g., "The dog chased the bus," and "The little girl tripped over the pumpkin"). Subjects were required to recall the direct object of the sentence at testing. For instance, subjects were asked, "What did the dog chase?" and "What did the little girl trip over?" There were three conditions in the experiment. As they listened to the sentences, subjects either saw pictures matched to the sentences, viewed pictures that contained incorrect direct objects (e.g., a dog chasing a train, a little girl tripping over a basket), or received no exposure to illustrations. Subjects in the pictures conditions were made completely aware of the nature of the illustrations that they would see. All subjects were instructed before study about the subsequent recall requirements. As usual, matched-picture subjects answered more questions than story-only subjects. Consistent with the Pressley et al. (1982) results, there was no significant difference in recall between story-only and mismatched-picture conditions, with the trend favoring sentence-only subjects at the third-grade level and mismatched-picture subjects at the second-grade level.

The Pressley et al. (1983, Experiment 2) study was aimed at determining whether the effects of mismatched pictures might be more pronounced when instructions about the task and memory requirements were not so obvious. Experiment 2 included the same three conditions that occurred in Pressley et al. (1983, Experiment 1) plus three identical conditions except that subjects in these conditions were told neither about the picture–text relationship nor about the nature of the test that was to follow. At testing they were told to answer on the basis of the "stories" they had heard.

When instructions were explicit, the pattern of mean differences was identical to that obtained in the first experiment, matched picture (80%) > mismatched picture (54%) ≈ sentence only (46%) (i.e., mismatched-pictures and sentence-only means did not differ significantly). With less explicit instructions, there was a mismatched-picture effect such that matched pictures (80%) > sentences only (52%) > mismatched pictures (31%).

Thus, when instructions were vague, mismatching produced interference. After the initial test was completed, subjects in the mismatched-picture conditions were asked to recall the content of the pictures that accompanied each sentence. They could do so 57% of the time in both the explicit and implicit instruction conditions. That recall of sentence and picture contents did not differ in the explicit-instruction/mismatched-picture condition made clear that subjects could code two objects for the same semantic context, yet keep them separate on the basis of modality. This result is completely consistent with dual-coding theory.

Pressley et al. (1983) realized that the nonexplicit versus explicit contrast in their Experiment 2 was confounded in that the experimenter was vague about both what was to be encoded and what was to be retrieved. Specifically, it was possible that the nonexplicit subjects did not realize that the "story" referred to at testing referred to only verbal content and not to the picture since the experimenter never distinguished between verbal and pictorial content. In a followup experiment, Pressley et al. (1983) obtained evidence that mismatched-picture subjects only require explicit instructions *at testing* in order to answer correctly on the basis of the text. In that study second- and third-grade children were given the nonexplicit coding instructions used in Pressley et al. (1983, Experiment 2). After study and before testing, however, subjects were told explicitly to base answers on the text and not on the pictures. Consistent with the hypothesis that explicit test directions alone would reduce mismatching effects, there was no significant difference in the recall of sentence-only and mismatched-picture subjects.

Summary

There was little evidence in the Pressley et al. (1982) or Pressley et al. (1983) experiments that mismatched pictures reduced children's recall of prose. The outcomes reported in these experiments are consistent with other reports of children's encoding not being affected by distracting stimuli (e.g., Baker-Ward, Ornstein, & Holden, 1984; Day, 1980; Wellman, Ritter, & Flavell, 1975; Yussen, 1974). Children can control their attention when confronted with distraction (Pressley, Borkowski, & Schneider, in press). Even children as young as 2 years of age can manage their attention skillfully *when it is clear what content should be encoded* (e.g., DeLoache, Cassidy, & Brown, 1985). Notably, the only hint of mismatched-picture interference occurred when children were left in the dark about what they were to learn *and* what they were to recall on the test.

CLOSING COMMENTS ABOUT LESS-THAN-COMPLETE PICTURES

There are a number of less-than-complete picture presentations that can be used to enhance children's learning of prose. What is also obvious from these data, however, is that great care must be taken if less-than-complete illustration effects on learning are to be obtained. Usually, a lot of the to-be-remembered content must be coded into the incomplete illustrations. In most of the studies, subjects were explicitly instructed to use the partial illustrations to construct more complete images, and thus little is known about occasions when pictures occur without accompanying directions as to how to use them. Work like Pressley et al. (1982) and Digdon et al. (1985) is a start on this problem.

On the other hand, the training about how to use partial pictures has been far from extensive in these studies. Exploring how to train children to use partial pictures would be an especially productive direction for additional partial-picture research. One tactic is the type of extensive training used by Higgins (1979). Alternatively, briefer training may be all that is required. In fact, we are currently training preschoolers to "guess what the artist forgot to put in the pictures" and to "imagine what the picture would look like if the artist hadn't forgotten the missing piece." Perhaps even more optimistic evaluations of less-than-complete pictures will follow from this new line of work.

Discussion: Where to Go from Here?

There has been substantial progress in understanding how pictures affect comprehension and memory of prose. Nonetheless, researchers have only scratched the surface of the many concerns relevant to pictorially mediated prose learning, concerns that blend into one another. In addition to some of the limitations that were already covered in the overview of methodological issues presented earlier in the chapter, several other issues are apparent following the review of the literature.

Most of the analytical work touched on here focused on pictures that literally retold the story, with this emphasis due largely to cognitive researchers' interests in dual-coding theory and the specific hypothesis that two codes are better than one. This research approach has paid off, for at every turn, support has been found for the dual-coding position. Illustrations in real children's books, however, often go far beyond the information contained in the text, largely because artists intentionally try to complement and expand on the written word. As Maurice Sendak, the prominent illustrator of children's books puts it:

... it's an expansion of the text. It's your version of the text as an illustrator, it's your interpretation. It's why you are an active partner in the book and not a mere echo of the author. To be an illustrator is to be a participant, someone who has something equally important to say as the writer of the book—occasionally something more important, never the writer's echo. (Lorraine, 1977, p. 152)

That a picture can be worth 1,000 words suggests that those who are interested in illustration effects need to shift their focus a bit. What are the relative contributions of the picture and the text? What variables can be manipulated to enhance children's coding of either the picture or text version of tales being told?

Although most of the researchers who conducted the research reported here claimed that their work tapped memory *and* comprehension, the memory component was emphasized more in these studies than were understanding and interpretation. We believe that the time has come to shift emphases. Particularly relevant to this point is the development of theories of illustration that make very explicit predictions about the impact of many specific picture variables on what the reader codes from illustrations (Goldsmith, 1984; Twyman, 1985). What is notable about these theories, especially Goldsmith's, is that they have been developed in light of substantial bodies of data (including the work reviewed in this chapter) about basic picture perception and processing. These theoretical advances should stimulate many new lines of investigation that establish more clearly the connections between picture interpretation and picture memory.

The need for knowledge about illustration effects extends beyond childhood, even though most picture-effects-on-prose work conducted to date has focused on children's performance. Consider, for example, the learning and understanding of prose that many adults consider difficult, such as Shakespeare's drama. That illustrated versions of these plays might make them more accessible to more people is suggested by the considerable successes of Sir Laurence Olivier's filmed versions of *Hamlet* and *Henry V*, Roman Polanski's *MacBeth*, and, most notably, Franco Zeffirelli's *Romeo and Juliet*. Recently, extensive sets of illustration have been developed for several Shakespearean plays: *MacBeth* (Von, 1982); *Romeo and Juliet* (Von, 1983); *Othello* (Zarate, 1983); and *King Lear* (Pollock, 1984). There are over 600 cartoon-like pictures for each play, with each illustration accompanying between one and ten lines of text. These illustrations are advertised as being "very valuable for those students initially staggered by Shakespeare" (Peggy O'Brien, Folger Shakespeare Library, quoted on cover of Pollock, 1984), with "comprehension aided through the marvelous illustrations not through a simplified text" (*Library Journal* quotation on cover of Pollock, 1984). Whether such pictures actually aid understanding and learning at all, let alone differentially aid poorer learners, are empirical questions, ones that are currently being addressed by Pressley and his colleagues. In addition to memory and comprehension, current investigations are also focusing on whether the illustrations are perceived to make the plays more interesting and more engaging. If illustrated Shakespeare produces more memory with less effort and more joy, there will be great motivation for both cognitive researchers and publishers to consider more carefully the potential of illustrative accompaniments.

Finally, some of the major investigators who have studied illustration effects have also been concerned with intellectual training. Yet teaching children to use illustrations accompanying prose was brief in the studies reviewed in this chapter. When it occurred at all, training usually consisted of 10–20 seconds of instruction to construct internal, representational images using the text pictures as a starting point. Thus, despite the generally negative findings for partial pictures, we still seriously entertain the hypothesis that preschool-age children may be able to use single illustrations to advantage. The additional resources required to determine children's full competence to exploit less-than-complete pictorial adjuncts seem worthwhile since there are so many partially complete illustrations in the world of children's literature. Not making the most of them would be a waste of a potentially valuable resource.

Acknowledgments. Financial support for the writing of this chapter was provided by a grant to the first author from the Natural Sciences and Engineering Research Council of Canada.

References

Anderson, R. C. (1972). How to construct achievement tests to assess comprehension. *Review of Educational Research, 42,* 145-170.

Baggett, P. (1984). Role of temporal overlap of visual and auditory material in forming dual media associations. *Journal of Educational Psychology, 76,* 408-417.

Baggett, P., & Ehrenfeucht, A. (1983). Encoding and retaining information in the visuals and verbals of an educational movie. *Educational Communication and Technology Journal, 31,* 23-32.

Baker-Ward, L., Ornstein, P. A., & Holden, D. J. (1984). The expression of memorization in early childhood. *Journal of Experimental Child Psychology, 37,* 555-575.

Beagles-Roos, J., & Gat, I. (1983). Specific impact of radio and television on children's story comprehension. *Journal of Educational Psychology, 75,* 128-137.

Bender, B. G., & Levin, J. L. (1978). Pictures, imagery, and retarded children's prose learning. *Journal of Educational Psychology, 70,* 583-588.

Bland, D. (1962). *The illustration of books.* London, England: Faber and Faber.

Bland, D. (1969). *A history of book illustrations: The illuminated manuscript and the printed book.* Berkeley: University of California Press.

Brainerd, C. J. (1978). Learning research and Piagetian theory. In L. S. Siegel & C. J. Brainerd (Eds.), *Alternatives to Piaget: Critical essays on the theory* (pp. 69-109). New York: Academic Press.

Ciancolo, P. J. (1973). *Picture books for children.* Chicago: American Library Association.

Cimino, M. (1947). Foreign picture books in a children's library. In B. E. Mahony, L. P. Latimer, & B. Folmsbee (Eds.), *Illustrations of children's books* (pp. 1744-1945). Boston: Horn Book Inc.

Day, M. C. (1980). Selective attention by children and adults to pictures specified by color. *Journal of Experimental Child Psychology, 30,* 277-289.

DeLoache, J. S., Cassidy, D. J., & Brown, A. L. (1985). Precursors of mnemonic strategies in very young children's memory. *Child Development, 56,* 125-137.

Digdon, N. L. (1982). *Picture and imagery effects on preschoolers' recall of long passages.* Unpublished master's thesis, University of Western Ontario, London, Ontario.

Digdon, N., Pressley, M., & Levin, J. R. (1985). Preschoolers' learning when pictures do not tell the whole story. *Educational Communication and Technology Journal, 33,* 139-145.

Duchastel, P. C. (1980). Research on illustrations in text: Issues and perspectives. *Educational Communication and Technology, 28,* 283-287.

Dunham, T. C., & Levin, J. R. (1979). Imagery instructions and young children's oral prose learning. *Journal of Educational Psychology, 69,* 473-480.

Feaver, W. (1977). *When we were young: Two centuries of children's book illustration.* London, England: Thames & Hudson.

Ghatala, E. S., & Levin, J. R. (1976). Children's recognition memory processes. In J. R. Levin & V. L. Allen (Eds.), *Cognitive learning in children: Theories and strategies* (pp. 61-100). New York: Academic Press.

Glaser, R. (1984). Education and thinking: The role of knowledge. *American Psychologist, 39,* 93-104.

Goldsmith, E. (1984). *Research into illustration: An approach and a review.* Cambridge, England: Cambridge University Press.

Goldston, D. B., & Richman, C. L. (in press). The effects of partial pictures and imagery instructions on the recall of young children. *Journal of Experimental Child Psychology.*

Guttmann, J., Levin, J. R., & Pressley, M. (1977). Pictures, partial pictures, and young children's oral prose learning. *Journal of Educational Psychology, 69*, 473-480.

Hannafin, M. J. (1983). The effects of instructional stimulus loading on the recall of abstract and concrete prose. *Educational Communication and Technology Journal, 31*, 103-109.

Harris, R. J. (Ed.). (1983). *Information processing research in advertising.* Hillsdale, NJ: Erlbaum.

Hayward, L. (1980). *The Sesame St. dictionary.* New York: Random House.

Higgins, L. C. (1979). Effects of strategy-oriented training on children's inference drawing from pictures. *Educational Communication and Technology Journal, 28*, 99-119.

Higgins, L. C. (1980). Literalism in the young child's interpretation of pictures. *Educational Communication and Technology Journal, 28*, 99-119.

Kobasigawa, A. (1974). Utilization of retrieval cues by children in recall. *Child Development, 45*, 127-134.

Levie, W. H., & Lentz, R. (1982). Effects of text illustrations: A review of research. *Educational Communication and Technology Journal, 30*, 195-232.

Levin, J. R. (1976). What have we learned about maximizing what children learn? In J. R. Levin & V. L. Allen (Eds.), *Cognitive learning in children: Theories and strategies* (pp. 105-134). New York: Academic Press.

Levin, J. R. (1981). On functions of pictures in prose. In F. J. Pirozzolo & M. C. Wittrock (Eds.), *Neuropsychological and cognitive processes in reading* (pp. 203-228). New York: Academic Press.

Levin, J. R., Bender, B. G., & Lesgold, A. (1976). Pictures, repetition, and young children's oral prose learning. *AV Communication Review, 24*, 367-380.

Levin, J. R., Bender, B. G., & Pressley, M. (1979). Pictures, imagery, and children's recall of central versus peripheral sentence information. *Educational Communication and Technology Journal, 27*, 89-95.

Levin, J. R., & Berry, J. K. (1980). Children's learning of all the news that's fit to print. *Educational Communication and Technology Journal, 28*, 177-185.

Levin, J. R., & Lesgold, A. M. (1978). On pictures in prose. *Educational Communication and Technology Journal, 26*, 233-243.

Lorraine, W. (1977). An interview with Maurice Sendak. *Wilson Library Bulletin, 52*, 152-157.

Meringoff, L. K. (1980). Influence of the medium on children's story apprehension. *Journal of Educational Psychology, 72*, 240-249.

Meyer, S. E. (1983). *A treasury of the great children's book illustrators.* New York: Abrams.

Miller, G. E., Pressley, M., Caldwell, C., & Hackling, M. (1985 April). *Developmental differences in children's memory for prose when part of the picture is missing.* Paper presented at the annual meeting of the American Educational Research Association, Chicago.

Morton, J. (1969). Interaction of information in word recognition. *Psychological Review, 76*, 165-178.

Muir, P. (1971). *Victorian illustrated books.* New York: Praeger.

Norman, D. A. (1982). *Learning and memory.* San Francisco: Freeman.

Norton, D. E. (1983). *Through the eyes of children: An introduction to children's literature.* Columbus, OH: Merrill.

Paivio, A. (1986). *Mental representations: A dual coding approach.* New York: Oxford University Press.
Paris, S. G., & Lindauer, B. K. (1976). The role of inference in children's comprehension and memory. *Cognitive Psychology, 8,* 217–227.
Peng, C-Y., & Levin, J. R. (1979). Pictures and children's story recall: Some questions of durability. *Educational Communication and Technology Journal, 27,* 39–44.
Peppin, B. (1975). *Fantasy: The golden age of fantastic illustration.* New York: Watson-Guptill.
Pezdek, K., & Stevens, E. (1984). Children's memory for auditory and visual information on television. *Developmental Psychology, 20,* 212–218.
Pitz, H. C. (1963). *Illustrating children's books: History–technique–production.* New York: Watson-Guptill.
Pollock, I. (1984). *William Shakespeare's King Lear.* New York: Workman Publishing.
Pressley, M. (1976). Mental imagery helps eight-year-olds remember what they read. *Journal of Educational Psychology, 68,* 355–359.
Pressley, M. (1977). Imagery and children's learning: Putting the picture in developmental perspective. *Review of Educational Research, 47,* 585–622.
Pressley, M. (1982). Elaboration and memory development. *Child Development, 53,* 296–309.
Pressley, M., Borkowski, J. G., & Schneider, W. (in press). Cognitive strategies: Good strategy users coordinate metacognition and knowledge. In R. Vasta & G. Whitehurst (Eds.), *Annals of child development* Vol. 4. Greenwich, CT: JAI Press.
Pressley, M., & Levin, J. R. (1977). Task parameters affecting the efficacy of a visual imagery learning strategy in younger and older children. *Journal of Experimental Child Psychology, 24,* 53–59.
Pressley, M., & Levin, J. R. (1978). Developmental constraints associated with children's use of the keyword method of foreign language vocabulary learning. *Journal of Experimental Child Psychology, 26,* 359–372.
Pressley, M., & Levin, J. R. (1980). The development of mental imagery retrieval. *Child Development, 51,* 558–560.
Pressley, M., Levin, J. R., Pigott, S., LeComte, M., & Hope, D. J. (1983). Mismatched pictures and children's prose learning. *Educational Communication and Technology Journal, 31,* 131–143.
Pressley, M., & MacFadyen, J. (1983). The development of mnemonic mediator usage at testing. *Child Development, 54,* 474–479.
Pressley, M., Pigott, S., & Bryant, S. L. (1982). Picture content and preschooler's learning from sentences. *Educational Communication and Technology Journal, 30,* 151–161.
Purkel, W., & Bornstein, M. H. (1980). Picture and imagery both enhance children's short-term and long-term recall. *Developmental Psychology, 16,* 153–154.
Rohwer, W. D., Jr. (1973). Elaboration in childhood and adolescence. In H. W. Reese (Ed.), *Advances in child development and behavior* (Vol. 8, pp. 1–57). New York: Academic Press.
Rohwer, W. D., Jr., & Harris, W. J. (1975). Media effects on prose learning in two populations of children. *Journal of Educational Psychology, 67,* 651–657.
Ruch, M. D., & Levin, J. R. (1977). Pictorial organization versus verbal repetition of children's prose: Evidence for processing differences. *AV Communication Review, 25,* 269–280.
Ruch, M. D., & Levin, J. R. (1979). Partial pictures as imagery-retrieval cues in young children's prose recall. *Journal of Experimental Child Psychology, 28,* 268–279.

Schallert, D. L. (1980). The role of illustrations in reading comprehension. In R. J. Spiro, B. C. Bruce, & W. F. Brewer (Eds.), *Theoretical issues in reading comprehension: Perspectives from cognitive psychology, linguistics, artificial intelligence, and education* (pp. 503-524). Hillsdale, NJ: Erlbaum.

Shimron, J. (1975). Imagery and the comprehension of prose by elementary school children. *Dissertation Abstracts International, 36,* 795-A. (University Microfilms No. 75-18, 254)

Shriberg, L. K., & Shriberg, L. D. (1974). Basal adaptations of trade literature: A descriptive study. *The Reading Teacher, 27,* 685-693.

Silvern, S. B. (1980). Play, pictures, and repetition: Mediators in aural prose learning. *Educational Communication and Technology, 28,* 134-139.

Slythe, R. M. (1970). *The art of illustration 1750-1900.* London: The Library Association.

Tulving, E. (1983). *Elements of episodic memory.* New York: Oxford University Press.

Twyman, M. (1985). Using pictorial language: A discussion of the dimensions of the problem. In T. M. Duffy & R. Waller (Eds.), *Designing usable texts* (pp. 245-312). Orlando, FL: Academic Press.

Von. (1982). *William Shakespeare's Macbeth.* New York: Workman Publishing.

Von. (1983). *William Shakespeare's Romeo and Juliet.* New York: Knopf.

Vygotsky, L. (1978). *Mind in society: The development of higher psychological processes.* Cambridge, MA: Harvard University Press.

Waters, H. S., & Andreassen, C. (1983). Children's use of memory strategies under instruction. In M. Pressley & J. R. Levin (Eds.), *Cognitive strategy instruction: Psychological foundations* (pp. 3-24). New York: Springer-Verlag.

Wellman, H. M., Ritter, K., & Flavell, J. H. (1975). Deliberate memory behavior in the delayed reactions of very young children. *Developmental Psychology, 11,* 780-787.

Whalley, J. I. (1974). *Cobwebs to catch flies: Illustrated books for the nursery and schoolroom 1700-1900.* London, England: Elek Books.

Wood, E., Pressley, M., Turnure, J. E., & Walton, R. (1986, April). *Enriching children's recall of picture-dictionary definitions with interrogation and elaborated pictures.* Paper presented at the annual meeting of the American Educational Research Association, San Francisco.

Woolridge, P., Nall, L., Hughes, L., Rauch, T., Stewart, G., & Richman, C. L. (1982). Prose recall in first-grade children using imagery, pictures, and questions. *Bulletin of the Psychonomic Society, 20,* 249-252.

Yussen, S. R. (1974). Determinants of visual attention and recall in observational learning by preschoolers and second graders. *Developmental Psychology, 10,* 93-100.

Zarate, O. (1983). *William Shakespeare's Othello.* New York: Workman Publishing.

4
The Role of Illustrations in Processing and Remembering Illustrated Text

JOAN PEECK

Introduction

This chapter deals with the differences that may be observed when a text is read with illustrations instead of without. Until the early 1970s an account of these differences necessarily had to remain largely speculative because—in spite of the frequent use of pictures in text—there were relatively few research data available. In recent years, however, the effects of illustration have increasingly become the subject of thorough investigation in psychology and education, and as a result a good deal more can be said now than was previously possible.

The chapter consists of three parts. *Part 1* gives an overview of the various functions that illustrations in a text may fulfill. These roles are grouped into two broad clusters: an affective-motivational one that indicates how readers' enjoyment of a text, their attention, motivation, and so on may be affected, and a cognitive one that mainly deals with effects on comprehension and retention of the illustrated text. The roles are discussed on the basis of the time of their assessment: during reading or after the text has been read.

Whether or not illustrations do in fact fulfill these roles depends on a number of factors or variables and these are discussed in *Part 2*. Here again two broad categories are distinguished. The first group pertains to the reader of the text and deals with such characteristics as age and reading ability. The second group of variables pertains to the characteristics of pictures (e.g., qualitative aspects such as color and complexity), text (e.g., the degree of abstraction), and their interrelationship (e.g., the degree of informational overlap between pictures and text).

The chapter ends with a brief *Part 3* focusing on some of the gaps in the present knowledge concerning the role of illustration and on some of the ways this state of affairs may be improved.

The review is limited mostly to one type of illustration: the type that is usually referred to as "realistic" (Knowlton, 1966) or "representational" (Levie & Lentz, 1982; Alesandrini, 1984); that is, pictures that "share a physical resemblance with the thing or concept that the picture stands for" (Alesandrini, 1984). Within this one type, however, the pictures in the experiments reviewed differ on many dimensions, although an accurate assessment is not always easy because most research reports are not illustrated.

Considerable variation can also be found in the type and length of text. The emphasis in this review is on meaningful prose that usually exceeds the length of one sentence, although occasionally other kinds of text may be discussed (e.g., one-sentence "mini-stories").

Finally, the chapter deals mainly with texts that are read rather than heard. Since this requires a certain degree of reading ability, functions of illustration for children under school age are not considered in this review. Likewise, the chapter is not concerned with effects of illustrations on learning to read.

Part 1: Roles and Effects of Illustrations

In recent years, several authors (e.g., Duchastel, 1978; Levie & Lentz, 1982; Levin, 1981) have stressed the importance of a functional approach to the study of effects of text illustrations and offered lists of possible functions. Although the emphasis on this perspective is a fairly recent phenomenon, various earlier instances of interest in functions of pictures exist. In the United States, for instance, detailed descriptions of functions were provided by K. U. Smith (e.g., Smith & Smith, 1966) and Travers (e.g., Travers, 1969), while in Europe similar accounts may be found in Jagodzinska (1976) and Peeck (1972; 1974a). In addition, many textbooks on audio-visual methods and techniques have traditionally described a variety of roles that text illustrations and still pictures in general can play in education (e.g., Brown, Lewis, & Harcleroad, 1969; Dale, 1969; Kinder, 1959; Wittich & Schuller, 1967). The origin of the proposed functions and effects in these early studies often is not very clear; most of them are probably based on educational practice, personal experience, common sense, and—one sometimes fears—wishful thinking, but in many cases they are not based on adequate empirical research. They seem generally quite plausible, however, and tend to fit in nicely with one's experience as a user of illustrated texts—be it reader or teacher. Yet, it should be realized that it is uncertain whether some of the effects do in fact occur.

Basically, all functions and effects of illustrations may be derived from two characteristics of pictures in text. The first is that they depict some elements from the text; that is, they show what something or someone treated in the text looks like. But in doing so, they will do something more, and this establishes the second characteristic: that of providing additional information. Thus, when a history text that relates, say, the execution of some historical person is accompanied by a picture of the event, the illustration necessarily contains all kinds of information about such aspects as how the occurrence took place and about the appearance, clothes, and behavior of the people present.

Inspection of illustrated texts reveals that pictures may differ widely in the number of text elements depicted and the amount of additional information provided. In fact, sometimes it is hard to find any text content represented in the accompanying illustration, while on other occasions the amount of additional information may be so small as to be virtually negligible. In most text illustrations, however, both characteristics may be observed and they form the basis of the roles that pictures may fulfill.

In discussing these roles, a distinction is made between effects of pictures that may be obtained when an illustrated text is being read or studied and effects that are assessed after the text has been read, for example, when a reader tries to recall information from the text.

The functions to be discussed may be further divided into two broad categories. On the one hand there are what have been called the "incentive-motivational" functions (Travers, 1969) and "attentional" and "affective" functions (Levie & Lentz, 1982). On the other hand there is a cluster of more "cognitive" (Levie & Lentz, 1982), "explicative," and "retentional" (Duchastel, 1978) functions.

Affective-Motivational and Cognitive Effects During Reading

Regarding the first category, the literature on audio-visual communication contains many references to the affective-motivational effects that occur when text is read. Thus, it is suggested that pictures arouse interest (Dale, 1946), create a mood of emotion (Dale, 1946), vitalize learning (Alcorn, Kinder, & Schunert, 1964), and arouse curiosity (Smith & Smith, 1966), among other things.

In addition, it is thought that illustrations may make reading a text more enjoyable, result in positive attitudes toward reading in general and in "approaching tendencies" to the illustrated text in particular.

Although the proposed roles sound quite plausible, educational research has not come up with much evidence in support of these claims—perhaps because researchers considered the interest and enjoyment effects too obvious for serious investigation. Moreover, the few supportive studies that do exist (e.g., Bryant, Brown, Silberberg, & Elliott, 1981; Sewell & Moore, 1980) tell us what subjects thought of the text some time after they had read it, rather than their enjoyment ratings at the time of reading. It may be assumed, however, that the obtained measures give a reasonably adequate reflection of the enjoyment experienced during reading. When investigated in some detail, the focus of the positive feelings may turn out to be a narrow one. For instance, in an experiment with fifth graders (Peeck, 1972; for a summary, see Peeck, 1978), children thought their illustrated booklets more attractive than control subjects their unillustrated text, but they did not differ in the ratings of the story itself or in their rated enjoyment in participating in the experiment.

Apart from these affective functions, pictures may serve both general and more specific attentional roles. Various suggestions to this effect may be found in the literature. Smith and Smith (1966), for instance, indicate that "a primary purpose of visual illustration is to regulate orientation and to maintain a high level of concentration on the symbolic response patterns" (p. 334). Pictures could thus be facilitative in extending the time readers are willing to spend on a text and play a role in the distribution of this time, that is, in the allocation of the readers'

118   Joan Peeck

> A little girl ran out of a white house into a big yard. "Mother," she said, "my pet bird is gone. It went out of the open door."
>
> Mother laughed and said, "Look on the steps." When the girl looked she had a big surprise. A yellow bird with blue wings was sitting on the steps. Then the bird started to sing. It was the bird that had flown away.
>
> The little girl carefully put the bird in her pocket and took it back into the house. She made sure that she closed the door behind her.

FIGURE 4.1. Children's story used by Willows with (a) the original illustration and (b) another illustration that depicts largely the same text content. From *Reading Comprehension of Illustrated and Nonillustrated Aspects of Text* by D. M. Willows, 1979. Paper presented at the annual meeting of the American Educational Research Association, San Francisco. Reprinted and adapted by permission.

attention to parts of the text. Again, the educational research literature offers little evidence, but clear support may be found in a study by Paradowski (1967). In this study, undergraduates read passages that could be used to describe either curiosity-arousing animals ("a pichiciago") or low-arousal animals ("a sheep"). Recall of the passages was significantly better when paired with strange-animal illustrations than when read with pictures of normal animals.

It should be noted that these attentional roles are not necessarily beneficial. As with adjunct aids such as prequestions (Andereson & Biddle, 1975), increased attention for some text elements may be detrimental for attention to other elements. Furthermore, too much attention may be deployed to the illustrations themselves rather than to the accompanying text (Willows, 1978). Facilitation will therefore depend on the information to be learned from the text and the overlap between text and illustrations.

Regarding the category of cognitive roles, again numerous effects are suggested in the literature—without a great deal of evidence to support the suggestions. Presented in advance of the reading passage they could serve functions (Bernard, Petersen, & Ally, 1981; Weisberg, 1970) somewhat akin to the "advance organizers" designed by Ausubel (1960). In addition, they could act as "perspective inducing" devices (Peeck & Goud, 1985), suggesting to the reader what a text is about and also how the subject of the text is treated. Pictures may also serve to enhance the reality of the material for the reader (Smith & Smith, 1966), enrich reading (Dale, 1969; Jagodzinska, 1976), make reading material more concrete, add something that is not clearly expressible in words (Duchastel,

A little girl ran out of a white house into a big yard. "Mother," she said, "my pet bird is gone. It went out of the open door."

Mother laughed and said, "Look on the steps." When the girl looked she had a big surprise. A yellow bird with blue wings was sitting on the steps. Then the bird started to sing. It was the bird that had flown away.

The little girl carefully put the bird in her pocket and took it back into the house. She made sure that she closed the door behind her.

FIGURE 4.1. *Continued.*

1978; Travers & Alvarado, 1970; cf. Dale, 1969: "What is a bivouac? A picture may show it"), standardize the way a text is comprehended (O'Donnell, 1983), and correct mistaken impressions (Dale, 1954).

All this may subserve a function that is mentioned in recent surveys, namely, that of facilitating comprehension of text. As various authors (e.g., Duchastel, 1981; Levie & Lentz, 1982) have observed, this role may be especially important when the text deals with information that is relatively abstract or difficult to understand. It should be noted, however, that with easy material, too, illustrations will affect the way the text is understood, interpreted, and represented in memory. For instance, it will make a difference whether a child reads the story presented in Figure 4.1a or the story as it is given in Figure 4.1b: Under the influence of the illustration the child will think of a different mother, a different girl, a different bird—perhaps even a different song.

Direct evidence for comprehension facilitation is surprisingly scarce, with most studies measuring retention of learning material rather than comprehension per se. Even in the Rankin and Culhane (1970) study, that is often cited as one of the few to measure comprehension directly, the illustrations were studied prior to the comprehension-assessing text. In that study, graduate students performed significantly better on a cloze test when provided with pictures illustrating the reading material than controls without such pictures. No differences in cloze-test performance, however, were found for sixth graders in the same experiment, nor for 14-year-old children in a recent study by Reid, Briggs, and Beveridge (1983). Another example of facilitation of comprehension was reported by Koenke and Otto (1969) with sixth graders who were asked to give the main idea of a passage read with either a specifically relevant or a generally relevant picture, or without supplemental illustration. Subjects were significantly more able to produce the main idea (with the reading material present) in the illustrated than in the unillustrated conditions.

In addition, there are several studies that show increased recall with text illustrations which may well be accounted for by differences in comprehension at the time of reading. However, since they demonstrate primarily effects on retention rather than on comprehension, they are discussed later. An exception is made for the well-known study by Bransford and Johnson (1972), which presented high school subjects with a seemingly obscure taped text ("If the balloons popped the sound would not be able to carry since everything would be too far away from the correct floor . . ."). This passage was rendered meaningful and was much better recalled when a picture (see Figure 4.2) showed that it dealt with a "modern-day Romeo" who had devised an ingenious way of serenading his lady perched high up in an apartment building. When asked to rate the overall comprehensibility of the passage, subjects who had seen the picture prior to hearing the text gave significantly higher ratings than subjects who had seen the picture after the passage or had not seen it at all. Replication of these results was reported by Borges and Robins (1980).

Apart from affecting literal comprehension, it has been suggested (Donald, 1979, 1983) that illustrations may also facilitate inferential comprehension. According to Moore and Skinner (1985), inferential comprehension could be either "text based" or "script based," that is, the illustration could help the reader interpret information in the text or go beyond the text. Children (11 years old) answering both types of inference question immediately after reading illustrated passages obtained significantly higher scores than children who had not seen the illustrations, but only when the passage was an abstract one.

Yet another measure of comprehension was used in the studies by Stone and his colleagues (Stone & Crandell, 1982; Stone & Glock, 1981) with a text consisting of directions for the assembly of a loading cart. Comprehension was operationally defined as the accuracy with which the subjects (undergraduates) followed the directions when they were asked to assemble the model as they read. The presence of the illustrations was found to produce significantly more accurate performance of the task (Stone & Glock 1981).

As indicated above, the facilitation of comprehension may be the result of any—or a combination—of a number of factors. Thus, an increase in interest and curiosity brought about by the pictures may lead subjects to invest more cognitive effort in studying the illustrated text, lengthen the time they are willing to spend on the reading material, or enhance and elaborate their semantic processing.

FIGURE 4.2. Context picture used in the Bransford and Johnson study. From "Contextual prerequisites for understanding: Some investigations of Comprehension and Recall" by J. D. Bransford and M. K. Johnson, 1972, *Journal of Verbal Learning and Verbal Behavior*, *11*, p. 718. Copyright 1972 by Academic Press. Reprinted by permission.

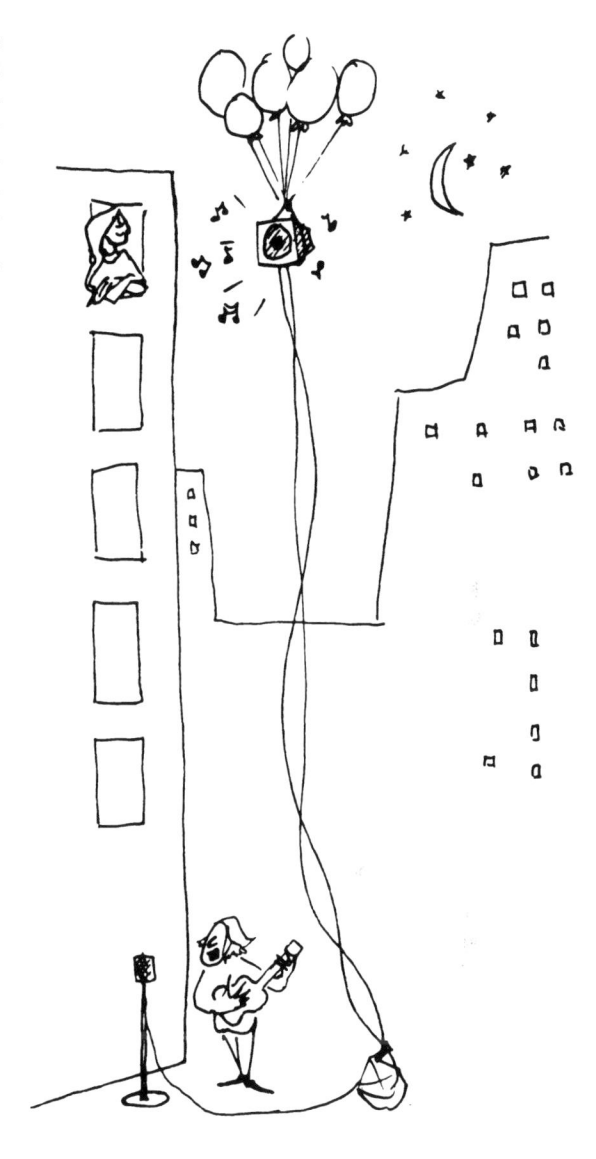

Other reasons are indicated by the Bransford and Johnson study: an illustration may be important in providing a context that allows people "to interpret meaningfully and to connect or organize sentences" (Bransford & Johnson, 1972, p. 132) they hear or read. Note that several distinct factors are involved here: The illustration enables one to bring to bear relevant prior knowledge to make sense of each individual sentence, but it also brings together all information into a meaningful whole, depicting the spatial and structural relationships that are mentioned in the text (cf. Dean & Enemoh, 1983).

Affective-Motivational and Cognitive Effects After Reading

On the basis of the processes that go on during inspection of illustrated prose, certain affective-motivational and cognitive effects may be expected when an assessment is made after the reading has finished, and it is this assessment with which most illustrated-prose studies are concerned.

Only a small part of this research has dealt with the affective-motivational category. In some studies emotional impact and attitudinal change due to the presence of illustrations are reported. Vernon (1953), for instance, found "considerable emotional impact" with the pictures when grammar-school pupils were presented with a text on the causes and cure of tuberculosis, illustrated by "rather striking photographs of, for instance, living conditions in the slums" (p. 181). Change in racial attitudes through the use of text illustrations was shown in a study by Litcher and Johnson (1969). Apart from the enhanced enjoyment mentioned before, confrontation with the illustrations in the learning material may have awakened "new desires and interests" (Kinder, 1959) or may have motivated further interest in the subject matter of the illustrated text (Bryant et al., 1981). Unfortunately, research evidence for these possible effects is scant and, where existent, not very encouraging. In the study by Bryant et al. (1981), for instance, humorous illustrations in textbook type material provided undergraduates with "little impetus to continue independent or course-related inquiry in the educational area under consideration" (p. 54). A surprising result was obtained in a study by Peeck (1972) that assessed "extended curiosity" (Berlyne, 1966) of fifth graders after they had read a text on two fictional prehistoric animals (see Figure 4.3) with either well-designed informative illustrations, poorly designed, less informative illustrations, or no illustrations. Extended curiosity (measured by ratings of the desire to read more, or see motion pictures, about the animals) was significantly lower with those children who had seen the poor-quality illustrations as compared to those in the other two conditions. Although the importance of this incidental outcome should not be overrated, it does suggest a caveat against a too casual inclusion of pictorial material for motivational purposes. It should not be assumed that illustrations, though perhaps not beneficial, will surely not do any harm. A somewhat similar observation was made by Willows, Borwick, and Hayvren (1981) who pointed out that when a text contains less information than a picture, "the child may find the text disappointing and the presence of pictures may actually detract from, rather than stimulate interest in the text" (p. 162).

The majority of studies on text illustration have focused on the effects of pictures on the retention of text that they accompany. For a long time positive empirical support for this retentional role remained scarce, but more recent research has made it abundantly clear that illustrations are in fact capable of affecting retention of illustrated prose in several ways.

Useful in clarifying the nature of these effects was the approach advocated in Peeck (1974b), which distinguishes carefully between information provided by text only, illustrations only, or both text and illustrations, and investigates the fate

FIGURE 4.3. "Poor" (top) and "good" (bottom) picture of the fictional prehistoric animal "Triops" used as stimulus material in Peeck. From *Plaatjes in leerprocessen* (Pictures in Learning Processes) by J. Peeck, 1972. Doctoral dissertation, University of Utrecht.

of each category at retention testing. In the past decade an impressive number of studies has appeared illuminating the retentive fate of these categories (especially the latter), and the results have recently been evaluated in the excellent, comprehensive review by Levie and Lentz (1982).

For the last of the above-mentioned categories their conclusion is clear-cut and positive: "Learning illustrated text information was better with illustrated text than with text alone in 98% of the [46] experimental comparisons. For 81% of the comparisons the difference was statistically significant" (p. 213). As will be discussed later in this chapter, the kind of picture–text relations involved are of importance for the effect. For instance, the effect may be more pronounced when spatial relations from the text are depicted (Schallert, 1980), when main ideas rather than details are depicted (Haring & Fry, 1979), or when illustration-dependent texts (Hayes & Readence, 1983) or sentences (Bock & Milz, 1977) are used; more will be said about this in Part 2.

The fate at retention testing of text information not incorporated in the illustration(s) is more complicated. Early speculations (e.g., Peeck, 1974b) suggested that both positive and negative effects could be expected: Pictures could serve as conceptual pegs (Paivio, 1969) facilitating the retention of information associatively connected to what is shown in the picture, but they could also distract the attention from the written word (cf. Samuels, 1970) or inhibit retention of picture-irrelevant text content the same way as prequestions may inhibit retention of question-irrelevant information (cf. Anderson & Biddle, 1975).

The experimental evidence brought together by Levie and Lentz led these authors to the conclusion that pictures neither help nor hinder learning of nonillustrated text information. It is not quite clear, however, how this failure to obtain effects should be interpreted. As Levie and Lentz (1982) suggest, it could mean that the presence of illustrations simply does not affect retention of nonillustrated text information, but it could also mean that positive and negative influences are simultaneously effective (on different text elements) and cancel each other out. In that case, experiments could perhaps be arranged in such a way that significant (positive and negative) effects could be obtained.

One such way is to make a distinction at testing between unillustrated elements from the text bearing some relationship to illustrated text content and those with none. This was attempted in a study reported by Peeck (1972). Fifth graders read an 850-word story on the life of a Mexican boy, Manolo, with or without two illustrations that depicted some of the text content. The retention test comprised the two types of question indicated above: questions on nonillustrated information related to illustrated text content (e.g., the value of a depicted washing machine that Manolo's parents won in a lottery) and questions on information not related to anything that could be seen in the pictures. The test, taken immediately or after a week, rendered no significant differences between experimental subjects and controls on either of these categories. Apparently, the critical relationship did not make a difference to the amount of information retained, but the issue should perhaps be explored a bit further.

Another, more productive, way may be to assess the learning result by different kinds of test. In one recent experiment, for instance, Van Dam, Brinkerink-Carlier, and Kok (1986) obtained inhibition of retention of unillustrated text content when university students read and gave oral recall of a 560-word text on "Egypt at the time of Thutmose III" that consisted of 20 paragraphs (called "scenes") dealing with subtopics. Illustration of half the subtopics with drawings that depicted "the gist of each scene" led to a moderate facilitating effect on gist recall of these scenes at the expense of the unembellished ones, in comparison to recall for the same scenes when presented without pictures. Thus, illustrations did not enhance the total amount of information retained, but it created mainly a different division of knowledge acquired from the text—a result that has also been obtained with other adjunct aids, such as prequestions (e.g., Peeck, 1970).

A recent study by Peeck and Goud (1985) indicates that the presence of illustrations may also lead subjects to recall unillustrated information congruent with a certain perspective on a text. In that study, grammar school pupils (15–16 years old) read a 1,700-word text on the Industrial Revolution that discussed positive, neutral, and negative aspects of a number of topics. In one condition, the text was illustrated with pictures representing negative aspects (e.g., a gloomy picture of child labor), in the other with pictures illustrating positive aspects (e.g., a charming picture of an early train). A week later there were several differences between the conditions in subjects' memory of the text. Differences in accordance with the induced perspective were obtained, for instance, when subjects were asked to write down the first five things they remembered from the text, and when they were required to produce a 10-line summary. Even though illustrated elements from the text (e.g., child labor) made up a substantial part of subjects' performance, it could be demonstrated that the retention effects of perspective also spread to nonillustrated text content. Obviously more research is needed to clarify the retentional fate of text-only information.

Before proceeding to the memory for pictorial information, it should be pointed out that effects on retention have also been found when illustrations were only generally relevant or vaguely related to text content (Levie & Lentz, 1982). This may be the case, for instance, when illustrations are used to provide a context to facilitate interpretation (Weinberg, 1970; Royer & Cable, 1976) or to provide a certain perspective on a text without specifically illustrating elements from the text (Peeck, in preparation).

As for the third category of information, that presented by pictures only, research evidence from illustrated-text studies is surprisingly scarce—perhaps reflecting the "literate bias of schooling" (Olson, 1977) and the tendency to see pictorial information as of only secondary importance. This is unfortunate because it is useful to establish the amount of pictorial information subjects remember when they have read an illustrated text—if only for the interpretation of effects on retention of text content. Experiments investigating retention for pictures presented without text have shown picture memory to be remarkable in both duration and capacity. Very high recognition rates, for instance, were obtained when subjects were briefly exposed to a large number of pictures (Nickerson, 1968; Shepard, 1967; Standing, Conezie, & Haber, 1970) even when tested after a few days. Although more recent research has indicated that these memory feats may be limited to recognition of certain types of information from the pictures (Mandler & Johnson, 1976; Friedman, 1979) and may be less impressive with other testing modes such as recall (see Spoehr & Lehmkuhle, 1982), substantial memory for pictorial information in illustrated texts may well be expected.

In accordance with this expectation, fourth graders who had read an illustrated text answered picture-only questions at various retention intervals significantly better than controls who had read the text without illustrations (Peeck, 1974b; for a replication, see Peeck, 1985). Strong evidence for long-term retention of pictures was also obtained by Read and Barnsley (1977) who tested adults for recognition of pictures from elementary school readers after retention intervals of 20-30 years. In a cross-cultural study involving secondary school subjects from various African and European countries, Jahoda, Cheyne, Deregowski, Sinha, and Collingbourne (1976), however, reported that "little if anything was learned from information presented in pictures but not also in text" (p. 311). The learning material in this study comprised short passages on animals or dwellings with or without black-and-white drawings illustrating passage content and some additional information. The result was obtained by comparing subjects who had read the illustrated text with subjects who took the test without prior exposure to the stimulus materials. Again, more research is needed to establish the extent to which information solely provided by illustrations is retained.

Although most studies have found some degree of facilitation, it should be noted that pictures also may affect retention of text in a less positive way, even where illustrated text elements are concerned. In particular, this may occur with a somewhat curious instance of the category of illustrated text content—namely, information from the text depicted more or less incorrectly. Retention for this type of information was studied in an experiment by Peeck (1974b), who presented fourth graders with a 19-page Rupert Bear story with or without illustrations (see Figure 4.4) containing occasional mismatches between pictures and text. Retention was tested after varying delays using a multiple choice test that included items dealing with the incongruously illustrated information. These items included both an alternative corresponding to the text and an alternative corresponding to the pictures. Subjects were not informed of the occurrence of the mismatches and, at the test, were free to select the response alternative they thought best. Considerable effects of the pictures were found: In the illustrated-text condition, subjects tended to select picture responses more frequently than text responses. Furthermore, they selected somewhat fewer text alternatives and, of course, far more picture alternatives than children who had not seen the illustrations. Similar results were obtained by Willows (1979) in a study with much shorter reading passages.

The pejorative effect of mismatched pictures on memory for text content sug-

All of the sudden the bird has disappeared. Rupert does not where to go, but he sees a fisherman coming smoking a little cigar. The fisherman asks Rupert: "Hello, would you like to go out to sea with me, young man? We'll go to the bed of the sea. Do you see that round thing floating there? That's my diving bell. We can sit in it for a while and see everything that goes on at the bottom of the sea." Excitedly Rupert says: "Oh, I'd love to come with you"!

FIGURE 4.4. Example of illustrated passage from Rupert Bear story used by Peeck. From *Rupert Bear Revisited: Memory for Modality and Awareness of Inconsistencies in Processing Illustrated Prose* by J. Peeck, 1983. Paper presented at the annual meeting of the American Educational Research Association, Montreal.

gested by these studies has recently been questioned by Pressley and his associates (Pressley, Levin, Pigott, LeComte, & Hope, 1983). In their study, Pressley et al. indicate that with some procedural changes in the design of mismatched-picture experimentation, no reduction of children's retention of prose will occur. More particularly, using cued-recall measures instead of recognition tests and warning subjects at testing to recall only from the text and not from the pictures appeared sufficient to neutralize interference effects from the mismatched pictures. A recent study by Peeck (1985), however, shows that the effects of mismatched illustrations are a good deal more complex than is apparent from the paper by Pressley et al., especially when retention is assessed after a delay. Complications arise, for instance, because inconsistencies between text and pictures are often not detected, even though there is strong evidence that quite often both the verbal and pictorial elements were initially encoded. In addition, after a while subjects tend to forget inconsistencies that they did originally detect. On these undetected, or no longer identified, mismatched items, subjects appeared strongly inclined to respond according to what they had seen in the illustrations, as did subjects in the original experiments by Peeck (1974b) and Willows (1979).

To end this section on picture effects, it should be noted that research has also occasionally probed the possibility of other effects in the cognitive realm. For example, as indicated earlier, illustrations may enhance the ability to draw inferences beyond the explicitly stated information (Donald, 1979, 1983; Moore & Skinner, 1985) or may produce facilitative transfer in the recall of related new passages (Royer & Cable, 1977; Hayes & Readence, 1983).

Causes of Cognitive Effects

The various cognitive roles of illustrations related above may be due to a number of factors, some of which were mentioned before in the discussion of comprehension effects. Comprehension and subsequent retention may thus be facilitated by the willingness to invest more time and cognitive effort in studying the reading material, the enhancement or elaboration of semantic processing, the availability of a context and the activation of relevant prior knowledge enabling a more meaningful interpretation and a more effective storage of the text, the availability of an organizing scheme clarifying and representing spatial and structural relationships of elements in the text, and so on.

Apart from these factors, much of the retentional role may be a result of the fundamental characteristic of illustration: to give a visual image of information provided by the text. As Levin (1981) put it, text-relevant illustrations "take information that was represented in one mode (verbal) and represent it in another (pictorial)" (p. 214).

The importance of the availability of such a visual code in addition to a verbal one may be derived from various theoretical positions, such as the "dual-coding" theory (e.g., Paivio, 1971) and the "superior sensory code" hypothesis proposed by Nelson and his colleagues (Nelson, Reed, & Walling, 1976). Paivio's model, for instance, proposes the existence of two qualitatively different memory stores, one visual and one verbal in nature, and predicts that information encoded in both stores will be better remembered than information encoded in only one. Apart from that, the pictorial image code may be "mnemonically superior" (Paivio & Csapo, 1973), or it may be "a qualitatively superior sensory code" in comparison to the corresponding label (Nelson et al., 1976).

Several of the retention effects reviewed above are in agreement with an interpretation along these lines, especially the outcome that retention of depicted text information is facilitated, whereas unillustrated text information is not. Support for the availability of visual and verbal modes can also be found in some of the mismatch-illustration studies. Due to their peculiar nature, these studies give an insight into the use that subjects make of the pictorial and verbal modes that is generally missing when text content is depicted correctly. The studies consistently show (Peeck, 1974b, 1983, 1985) that, especially with growing delay, subjects increasingly tend to base their retention-test responses on what they have seen in the pictorial supplements. One is tempted to relate this increased reliance on the visual rather than on the verbal mode to differential forgetting curves for pictures and words that have been reported in picture-memory experiments (e.g.,

Shepard, 1967). Increased reliance on pictorial information could also be at the basis of the finding by Levie and Lentz (1982) that in 24 cases where facilitation due to illustrations could be directly compared, 19 showed that pictures helped more in delayed than in immediate recall. Similar results were obtained in two separate experiments reported in Peeck (1972; see also Peeck, 1978).

The gradually increasing reliance on the information provided by illustrations that is suggested by these data does not necessarily mean that subjects can accurately report whether information they remember originated from the verbal or pictorial mode. In fact, some evidence shows that correct modality identification of information recalled deteriorates considerably after a few days (Peeck, 1983, 1985; cf. Pezdek, 1977). In addition, after a delay there is in the case of mismatched items an intriguing bias to think that verbal information was presented pictorially in the original reading materials (Peeck, 1983).

Finally, in the present context it is perhaps of interest to mention a finding from the Peeck and Goud (1985) experiment mentioned previously. When the subjects were required to write down in keywords the first five things they remembered from the illustrated text that they had read a week before, many of the responses could be directly related to what they had seen in the pictures. Once again, this suggests the importance of the availability of pictorial representation in memory for an illustrated text.

Although several findings of the illustrated-text research can thus be accounted for, many effects of facilitation of retention may also be explained without resorting to the visual mode of the information stored. The presence of the illustration could lead to an increase in attention for the depicted text elements amounting to a rehearsal of the information, perhaps with enhanced semantic or deeper-level processing as suggested above. Mere rehearsal, however, seems unsatisfactory as an explanation in view of results by Levin and his associates (e.g., Levin, Bender, & Lesgold, 1976; Ruch & Levin, 1977) which showed a stronger facilitation for recall of oral prose with pictures than through repetition. Furthermore, it should be noted that the virtual absence of inhibitory effects for unillustrated text information is somewhat difficult to reconcile with a differential deployment of attention and processing activities over the information in the text.

Part 2: Factors Influencing Text–Illustration Effects

In discussing the various roles of text illustrations in Part 1, little attention was paid to factors that influence the occurrence and magnitude of the effects under consideration. In a way this negligence is justified because inspection of the literature reveals that picture effects have been found, with considerable consistency, across a wide range of learner characteristics, pictures and texts, and picture–text relationships. At the same time, however, research results have shown that each of these sets of factors affects picture effects in ways that deserve closer scrutiny.

In this part of the chapter the influence of some of these variables on the outcome of reading illustrated text is examined. The variables are treated separately without much reference to the interaction with other variables that may occur. It should be realized, however, that the sets of factors indicated above never operate in isolation. In every situation where an illustrated text is read, all sets of variables will affect the outcome.

Learner Characteristics

In their review of research on pictures in oral prose, Levin and Lesgold (1978) note that positive picture effects were obtained with students representing different levels within each of a number of learner characteristics, such as age, intellectual ability, and sex. The same can be said for studies of illustrated written prose. In fact, in several studies allowing a direct comparison of subjects differing in one characteristic (e.g., Haring & Fry, 1979), no differences in magnitude or kind of picture effects were found. The outcome of other studies (e.g., see Hanes, 1973), however, indicates that a closer look at some of these learner characteristics, in particular the reader's age, is desirable.

Age differences relevant to motivational-affective roles were observed in a number of early studies and summarized in reviews by Spaulding (1955), Travers and Alvarado (1970), and others. Thus, it was found that young children prefer realistic pictures with color and relatively simple design, whereas older children and adults prefer more complex pictures, perhaps because of an increased capacity to handle perceptual complexity (Travers & Alvarado, 1970).

Of more importance, especially for cognitive effects, are differences between children and adults in approach, interpretation, and use of illustrations. Before discussing these differences, some general comments on learner activities in relation to text illustrations will be made.

Of primary importance for the effect that illustrations may have is, of course, what the reader *does* with a picture that goes with the text. Does he or she look at the picture and, if so, for how long and what kind of inspection occurs? Though a brief glance is sufficient to recognize a picture at a later date (Potter & Levy, 1969), longer inspection times are needed when more information has to be extracted than is necessary for simply identifying a picture well enough to distinguish it from others (Potter, 1976). In this respect, it has been shown that it is not so much the length of viewing time per se, as the number of fixations the subject makes during that time that determines what is remembered (Loftus, 1972; see also Spoehr & Lehmkuhle, 1982).

Given the dependence of picture effects on length and nature of inspection, it is not surprising that some investigators (e.g., Hayes & Readence, 1983; Moore & Skinner, 1985) have tried to augment the possible effects of illustrations by instructing subjects to pay attention to the pictures as they studied the reading material in their experiments. Studies allowing a comparison of intentional attention to illustrations with incidental attention in other conditions (Rasco, Tennyson, & Boutwell, 1975; Hayes & Readence, 1983), however, suggest—somewhat surprisingly—that such instructional interventions do not significantly increase the effect of illustrations. Nevertheless, as research evidence is scarce, Hayes and Readence (1983) are probably right in commenting that "as a matter of sound educational practice, teachers would be well advised to continue to call readers' attention to illustrations in their text" (p. 248).

Merely calling attention to an illustration, however, may not be sufficient. One way to achieve adequate attention could be to force readers to study illustrations in a text. There are several indications in the literature that the effects of illustrations are indeed stronger when readers are made to process pictures more

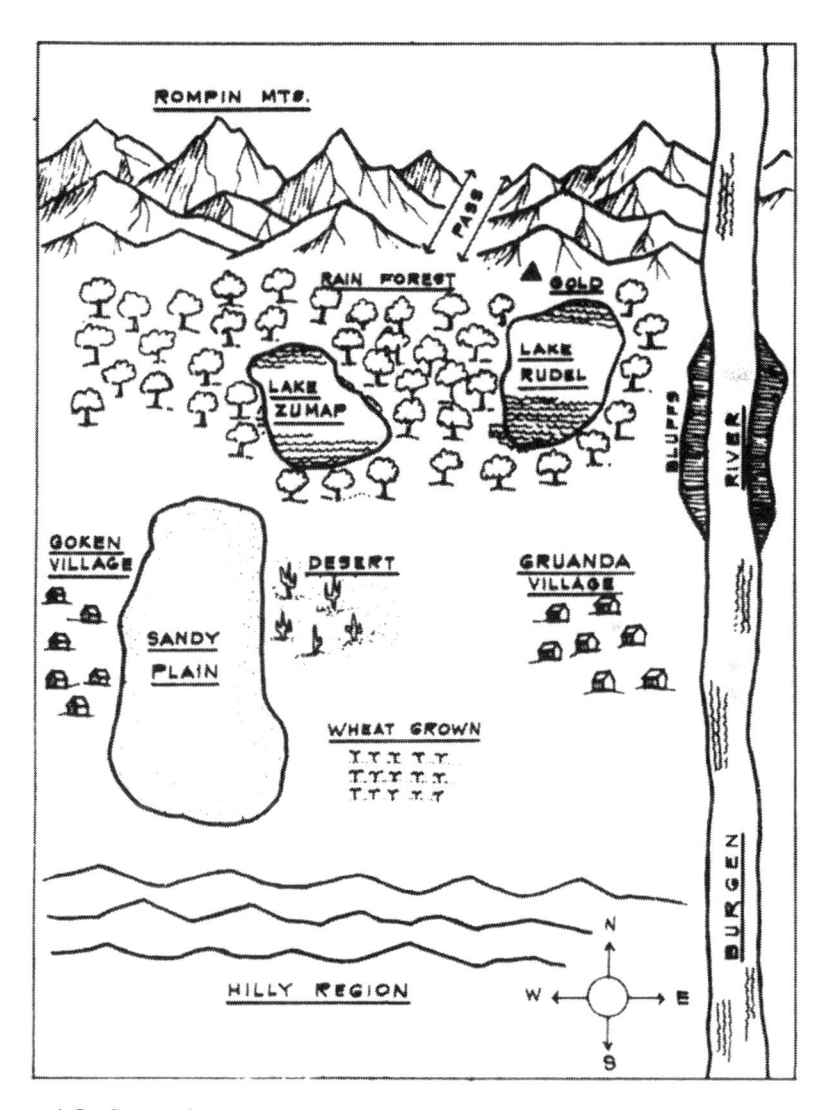

FIGURE 4.5. Composite map showing topological referents used in Dean and Kulhavy (Experiment 2). From "The Influence of Spatial Organization in Prose Learning" by R. S. Dean and R. W. Kulhavy, 1981, *Journal of Educational Psychology*, 73, p. 60. Copyright 1981 by the American Psychological Association. Reprinted by permission of the author.

132   Joan Peeck

thoroughly. In an experiment by Dean and Kulhavy (1981), for instance, subjects benefited more from a map (see Figure 4.5) showing topological features from a text when they were required to label each feature than when the map was presented with the labels already provided. A similar result was obtained by Verhaegen (1983) with fifth and sixth graders who read a text on the design, operation, and history of air balloons (cf. Peeck, 1980; see Figure 4.6). Children who studied the text with a drawing that showed a balloon with 15 labeled parts discussed in the text remembered less of the location of these parts than subjects who were given the drawing and told to put in the labels themselves. A different, perhaps somewhat curious way of achieving active processing of an illustration was used by Dean and Enemoh (1983) who required undergraduates "to trace and study" a picture (see Figure 4.7) for 5 minutes prior to, or after, reading a text.

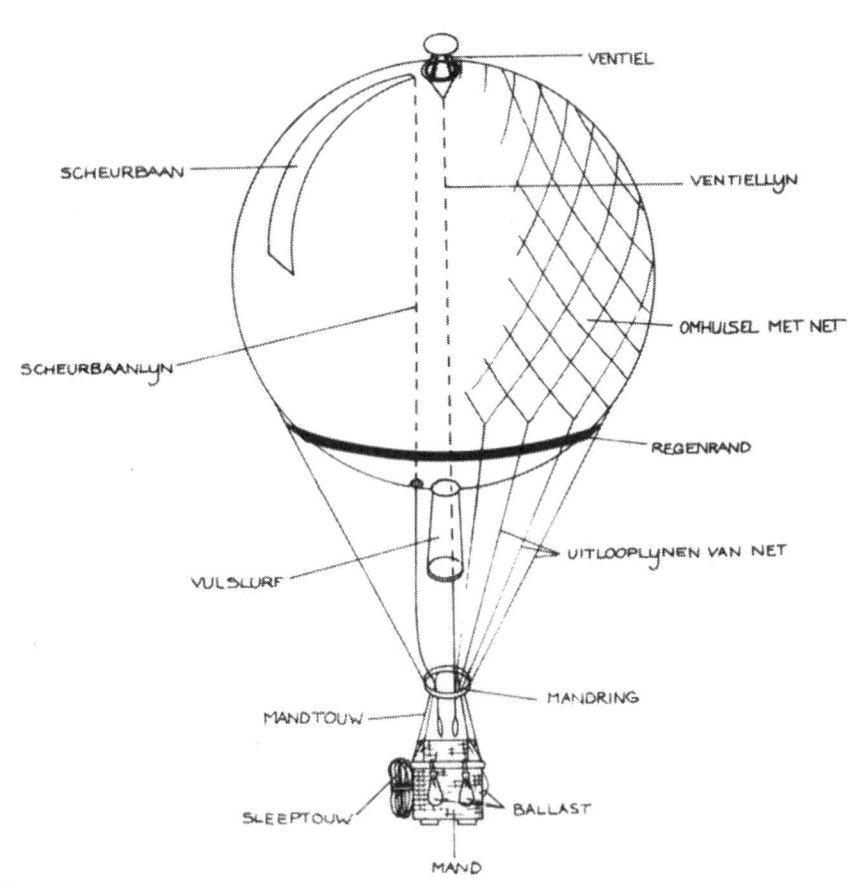

FIGURE 4.6. Experimenter-provided drawing of air balloon used by Peeck. From *Experimenter-Provided and Learner-Generated Pictures in Learning from Text* by J. Peeck, 1980. Paper presented at the annual meeting of the American Educational Research Association.

FIGURE 4.7. Photograph of meandering river presented as "pictorial organizer" in the study by Dean and Enemoh. From "Pictorial Organization in Prose Learning" by R. S. Dean and P. A. Enemoh, 1983, *Contemporary Educational Psychology, 8*, p. 23. Copyright 1983 by Academic Press. Reprinted by permission.

In all these attempts there is the implicit assumption that subjects are capable of adequate processing of the illustrative material when they are simply told to do so. This assumption is questionable, especially when young children are concerned. It seems likely that, not only in the case of more obviously complicated illustrations such as diagrams and graphics but also with representational pictures, competency in adequately dealing with illustrations develops only gradually.

An account of the development of picture interpretation in children was given many years ago by the French psychologist Binet (e.g., Binet & Simon, 1908; see Figure 4.8), who distinguished three stages. (For a similar but more rapidly progressing development see Stern, 1930.) When presented with a picture of a scene or event, children at the first stage will merely enumerate persons or objects in the picture. At the second stage, when the child is about 7 years old, a more complete description can be given including some mention of relations between pictured objects or persons ("The bread is on the table") and descriptions of human actions ("The man is chopping wood"). The last stage is reached when children are about 12 years old (or some years younger according to Stern, 1930), and only then are they capable of a more complete and correct interpretation of the picture and an identification of its central theme. Recent research has confirmed and elaborated these findings, indicating interactions with the kind of

FIGURE 4.8. Reproduction of engraving used by Binet and Simon in their research on the development of picture interpretation. From "Le développement de l'intelligence chez les enfants" by A. Binet and Th. Simon, 1908, *l'Année Psychologique, 14*, p. 9. Copyright 1908 by *l'Année Psychologique*. Reprinted by permission.

picture shown and with factors such as the child's home experience with being shown picture books (Danset-Léger, 1980).

But even when the last stage is reached, there are likely to remain differences between the way adults and children approach and understand pictures. A number of these differences have recently been listed by Van Parreren (1983). An important difference, according to Van Parreren, is that adults look at pictures in a more systematic and active way. They approach pictures with certain expectations (cf. Jörg, 1977) that change and develop in the course of inspection, their eye movement patterns appear to be more meaningful and effective than those of younger children (Mackworth & Bruner, 1970), and they are more capable of systematically and sequentially deploying attention to separate parts of the picture (cf. Neisser, 1979). Van Parreren (1983) also points out that adults make far more inferences from what is shown visually: "In the same way as we read between the lines when confronted by a written text, we conclude from that which is visible in a picture states of affairs which cannot strictly be seen in the picture" (Van Parreren, 1983, p. 67). A final difference mentioned by Van Parreren is that adults, in comparison with children, do not treat an illustration as an isolated item but apprehend it within a context (i.e., make use of the caption, read the accompanying text, look at other pictures).

In view of these imperfections in children's use and interpretation strategies, several attempts have been made to teach children how to deal with pictures in a more productive way. One such attempt is the TAP (Thinking About Pictures) program developed by Higgins (1979) in Australia. In this program, children are taught guidelines and their application for drawing and evaluating inferences from pictures depicting various forms of human interaction. In one recent study (Higgins, 1979), the program was shown to increase significantly the productivity of inference drawing among fourth graders, but it failed to enhance their evaluation of the quality of the inferences that were produced.

In the Netherlands, Van den Bosch (1979) tried to enhance effects of text illustrations by making children aware of the three categories of information that are usually present in an illustrated text (see p. 120). In the program (six sessions of 40 minutes duration), children were presented with line drawings and captions of increasing complexity and length and were shown how the information in text and picture could be assigned to one of the three categories. Care was taken to point out the mutual influence of text and illustrations: Through pictures we can know a lot more about the text, while, at the same time, the text can help us to interpret the pictures. In addition, guidelines were given to promote depth of processing of the illustrations and to help the children to relate the pictures to relevant prior knowledge. In one exploratory study (Van den Bosch, 1979), some improvement in retention of illustrated text could be demonstrated for fifth graders who had taken the course in comparison with controls who had not.

Apart from these training programs, there are, of course, more ordinary ways of aiding people to profit from the presence of illustrations. Effects of illustrations may be enhanced, for example, by the use of captions. As Spaulding (1956) noted in his study of inhabitants of rural areas in Mexico and Costa Rica, captions serve important functions in helping viewers to correctly interpret illustrations. In particular, they can aid in directing attention to specific aspects of pictures (cf. Fleming, 1979). Evidence for the notion that verbal descriptions modify visual encoding processes and recognition memory in adults and children of various age groups can be found in a number of studies (e.g., Bacharach, Carr, & Mehner, 1976; Carr, Bacharach, & Mehner, 1977; Jörg & Hörmann, 1978, 1983), but research into caption effects in illustrated prose is largely lacking. Focusing attention may also be achieved by other cueing techniques, such as arrows, adjunct questions, and color (Dwyer, 1972; Holliday, 1981; Winn, 1981).

Apart from the age-related learner-activity variables discussed above, various other learner characteristics could affect the outcome of studies using illustrated text. One of the subject variables that has been studied in some detail is reading ability. As Willows et al. (1981) have speculated, reading ability could influence illustration effects in several ways. Children who are relatively low in reading ability, for instance, may direct more attention to pictorial accompaniments because they lack confidence in their ability to process text without regularly checking the illustration in search of "clues" to the text's meaning. They may also require the additional motivation that the pictures can provide to arouse their interest in reading text in the first place. In accordance with this, Goldstein and Underwood (1981) conclude in their recent review that the less competent or the younger a reader is, the greater the influence of picture information will be. They also point out that this may or may not be of benefit, "depending upon whether the picture is representative of the text, and to what extent it corresponds to the intended meaning" (p. 14). In their review of the literature, Levie and Lentz (1982) find some (albeit inconclusive) support for the contention that poor readers are helped more by illustrations than good readers. Levie and Lentz report that in the studies which they reviewed the average facilitation due to the presence of illustrations was 44% for poor readers and 23% for good readers. In only one study (Wardle, 1977), however, was the suggested interaction between reading ability and the presence or absence of pictures found to be significant. Also relevant in this aspect is the finding in a study by Rusted and M. Coltheart (1979) that the correlation between reading ability and text recall that was obtained in the no-pictures control condition appeared absent when children read the text with illustrations. This suggests again that the enhancing effects of pictures may be more pronounced for poor than for good readers. In other studies, however, substantial correlations between reading ability and performance were also obtained when illustrations were present (e.g., Goldberg, 1974; Moore & Skinner, 1985; Peeck, 1972).

Some additional evidence for the suggestion that poor readers may make more intensive use of text illustrations comes from an observation by Rusted and V. Coltheart (1979) that "poor readers frequently moved their eyes from the passage to the picture, apparently checking the features in the pictures as they read them. In contrast, the good readers paid little attention to the pictures during their reading" (pp. 521-522). No systematic relationships between viewing time and reading level, however, were found in the eye movement patterns registered by Flagg and associates (Flagg, Weaver, Fenton, Gelatt, & Pray, 1980).

Apart from reading ability, in some investigations verbal ability (Dean & Kulhavy, 1981; Holliday, Brunner, & Donais, 1977) and reasoning ability (Koran & Koran, 1980) have been related to the effects that illustrations may have. These studies generally suggest that low-ability students may obtain more benefit from the presence of pictorial adjuncts than high-ability students.

There are a number of other subject variables that could well be related to pictorial effects, but, although some research data have been collected, the evidence is generally insufficient for drawing any definitive conclusions. For instance, as it has been shown that good visualizers are able to recall pictures more accurately than poor visualizers (Marks, 1983), the ability to visualize could well influence retention effects of illustrations. It has also been suggested that performance may be affected by cognitive style variables, such as field dependence (Carrier, Joseph, Krey, & LaCroix, 1983) or by the extroversion–introversion dimension (Riding & Wicks, 1978), but again the issue has not been studied in sufficient detail to permit conclusions.

Finally, mention should be made of a learner variable that has not been the subject of much investigation, although it is known to be of crucial importance in (prose) learning (see Ausubel, 1963; Bransford, 1979). This is the level of prior knowledge of, and experience with, the subject matter of the illustrated text. It may reasonably be assumed that this variable will substantially affect the interpretation and understanding of the illustrations, the length of viewing time required, and the amount and quality of information extracted. Some research on this issue has recently been published by Joseph and Dwyer (1984). They presented tenth-grade public school students who differed in degree of prior knowledge of general physiology with a text on the physiology of the human heart illustrated with pictures varying in level of realism and abstraction. In both externally paced (taped) and self-paced (printed) presentation formats, students with a high level of prior knowledge generally outperformed students with a lower level. An interesting finding of this study was that high-level students in the self-paced condition benefited most from the realistic and abstract visuals; no difference in effectiveness of the kind of illustration was found for the low-level learners.

Picture, Picture/Text, and Text Variables

Picture Variables

As Willows (1980; see also Willows et al., 1981) and other authors reviewing the literature (e.g., Brody, 1981) have pointed out, there is little consistency in the pictures used in studies that investigate influence of text illustrations. Although examples of the illustrations used are generally not reproduced in journals, the pictures apparently vary in type, number, the presence or absence of color, size, density of information presented, and so on. And yet, as Willows (1980) puts it, researchers often act as though "a picture is a picture is a picture."

Although the finding—despite these differences—of consistent influences across the studies gives an indication of the robustness of the effects, it is obvious that uncontrolled variability is generally not very helpful, for example, in furthering insight into the relationship between picture variables and effects obtained.

That effects of illustration may be influenced by qualitative aspects of the pictures used is intuitively plausible and has long been stressed by authors of textbooks on the use of audio-visual aids (e.g., Dale, 1954; Kinder, 1959; Wittich & Schuller, 1967). These texts often contain lengthy discussions of a number of relevant picture variables and of criteria with which the usefulness of pictures may be assessed. Some of these are:

The aesthetic, artistic, and technical quality; with photographs, for instance, this concerns such topics as contrast, viewpoint, use of color, and composition

Authenticity and validity; this refers, for instance, to the demand that "the impression left in the learner's mind be correct and accurate" (Dale, 1954) and that the picture "will not lead to wrong inferences" (Wittich & Schuller, 1969)

Density of information; this aspect refers to both the number of picture elements or objects and to the degree of detail with which each element is depicted. For example, it is suggested that with too many details the eye "does not know where to go" (Wittich & Schuller, 1967) and the central idea may accordingly be obscured.

On some of these issues more research data have by now become available. Thus, the influence of color has been the subject of a number of studies, in particular by Dwyer (for summaries, see Dwyer, 1970, 1972), although most of these have been concerned with color pictures in slide/tape or programmed instruction presentations rather than in ordinary written text (for a review, see Chute, 1979). The results indicate that color may help to direct attention to specific properties of elements and to detect interrelationships or make discriminations. Furthermore, color may make pictures more attractive and motivate students (especially low-ability learners, see Willows, 1980) to study them more attentively. Color, however, may also add to the complexity of a picture and may give the learner more information than he or she is able to process, especially when looking time is restricted. In addition, it may serve to direct attention to irrelevant parts of the picture (cf. Rudnick, Porter, & Suydam, 1973).

A number of research studies have dealt with a cluster of variables concerning the type of illustration in terms of the amount of information and detail they contain and their complexity and concreteness. Some of these studies were inspired by a controversy arising from the recommendation by Dale (1946) that for instructional purposes the more realistic or lifelike the stimulus material is, the greater the probability that it may facilitate learning. The suggested emphasis on realism in pictures with the complexity and detail that this implies has been disputed by a number of authors, for instance, by Travers (1964) who called it "the worship of a false god" (p. 380).

The issue has been studied in several experiments, particularly in a series of investigations by Dwyer (summarized in Dwyer, 1970, 1972). He compared the effects of different types of visuals (see Figure 4.9) accompanying a 2,000-word text on the human heart on four different dependent measures. The four types of picture were simple line drawings, detailed shaded drawings, photographs of models of the heart, and photographs of heart specimens. They displayed "relatively the same information . . . differing only in the amount of detail they contained" (Dwyer, 1970, p. 238). The visuals could be either black-and-white or in color. Students in the oral/verbal control conditions viewed displays containing the names of the parts and processes of the heart as they were mentioned in the instructional presentation.

The results of Dwyer's work indicate that the effectiveness of realism and complexity is very dependent on the time and effort the reader is willing and able to invest in studying the pictures (see also Fleming & Sheikhian, 1972). If viewing time is limited, as may occur in externally paced conditions, then illustrations containing relatively small amounts of realistic detail, such as simple line drawings, tend to be most effective. With self-paced instruction, there is a better chance that students will take advantage of the additional information provided by the details, although there is some danger that, with too casual inspection, "excessive realistic detail may . . . detract attention from relevant and important learning cues" (Dwyer, 1972, p. 91). The effectiveness of the various types of picture also depends on the students' ability to deal with such detailed illustrations and the prior knowledge they bring to the task. In some cases, a combina-

4. Role of Illustrations in Processing   139

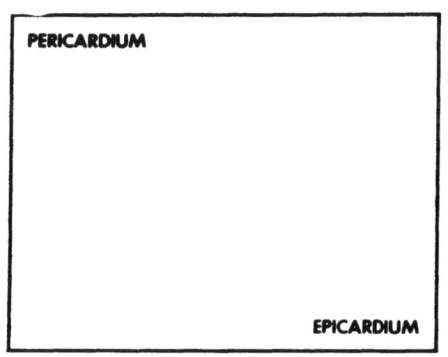

PLATE 1
Oral/verbal presentation

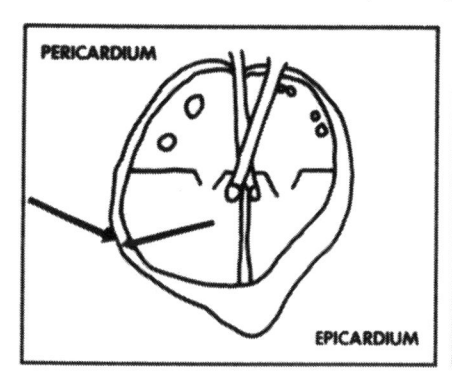

PLATE 2
Simple line drawing presentation (b & w)

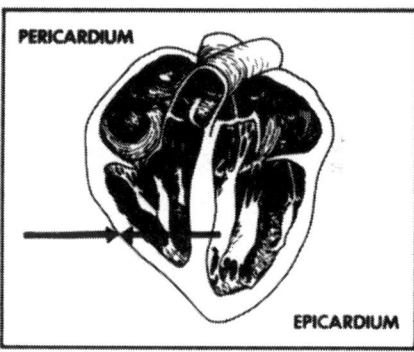

PLATE 3
Detailed, shaded drawing presentation (b & w)

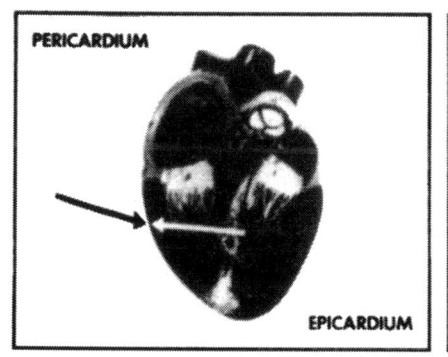

PLATE 4
Heart model presentation (b & w)

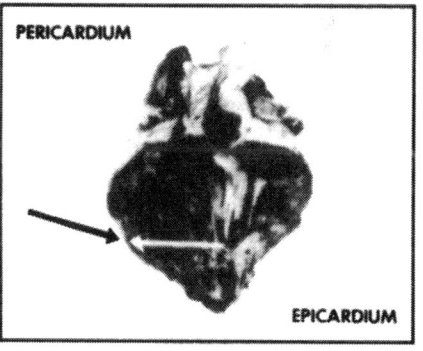

PLATE 5
Realistic photographic presentation (b & w)

FIGURE 4.9. Sample visuals (black and white) used to complement instructional treatments in research summarized by Dwyer. From *A Guide for Improving Visualized Instruction* (p. 16) by F. M. Dwyer, 1972, University Park, PA: State College, Pennsylvania State University, Learning Services Division. Copyright 1972 by Learning Services Division, Pennsylvania State University. Reprinted by permission.

140 Joan Peeck

tion of detailed and less detailed pictures, such as photographs and drawings (Holliday & Thursby, 1977)—perhaps combined in one "hybrid" illustration (Joseph & Dwyer, 1984)—may be the most effective presentation. A final factor regarding the suitability of realistic detail is the objective to be achieved. As a case in point, since students have been found to be appreciative of realistic detailed pictures (Spaulding, 1955), the use of such visuals may be appropriate when the main reason for illustration is promoting the enjoyment of the reading material. Achieving that objective does not imply, however, that other (e.g., cognitive) objectives are simultaneously served. As Dwyer (1972) has noted: 'Aesthetically pleasing visuals may be deceptive in their instructional value" (p. 90). Within the cognitive realm too, the degree of realistic detail that is most appropriate may depend on the specific learning objective to be attained. Support for this contention can again be derived from several of Dwyer's experiments (see Dwyer, 1970, 1972) in which the effectiveness of various types of visuals was compared for a number of different criterial tasks.

A variable that has occasionally received some attention (e.g., Bryant et al., 1981; Sewell & Moore, 1980) is the use of humor in illustrations. In their paper, Bryant et al. discuss a number of positive and negative effects humorous illustrations (see Figure 4.10) may have in terms of pedagogical effectiveness (especially recall of text content), appeal, motivations to sustain attention, and persuasion. In their study, 180 undergraduates read a 6-page booklet with a variable number of humorous cartoons and, after reading, evaluated the material on a number of dimensions and took a retention test. Humorous pictorial illustrations were found to have no effect on information acquisition and on motivation, positive

FIGURE 4.10. Humorous illustration used in the study by Bryant et al. From "Effects of Humorous Illustrations in College Textbooks" by J. Bryant, D. Brown, A. R. Silberberg, and S. C. Elliott, 1981, *Human Communication Research*, 8, p. 48. Copyright 1981 by Sage Publications, Inc. Reprinted by permission of the publisher.

effects on appeal (i.e., enjoyment and the likelihood of book purchase), and negative effects on persuasibility, that is, the credibility of the author appeared significantly diminished.

Finally, a rather different type of illustration that may be discussed—somewhat arbitrarily—in the present context are pictures drawn by learners themselves instead of being provided by teachers or experimenters. There has been little research on this subject, partly due perhaps to the methodological difficulties involved. One problem, for instance, has to do with time-on-task: Subjects required to draw tend to spend much more time on the learning material than subjects studying a text with or without experimenter-provided illustrations. This makes investigations, not controlling for reading time, somewhat difficult to interpret. In some studies (Alesandrini, 1981; Dean & Kulhavy, 1981; Rasco, Tennyson, & Boutwell, 1975; Snowman & Cunningham, 1975), subjects who had drawn aspects of the reading passage retained significantly more of the passage than subjects who just read the text; in other studies (Tirre, Manelis, & Leicht, 1979; Peeck, 1980) no facilitation was obtained. The results are therefore inconclusive.

A positive aspect of this pictorial strategy is the thoroughness of the processing of relevant text elements required to carry out the task. At the same time, however, it makes the result dependent on the quality of the drawing produced—its completeness, clarity, accuracy, and so on. (Since it may be assumed that, in general, only a correct drawing of elements will facilitate recall performance, the quality of the drawings should be incorporated into the analysis of research results in this area; unfortunately, most investigators fail to do this.) The failure of subjects, especially children (cf. Peeck, 1980), to produce complete and accurate drawings has perhaps the advantage of revealing comprehension gaps at an early stage in the learning process.

PICTURE/TEXT AND TEXT VARIABLES

In an earlier section it was shown that the relationship between pictures and text is a crucial one for several roles that illustrations may fulfill in processing and especially in remembering text. As the Levie and Lentz (1982) survey clearly indicates, much of the facilitative cognitive effect is restricted to the information in the text actually depicted in the illustrations.

It is not very clear what *kind* of information may profit most from illustration. On this issue the method section in the published research reports is often very inexplicit and when specification is given the characteristics of the illustrated features in terms of, for instance, level of importance are generally not provided. A few studies, however, have dealt directly with effects of illustration in relation to level of text importance. A study by Haring and Fry (1979) indicates that illustrations may be especially effective in representing main ideas. In this particular study, main ideas were operationalized as information high in the text hierarchy according to Meyer's (1975) system of prose analysis. In the Haring and Fry experiment, illustration did not facilitate immediate or delayed recall of lower-level text content. In a study involving oral prose (a series of one-sentence "ministories"), however, Levin, Bender, and Pressley (1979) obtained facilitation for recall of both central and peripheral sentence information, although the effect was statistically larger for central than for peripheral content. The issue is therefore not very clear and it seems too early to conclude, as Schallert (1980) does, that "pictures help the reader learn and comprehend a text when they illustrate information central to the text [and] when they represent new content which is important to the overall message" (p. 514).

Schallert also notes that illustrations are especially facilitative when they depict spatial–structural relationships in a text—an observation that is made by several other reviewers of the research literature (e.g., Levie & Lentz, 1982; Peeck, 1972) and is indeed supported by a good deal of evidence, in particular through the work of Dwyer (1970, 1972). As Levie and Lentz have shown, in Dwyer's experiments the overall facilitative effect of illustration was most pronounced when retention of spatial information in the learning material was tested.

Several authors (e.g., Dean & Enemoh, 1983; Duchastel, 1980b; Royer & Cable, 1976; Willows, 1979) have argued that the effects of pictures may depend on the difficulty level or the degree of abstractness of the text they illustrate. Thus, Royer and Cable (1976) speculate that the reason for inconsistent findings regarding the benefits of illustrations is "that illustrations are likely to prove beneficial only in the situation where the text material to be learned is difficult to comprehend" (p. 306). Studies addressing this issue (Moore & Skinner, 1985; Royer & Cable, 1976) tend to support this suggestion in that illustration facilitated learning in abstract but not in concrete passages.

In this respect, the work by Bock and his colleagues (Bock & Hörmann, 1974; Bock & Milz, 1977) should be mentioned because it shows that the effects of pictures on retention of sentences depend on the degree to which they can contribute to the understanding of the sentences. For example, while no facilitation occurred when a picture (see Figure 4.11) depicting a man, a bucket, and a car accompanied the sentence "the man has washed his car," a significant effect was found when the sentence read "he has washed it." Whereas the comprehensibility of the former sentence is not affected by the presence or absence of the picture, the latter sentence becomes more intelligible with the picture present and hence, according to Bock and his associates, is better retained. Another study relevant to this issue was done by Hayes and Readence (1983). In that study, seventh graders recalled information from transfer passages of texts varying in their level of dependence on illustrations, as established by a separate assessment procedure. Significant benefits of the presence of illustrations were found only for the texts for which illustration dependence was moderate or high.

Yet another factor of possible importance in determining illustration effects is the position of the pictures in the text. In the literature, several reasons are given for possible differential effects of pictures attributable to their position. Koran and Koran (1980), for instance, suggest that, when put in advance of text, "pictures may provide a scheme for organizing incoming textual material and may also have an attention-directing and controlling effect as the learner proceeds

FIGURE 4.11. Illustration used in the study by Bock and Milz. From "Pictorial Context and the Recall of Pronoun Sentences" by M. Bock and B. Milz, 1977, *Psychological Research*, *73*, p. 206. Copyright 1977 by Springer-Verlag. Reprinted by permission.

Er hat es gewaschen
(He has washed it.)

through the text" (p. 478). Conversely, pictures at the end of a segment of text may stimulate "a selective review and covert reorganization of previously processed material" (p. 478) or, alternatively, a review of "materials that are related to but not necessarily included in the picture" (Brody & Legenza, 1980, p. 28), comparable to the general backward or review process obtained with postquestions (cf. Rickards, 1979).

Research evidence in support of these speculations is as yet still scarce. Position of the illustrations did not appear to be of much significance in studies by Koran and Koran (1980) and Flagg and associates (Flagg et al., 1980). In an experiment by Brody and Legenza (1980), however, postpictures were more beneficial than prepictures for several types of incidental learning (i.e., that which cannot be learned directly from viewing the picture).

Finally, mention should be made of the rather special instance of the picture–text relationship discussed in an earlier section—that of illustrations which depict text content more or less incorrectly. At first glance, interest in these mismatched pictures may seem largely superfluous, as it may be assumed that text illustrations are usually made with so much care than inconsistencies are unlikely to occur. Although blatant mismatches may indeed be relatively scarce (although surely not wholly absent!), pictures quite often may suggest a different interpretation than the one that is derived from the text. As was argued in the earlier section, the possible consequences of such mismatched illustrations on what is retained from a text should not be underrated.

Part 3: Present Shortcomings and Future Avenues of Research

When one surveys the literature in the area of text–illustration studies, two somewhat contradictory conclusions suggest themselves. On the one hand, one is struck by the obvious progress that has been made since Samuels (1970) concluded, on the basis of the few (mostly retention!) studies then available "that pictures when used as adjuncts to the printed text, do not facilitate comprehension" (p. 405). As the very frequency of recent reviews (e.g., Alesandrini, 1982, 1984; Duchastel, 1980a; Levie & Lentz, 1982; Levin & Lesgold, 1978; Schallert, 1980) indicates, the growth of research and interest in this area has been considerable. As a result, a good deal more is now known about the various functions that text illustrations may fulfill and about the factors that influence these effects.

At the same time, however, it is clear that much remains to be done; much of what is said about the functions of illustrations is still speculative and many of the conditions and factors that affect these functions are not well understood. These gaps in our knowledge are to some extent likely to be filled as more studies of the type reviewed here become available.

Nonetheless, more of the same will not be sufficient. For new insights to occur, certain extensions in picture–text studies will be necessary, especially in the way the various roles are assessed. For instance, as studies have generally focused on the effects of pictures on the retention of text, more attention should be paid to possible, less-known effects in the affective-motivational domain and on comprehension per se (rather than on comprehension via retention).

More variety is also called for in the assessment procedures used. Most studies employ verbal multiple choice or cued recall measures, or, with short passages, free recall. Extension could be achieved in a variety of ways, for example, through nonverbal measures of the type used in studies by Dwyer (Dwyer & De Melo, 1984; cf. Magne & Parknäs, 1963), the use of cloze procedures, the assessment of inference drawing, or performance on transfer tasks.

Of particular importance in this respect is the time at which assessment takes place. Most studies investigate the effects of illustration immediately after a text has been read. On the one hand, this interval should be extended; ultimately, it is the long-term effect that counts, and far too little is known about this. On the other hand, assessment should focus on what goes on during the reading of a text. Investigating this may be especially helpful in view of a serious problem that also vexes research on other adjunct aids in prose learning (e.g., adjunct questions—see Duchastel, 1979), namely, the problem of ecological validity. In recent years, several authors (Brody, 1981; Willows et al., 1981) have noted that it is doubtful to what extent the outcome of picture–text studies may be generalized to the use of illustrations in educational practice. As Brody (1981) indicates, the problem arises because research and practice differ in such variables as types of picture, type, length and topic of text, and presentation conditions. More important than these differences may be the fact that not much is known, either in research studies or in real-life settings, about what subjects *do* with illustrated text, that is, how and when (or indeed whether at all) they use pictures. Further research should be especially concerned with remedying this state of ignorance. This will require the extension and more intensive use of already available methods, such as eye movement recordings and less accurate ways of observing individuals reading a text, as well as questioning students about their pictorial strategies, their interpretation, application, and evaluation of illustrations. It may also necessitate the invention and development of new assessment procedures.

From an extension of research along these lines both psychological theory and educational practice will profit. It will provide a better understanding of the processes involved in reading and remembering an illustrated text. It will also clarify how specific educational objectives may be served by including specific types of illustration in text and indicate the conditions under which specific types of learner can benefit.

References

Alcorn, M. D., Kinder, J. S., & Schunert, J. R. (1964). *Better teaching in secondary schools* (2nd ed.). New York: Holt, Rinehart & Winston.

Alesandrini, K. L. (1981). Pictorial–verbal and analytic–holistic learning strategies in science learning. *Journal of Educational Psychology, 73*, 358–368.

Alesandrini, K. L. (1982). Imagery-eliciting strategies and meaningful learning. *Journal of Mental Imagery, 6*, 125–140.

Alesandrini, K. L. (1984). Pictures and adult learning. *Instructional Science, 13*, 63–77.

Anderson, R. C., & Biddle, W. B. (1975). On asking people questions about what they are reading. In G. Bower (Ed.), *Psychology of learning and motivation* (Vol. 9, pp. 89–132). New York: Academic Press.

Ausubel, D. P. (1960). The use of advance organizers in the learning and retention of meaningful verbal material. *Journal of Educational Psychology, 51*, 267–272.

Ansubel, D. P. (1963). *The psychology of meaningful verbal learning*. New York: Grune & Stratton.

Bacharach, V. R., Carr, T. H., & Mehner, D. S. (1976). Interactive and independent contributions of verbal descriptions to children's picture memory. *Journal of Experimental Child Psychology, 22*, 492–498.

Berlyne, D. E. (1966). Conditions of prequestioning and retention of meaningful material. *Journal of Educational Psychology, 57*, 128–132.

Bernard, R. M., Petersen, C. H., & Ally, M. (1981). Can images provide contextual support for prose? *Educational Communication and Technology Journal, 29*, 101–108.

Binet, A., & Simon, Th. (1908). Le développement de l'intelligence chez les enfants [The development of intelligence in children]. *Année Psychologique, 14*, 1–94.

Borges, M. A., & Robins, S. L. (1980). Contextual and motivational cue effects on the comprehension and recall of prose. *Psychological Reports, 47*, 263–268.

Bock, M., & Hörmann, H. (1974). Der Einfluss von Bildern auf das Behalten von Sätzen [The influence of illustrations on memory for sentences]. *Psychologische Forschung, 36*, 343–357.

Bock, M., & Milz, B. (1977). Pictorial context and the recall of pronoun sentences. *Psychological Research, 39*, 203–220.

Bransford, J. D. (1979). *Human cognition*. Belmont, CA: Wadsworth.

Bransford, J. D., & Johnson, M. K. (1972). Contextual prerequisites for understanding: Some investigations of comprehension and recall. *Journal of Verbal Learning and Verbal Behavior, 11*, 717–726.

Brody, P. J. (1981). Research on pictures in instructional texts: The need for a broadened perspective. *Educational Communication and Technology Journal, 29*, 93–100.

Brody, P. J., & Legenza, A. (1980). Can pictorial attributes serve mathemagenic functions? *Educational Communication and Technology Journal, 28,* 25-29.

Brown, J. W., Lewis, R. B., & Harcleroad, F. F. (1969). *AV instruction, media and methods* (3rd ed.). New York: McGraw-Hill.

Bryant, J., Brown, D., Silberberg, A. R., & Elliott, S. C. (1981). Effects of humorous illustrations in college textbooks. *Human Communication Research, 8,* 43-57.

Carr, T. H., Bacharach, V. R., & Mehner, D. S. (1977). Preparing children to look at pictures: Advance descriptions direct attention and facilitate active processing. *Child Development, 48,* 22-27.

Carrier, C., Joseph, M. R., Krey, C. L., & LaCroix, P. (1983). Supplied visuals and imagery instructions in field independent and field dependent children's recall. *Educational Communication and Technology Journal, 31,* 153-160.

Chute, A. G. (1979). Analysis of the instructional functions of color and monochrome cueing in media presentations. *Educational Communication and Technology Journal, 27,* 251-263.

Dale, E. (1946). *Audio-visual methods in teaching.* New York: Dryden Press. (2nd ed., 1954; 3rd ed., 1969).

Danset-Léger, J. (1980). Aspects du déchiffrement des images de la littérature enfantine: Réactions d'enfants à l'image-unité [Aspects of deciphering illustrations in children's literature: Reactions of children to composite pictures]. *Bulletin de Psychologie, 33,* 913-922.

Dean, R. S., & Kulhavy, R. W. (1981). The influence of spatial organization in prose learning. *Journal of Educational Psychology, 73,* 57-64.

Dean, R. S., & Enemoh, P. A. (1983). Pictorial organization in prose learning. *Contemporary Educational Psychology, 8,* 20-27.

Donald, D. R. (1979). Effects of illustrations on early oral reading accuracy, strategies and comprehension. *British Journal of Educational Psychology, 49,* 282-289.

Donald, D. R. (1983). The use and value of illustrations as contextual information for readers at different progress and developmental levels. *British Journal of Educational Psychology, 53,* 175-185.

Duchastel, P. C. (1978). Illustrating instructional texts. *Educational Technology, 11,* 36-39.

Duchastel, P. C. (1979). *Adjunct question effects and experimental constraints* (Occasional Paper No. 1). Bryn Mawr, PA: The American College, Department of Research and Evaluation.

Duchastel, P. C. (1980). *Research on illustrations in instructional texts* (Occasional Paper No. 3). Bryn Mawr, PA: The American College, Department of Research and Evaluation. (a)

Duchastel, P. C. (1980). Research on illustrations in text: Issues and perspectives. *Educational Communication and Technology Journal, 28,* 283-287. (b)

Duchastel, P. C. (1981). Illustrations in text: A retentional role. *Programmed Learning and Educational Technology, 18,* 11-15.

Dwyer, F. M. (1970). Exploratory studies in the effectiveness of visual illustrations. *AV Communication Review, 18,* 235-249.

Dwyer, F. M. (1972). *A guide to improving visualized instruction.* University Park, PA: State College, Pennsylvania State University, Learning Services Division.

Dwyer, F. M., & De Melo, H. (1984). Effects of mode of instruction, testing, order of testing, and cued recall on student achievement. *Journal of Experimental Education, 52,* 86-94.

Flagg, B. N., Weaver, P. A., Fenton, T., Gelatt, R., & Pray, R. (1980). *Children's use of pictures in comprehending written text.* Paper presented at the annual meeting of the American Educational Research Association, Boston.

Fleming, M. L. (1979). On pictures in educational research. *Instructional Science, 8,* 235-251.

Fleming, M. L., & Sheikhian, M. (1972). Influence of pictorial attributes on recognition memory. *AV Communication Review, 20,* 423-441.

Friedman, A. (1979). Framing pictures: The role of knowledge in automatized encoding and memory for gist. *Journal of Experimental Psychology: General, 108,* 316-355.

Goldberg, F. (1974). Effects of imagery on learning incidental material in the classroom. *Journal of Educational Psychology, 66,* 233-237.

Goldstein, R., & Underwood, G. (1981). The influence of pictures on the derivation of meaning from children's reading materials. *Journal of Research in Reading, 4,* 6-16.

Hanes, M. L. (1973). The research on how children learn from pictures. *Viewpoints, 49,* 11-20.

Haring, M. J., & Fry, M. A. (1979). Effect of pictures on children's comprehension of written text. *Educational Communication and Technology Journal, 27,* 185-190.

Hayes, D. A., & Readance, J. E. (1983). Transfer of learning from illustration-dependent text. *Journal of Educational Research, 76,* 245-248.

Higgins, L. C. (1979). Effects of strategy-oriented training on children's inference drawing from pictures. *Educational Communication and Technology Journal, 27,* 265-280.

Holliday, W. G. (1981). Selective attentional effects of textbook study questions on student learning in science. *Journal of Research in Science Teaching, 18,* 283-289.

Holliday, W. G., Brunner, L. L., & Donais, E. E. (1977). Differential cognitive and affective responses to flow diagrams in science. *Journal of Research in Science Teaching, 14,* 129-138.

Holliday, W. G., & Thursby, P. M. (1977). *Teaching visual concepts in the classroom.* Paper presented at the annual convention of the Association for Educational Communication and Technology, Miami.

Jagodzinska, M. (1976). The role of illustrations in verbal learning. *Polish Psychological Bulletin, 7,* 95-104.

Jahoda, G., Cheyne, W. M., Deregowski, J. B., Sinha, D., & Collingbourne, R. (1976). Utilization of pictorial information in classroom learning: A cross cultural study. *AV Communication Review, 24,* 295-315.

Jörg, S. (1977). Charakteristische Merkmale der visuellen Wahrnehmungsentwicklung bis zum Beginn der Schulzeit [Characteristic traits of visual perception development up to the beginning of school entry]. *Fernsehen und Bildung, 11,* 35-52.

Jörg, S., & Hörmann, H. (1978). The influence of general and specific verbal labels on the recognition of labeled and unlabeled parts of pictures. *Journal of Verbal Learning and Verbal Behavior, 17,* 445-454.

Jörg, S., ¿ Hörmann, H. (1983). Sentences before and after pictures: How do verbal specifications influence recognition? *Psychological Research, 45,* 255-266.

Joseph, J. H., & Dwyer, F. M. (1984). The effects of prior knowledge, presentation mode, and visual realism on student achievement. *Journal of Experimental Education, 52,* 101-121.

Kinder, J. S. (1959). *Audio-visual materials and techniques.* New York: American Book Company.

Knowlton, J. Q. (1966). On the definition of picture. *AV Communication Review, 14,* 157-183.

Koenke, K., & Otto, W. (1969). Contribution of pictures to children's comprehension of the main idea in reading. *Psychology in the Schools, 6*, 298–302.

Koran, M. L., & Koran, J. J. (1980). Interaction of learner characteristics with pictorial adjuncts in learning from science text. *Journal of Research in Science Teaching, 17*, 477–483.

Levie, W. H., & Lentz, R. (1982). Effects of text illustrations: A review of research. *Educational Communication and Technology Journal, 30*, 195–232.

Levin, J. R. (1981). On functions of pictures in prose. In F. J. Pirozzolo & M. C. Wittrock (Eds.), *Neuropsychological and cognitive processes in reading* (pp. 203–228). New York: Academic Press.

Levin, J. R., Bender, B. G., & Lesgold, A. M. (1976). Pictures, repetition, and children's oral prose learning. *AV Communication Review, 24*, 367–380.

Levin, J. R., & Lesgold, A. M. (1978). On pictures in prose. *Educational Communication and Technology Journal, 26*, 233–243.

Levin, J. R., Bender, B. G., & Pressley, M. (1979). Pictures, imagery, and children's recall of central versus peripheral sentence information. *Educational Communication and Technology Journal, 27*, 89–95.

Litcher, J., & Johnson, D. (1969). Changes in attitudes towards Negroes and White elementary school students after use of multi-ethnic readers. *Journal of Educational Psychology, 60*, 148–152.

Loftus, G. R. (1972). Eye fixations and recognition memory for pictures. *Cognitive Psychology, 3*, 525–551.

Mackworth, N. J., & Bruner, J. S. (1970). How adults and children search and recognize pictures. *Human Development, 13*, 149–177.

Magne, O., & Parknäs, L. (1963). The learning effects of pictures. *British Journal of Educational Psychology, 33*, 265–275.

Mandler, J., & Johnson, M. (1976). Some of the thousand words a picture is worth. *Journal of Experimental Psychology: Human Learning and Memory, 2*, 529–540.

Marks, D. F. (1983). Mental imagery and consciousness: A theoretical review. In A. A. Sheikh (Ed.), *Imagery* (pp. 96–130). New York: Wiley.

Meyer, B. J. F. (1975). *The organization of prose and its effect on memory.* Amsterdam: North-Holland.

Moore, P. J., & Skinner, M. J. (1985). The effects of illustrations on children's comprehension of abstract and concrete passages. *Journal of Research in Reading, 8*, 45–56.

Neisser, U. (1979). The control of information pick up in selective looking. In A. D. Pick (Ed.), *Perception and its development* (pp. 201–219). Hillsdale, NJ: Erlbaum.

Nelson, D. L., Reed, V. S., & Walling, J. R. (1976). Pictorial superiority effect. *Journal of Experimental Psychology: Human Learning and Memory, 2*, 523–528.

Nickerson, R. S. (1968). A note on long-term recognition memory for pictorial material. *Psychonomic Science, 11*, 58.

O'Donnell, H. (1983). The use of illustrations in textbooks. *The Reading Teacher, 37*, 462–464.

Olson, D. R. (1977). The language of instruction: The literate bias of schooling. In R. C. Anderson, R. J. Spiro, & W. E. Montague (Eds.), *Schooling and the acquisition of knowledge* (pp. 65–89). Hillsdale, NJ: Erlbaum.

Paivio, A. (1969). Mental imagery in associative learning and memory. *Psychological Review, 76*, 241–263.

Paivio, A. (1971). *Imagery and verbal processes.* New York: Holt, Rinehart & Winston.

Paivio, A., & Csapo, K. (1973). Picture superiority in free recall: Imagery or dual coding. *Cognitive Psychology, 5*, 176–206.

Paradowski, W. (1967). Effect of curiosity on incidental learning. *Journal of Educational Psychology, 58,* 50-55.

Peeck, J. (1970). Effects of prequestions on delayed retention of prose material. *Journal of Educational Psychology, 61,* 241-246.

Peeck, J. (1972). *Plaatjes in leerprocessen* [Pictures in learning processes]. Unpublished doctoral dissertation, University of Utrecht.

Peeck, J. (1974). Het bestuderen van teksten [Learing from text]. In C. F. Van Parreren & J. Peeck (Eds.), *Informatie over leren en onderwijzen* (pp. 88-113). Groningen: Tjeenk Willink. (a)

Peeck, J. (1974). Retention of pictorial and verbal content of a text with illustrations. *Journal of Educational Psychology, 66,* 880-888. (b)

Peeck, J. (1978). Die Effekte von Illustrationen zu Texten [The effects of illustrations accompanying text]. In K. J. Klauer & H. J. Kornadt (Eds.), *Jahrbuch für Empirische Erziehungswissenschaft* (pp. 196-229). Düsseldorf: Schwann.

Peeck, J. (1980). *Experimenter-provided and learner-generated pictures in learning from text.* Paper presented at the annual meeting of the American Educational Research Association, Boston.

Peeck, J. (1983). *Rupert Bear revisited: Memory for modality and awareness of inconsistencies in processing illustrated prose.* Paper presented at the annual meeting of the American Educational Research Association, Montreal.

Peeck, J. (1985). *Effects of mismatched pictures on retention of illustrated prose.* Paper presented at the annual meeting of the American Educational Research Association, Chicago.

Peeck, J., & Goud, A. (1985). Perspective-inducing effects of text illustrations. *Human Learning, 4,* 243-249.

Pezdek, K. (1977). Cross-modality semantic integration of picture and sentence memory. *Journal of Experimental Psychology: Human Learning and Memory, 3,* 514-524.

Potter, M. C. (1976). Short-term conceptual memory for pictures. *Journal of Experimental Psychology: Human Learning and Memory, 2,* 509-522.

Potter, M. C., & Levy, E. I. (1969). Recognition memory for a rapid sequence of pictures. *Journal of Experimental Psychology, 81,* 10-15.

Pressley, M., Levin, J. R., Pigott, S., LeComte, M., & Hope, D. J. (1983). Mismatched pictures and children's prose learning. *Educational Communication and Technology Journal, 31,* 131-143.

Rasco, R. W., Tennyson, R. D., & Boutwell, R. C. (1975). Imagery instructions and drawings in learning prose. *Journal of Educational Psychology, 67,* 188-192.

Rankin, E. F., & Culhane, J. W. (1970). One picture equals 1,000 words? *Reading Improvement, 7,* 37-40.

Read, J. D., & Barnsley, R. H. (1977). Remember Dick and Jane? Memory for elementary school readers. *Canadian Journal of Behavioral Science, 9,* 361-370.

Reid, D. J., Briggs, N., & Beveridge, M. (1983). The effect of pictures upon the readability of a school science project. *British Journal of Educational Psychology, 53,* 327-335.

Rickards, J. R. (1979). Adjunct postquestions in text: A critical review of methods and processes. *Review of Educational Research, 49,* 181-197.

Riding, R. J., & Wicks, B. J. (1978). The effect of extraversion and presentation order on learning from picture–commentary sequences by children. *Educational Review, 30,* 255-257.

Royer, J. M., & Cable, G. W. (1976). Illustrations, analogies, and facilitative transfer in prose learning. *Journal of Educational Psychology, 68,* 205-209.

Ruch, M. D., & Levin, J. R. (1977). Pictorial organization versus repetition in children's prose: Evidence for processing differences. *AV Communication Review, 25*, 269-280.

Rudnick, M. F., Porter, M. C., & Suydam, E. L. (1973). Pictorial stimulus variables. *Viewpoints, 49*, 21-28.

Rusted, J., & Coltheart, M. (1979). Facilitation of children's prose recall by the presence of pictures. *Memory and Cognition, 7*, 354-359.

Rusted, J., & Coltheart, V. (1979). The effect of pictures on the retention of novel words and prose passages. *Journal of Experimental Child Psychology, 28*, 516-524.

Samuels, S. J. (1970). Effects of pictures on learning to read, comprehension and attitudes. *Review of Educational Research, 40*, 397-407.

Schallert, D. L. (1980). The role of illustrations in reading comprehension. In R. J. Spiro, B. C. Bruce, & W. F. Brewer (Eds.), *Theoretical issues in reading comprehension: Perspectives from cognitive psychology, linguistics, artificial intelligence, and education* (pp. 503-524). Hillsdale, NJ: Erlbaum.

Sewell, E. H., Jr., & Moore, R. L. (1980). Cartoon embellishments in informative presentations. *Educational Communication and Technology Journal, 28*, 39-46.

Shepard, R. N. (1967). Recognition memory for words, sentences and pictures. *Journal of Verbal Learning and Verbal Behavior, 6*, 156-163.

Smith, K. U., & Smith, M. F. (1966). *Cybernetic principles of learning and educational design*. New York: Holt, Rinehart & Winston.

Snowman, J., & Cunningham, D. J. (1975). A comparison of pictorial and written adjuncts in learning from text. *Journal of Educational Psychology, 67*, 307-311.

Spaulding, S. (1955). Research on pictorial illustration. *AV Communication Review, 3*, 22-45.

Spaulding, S. (1956). Communication potential of pictorial illustrations. *AV Communication Review, 4*, 31-46.

Spoehr, K. T., & Lehmkuhle, S. W. (1982). *Visual information processing*. San Francisco: Freeman.

Standing, L., Conezie, J., & Haber, R. N. (1970). Perception and memory for pictures: Single-trial learning of 2,500 visual stimuli. *Psychonomic Science, 19*, 73-74.

Stern, W. (1930). *Psychologie der frühen Kindheit bis zum sechsten Lebensjahre* [The psychology of early childhood up to age 6]. Leipzig: Quelle & Meyer.

Stone, D. E., & Crandall, T. L. (1982). Relationship of illustrations and text in reading technical material. In B. A. Hudson (Ed.), *Advances in reading/language research* (Vol. 1, pp. 283-307). Greenwich, CT: JAI Press.

Stone, D. E., & Glock, M. D. (1981). How do young adults read directions with and without pictures? *Journal of Educational Psychology, 73*, 419-426.

Tirre, W. C., Manelis, L., & Leicht, K. L. (1979). The effects of imaginal and verbal strategies on prose comprehension by adults. *Journal of Reading Behavior, 11*, 99-106.

Travers, R. M. W. (1964). The transmission of communication to human receivers. *AV Communication Review, 12*, 373-385.

Travers, R. M. W. (1969). *A study of the advantages and disadvantages of using simplified visual presentations in instructional materials*. Washington, DC: Final Report on USOE Grant No. OEG-1-7-070144-5235.

Travers, R. M. W., & Alvarado, V. (1970). The design of pictures for teaching children in elementary schools. *AV Communication Review, 18*, 47-64.

Van Dam, G., Brinkerink-Carlier, M., & Kok, I. (1986). The influence of visual and verbal embellishment on free recall of the paragraphs of a text. *American Journal of Psychology, 99*, 103-110.

Van den Bosch, A. B. (1979). *Geïllustreerde teksten in onderwijsleerprocessen* [Illustrated text in learning processes]. Unpublished master's thesis, University of Utrecht, Psychological Laboratory.

Van Parreren, C. F. (1983). Teaching pupils to "read" pictures. In R. Briel (Ed.), *Media science* (pp. 65–71). Durban: Butterworth.

Verhaegen, L. J. J. (1983). *Visuele hulpmiddelen bij het lezen van teksten* [Visual aids for the reading of text]. Unpublished master's thesis, University of Utrecht, Psychological Laboratory.

Vernon, M. D. (1953). The value of pictorial illustration. *British Journal of Educational Psychology, 23*, 180–187.

Wardle, K. F. (1977). *Textbook illustrations: Do they aid reading comprehension?* Paper presented at the annual convention of the American Psychological Association, San Francisco.

Weisberg, J. S. (1970). The use of visual advance organizers for learning earth science concepts. *Journal of Research in Science Teaching, 7*, 161–165.

Willows, D. M. (1978). A picture is not always worth a thousand words: Pictures as distractors in reading. *Journal of Educational Psychology, 70*, 255–262.

Willows, D. M. (1979). *Reading comprehension of illustrated and nonillustrated aspects of text*. Paper presented at the annual meeting of the American Educational Research Association, San Francisco.

Willows, D. M. (1980). *Effects of picture salience on reading comprehension of illustrated and nonillustrated aspects of text*. Paper presented at the annual meeting of the American Educational Research Association, Boston.

Willows, D. M., Borwick, D., & Hayvren, M. (1981). The content of school readers. In T. G. Waller & G. E. MacKinnon (Eds.), *Reading research: Advances in theory and practice* (Vol. 2, pp. 97–175). New York: Academic Press.

Winn, W. D. (1981). Effect of attribute highlighting and diagrammatic organization on identification and classification. *Journal of Research in Science Teaching, 18*, 23–32.

Wittich, W. A., & Schuller, C. F. (1967). *Audiovisual materials: Their nature and use* (4th ed.). New York: Harper & Row.

5
Charts, Graphs, and Diagrams in Educational Materials

BILL WINN

Introduction

The purpose of this chapter is to explore research into the ways in which charts, graphs, and diagrams can communicate and instruct. This requires, first, an examination of the general properties of charts, graphs, and diagrams and how they convey meaning. Then, research is reviewed which has attempted to discover relationships between these graphic forms and the success with which students learn from them. Independent variables of interest in this research are the characteristics of charts, graphs, and diagrams, the characteristics of students, and different learning tasks.

Unfortunately, researchers, like laypersons, use the terms "chart," "graph," and "diagram" very imprecisely. What to one is a "flowchart" is a "flow diagram" to another. What is a "pie chart" to a third might be a "pie graph" to a fourth. To forestall any confusion that might arise from this imprecision, we begin by defining, for this chapter, what charts, graphs, and diagrams are.

Definitions

Information can be presented to students using a variety of formats. Researchers typically have arranged these formats on a continuum with realistic pictures at one end and written and spoken language at the other (see Dale, 1946; Knowlton, 1966; Levie & Dickie, 1973; Fleming & Levie, 1978). The usual rationale for this arrangement is that pictures resemble what they stand for, while words are arbitrary and conventional (Knowlton, 1966), or that pictures describe phenomena, while words and more abstract forms name or explain them (Doblin, 1980).

Charts, graphs, and diagrams lie at the center of this continuum that extends from pictures to words. From words, they inherit the attribute of abstraction; but like pictures they exploit spatial layout in a meaningful way. Their abstract nature makes them well suited to explaining how processes work where realistic pictures would fail. A simplified diagram of the digestive system would be a more effective illustration of how it works than a realistic picture of the organs and tissues. Their spatial nature, on the other hand, opens up a whole range of possibilities for communication that are precluded when language is used alone. A graph of average monthly hours of sunshine over a year is much more effective than a written description.

Charts, graphs, and diagrams therefore comprise a family of graphic forms that have in common the attributes of abstraction and the exploitation of space. Research into the instructional effectiveness of these general attributes does not necessarily distinguish among the three separate forms. The terms "graphic" or "graphic form" are used when discussing research at this general level.

Within this general definition, we make the following distinctions:

Graphs are taken to be those graphic forms that illustrate relationships among variables, at least one of which is continuous. Thus, a plot of height with age (two continuous variables) or a histogram showing the Gross National Products of different countries (one continuous and one categorical variable) are both referred to as "graphs."

Charts are those graphic forms that illustrate relationships among categorical variables. Tables showing the sources and effects of different vitamins (Holliday & Benson, 1981), or stages in insect metamorphosis (Winn, 1981) are examples of charts (see Figures 5.1 and 5.2). Neither vitamin type nor stage of metamorphosis is a continuous variable in the sense that time or temperature are.

The difference between *diagrams* and the other two graphic forms is first and foremost one of function and then also often one of complexity. While the function of graphs and charts is to illustrate simple *relationships* among variables, the function of diagrams is to describe whole *processes* and *structures* often at levels of great complexity. Schematics showing the placement of electronic components in a circuit (Winn, 1986), illustrations of biochemical cycles (Holliday, 1976), and labeled line drawings showing how the human heart works (Dwyer, 1978) are all examples of diagrams.

We begin our examination of charts, graphs, and diagrams at the general level of graphic forms with some remarks about why these are considered to be successful in instruction. Then we move to the issue of how spatial factors, such as layout, can be used to convey meaning. We then look at research specific to graphic forms in instruction.

Advantages of Graphic Forms

Consider the following puzzle:

"A monk went to the temple at the top of a holy mountain to meditate and pray. He started out early one morning along the path that led up to the temple. Because he was an old man, and the way was steep and arduous, he frequently slowed his pace, and even sat and rested awhile beside the path. Toward evening, he came to the temple at the top.

After several days of meditation and prayer, it was time for him to leave. Early in the morning, he set off back down the path. Again, he frequently changed his pace and rested by the way. He arrived back at the bottom in the evening."

154   Bill Winn

VITAMIN CHART

Vitamin Letter	SOURCE		EFFECTS	
	One Name	One Food	Can help produce healthy	Lacking or too little can produce unhealthy
A	carotene	red peppers	lungs	night blindness
B_1	thiamine	organ meat	muscle	appetite loss
B_2	riboflavin	almonds	eyes	premature aging
B_3	niacin	rice bran	tissues	swelled tongue
B_4	pantothen	yeast	adrenals	sleep disturbances
B_5	biotin	egg yolks	fats	mental disorders
B_6	pyridoxine	nuts	antibodies	muscle weakness
B_7	choline	peas	nerves	liver problems
B_8	folacin	gland meat	babies	gray hair
B_{12}	cobalamin	soybeans	bones	fragile cells
C	ascorbate	parsley	capillaries	tooth loss
D	calciferol	fatty fish	cartilage	muscle spasms
E	tocophenol	margarine	skin	cell breakdown
K	naphthoquinone	alfalfa sprouts	liver	internal bleeding

FIGURE 5.1. Chart illustrating the characteristics of vitamins and showing the use of columns and rows. From *Using Questions to Focus Students' Attention on Non-prose Science Materials* by W. G. Holliday and G. Benson, 1981, April. Paper presented at the conference of the National Association for Research in Science Teaching, New York. Reprinted by permission.

Show that there is one single point on the path up the mountain where the monk will be at precisely the same time both when he goes up and when he comes down.

You may wish to pause here to try to solve the puzzle before reading on.

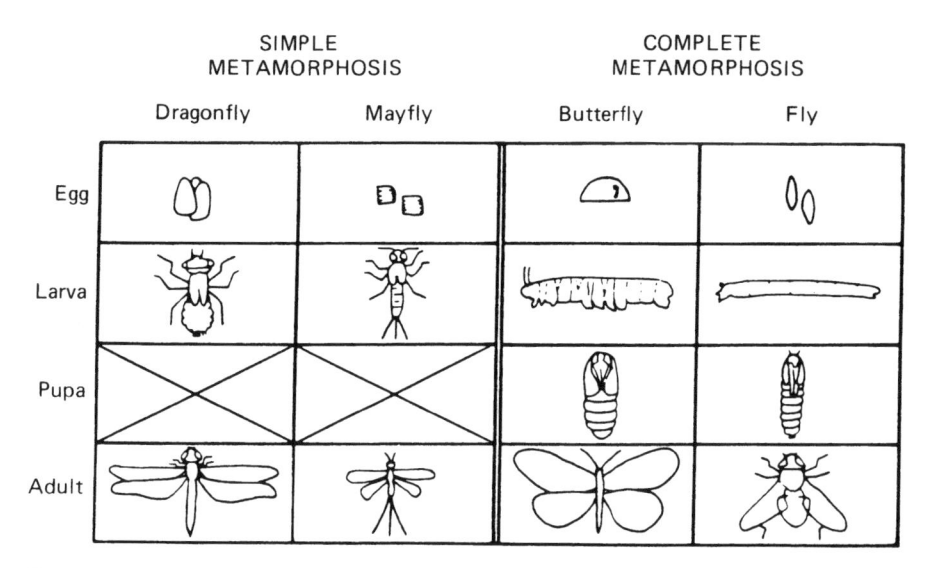

	SIMPLE METAMORPHOSIS		COMPLETE METAMORPHOSIS	
	Dragonfly	Mayfly	Butterfly	Fly
Egg				
Larva				
Pupa	×	×		
Adult				

FIGURE 5.2. Chart illustrating the stages and concept categories of insect metamorphosis. From "Design Principles for Diagrams and Charts" by W. D. Winn and W. G. Holliday. In D. Jonassen (ed.), 1982, *The Technology of Text, Vol. 1*, p. 291. Englewood Cliffs, NJ: Educational Technology Publications. Reprinted by permission.

People typically try one of two strategies when they attempt to solve this puzzle. The first is a mathematical strategy that requires a solution by either algebra or arithmetic through the manipulation of sets of various intuitive estimates of time and distance. However, because the monk's pace is not constant, and because we do not know the precise time he left or arrived, nor the distance he had to travel, neither of these mathematical approaches will produce a solution.

The second strategy is to represent the puzzle in graphic form, usually as a line graph plotting distance along the path against time. If the two days' journeys are superimposed on the same graph, the two lines have to cross. And where they cross is the unique point that is the solution to the puzzle. Variations in the monk's times of departure and arrival, or of his pace, only mean that the lines cross at a different place.

The graphic strategy, showing the solution to the puzzle, is illustrated in Figure 5.3. People who arrive at the solution this way often report that they suddenly "saw" the solution or that "something clicked." Why does this happen? It may be that simply changing the form of the puzzle, from text to diagram, is sufficient to make the solution "transparent" in the way that Simon (1981, p. 153) has described. However, many scholars would argue that there is more to it than that. There is a belief among researchers that the particular attributes of charts, graphs, and diagrams do in fact make it easier for people to understand and learn information that these graphic forms present. There are several approaches to looking at these advantages of graphic forms.

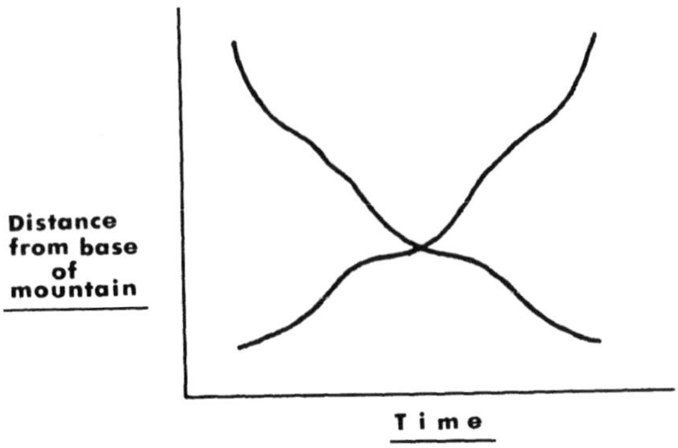

FIGURE 5.3. Graphic solution to the monk puzzle.

Visual Argument

What Waller (1981) has called "visual argument" involves the expression of ideas, the presentation of points of view, and the solving of problems by means of representations that convey meaning graphically rather than linguistically. Intuitively, we feel that some things are far better explained visually than verbally or in languages like mathematics. Often, it is easier to draw a map giving directions than to describe verbally the route to follow. Some types of information even seem impossible to understand without being represented visually (Macdonald-Ross, 1977a; Doblin, 1980). Macdonald-Ross (1979) has suggested that these visual representations use an entirely different type of logic based on the meaningful use of space and the juxtaposition of elements in a graphic.

A variety of explanations have been given for why this logic of visual argument, used in graphic forms, is often so effective. Some researchers have suggested that, quite simply, graphic forms offer more information than words alone. For example, Stewart, Van Kirk, and Rowell (1979) drew an interesting comparison between "concept maps" and roadmaps. A roadmap conveys much more information than would a list of the towns found on the map. In addition to telling us the names of the towns, the map gives us an indication of their sizes and their distances and directions from each other. In the same way, "concept maps" (Novak, 1979), in which domains of concepts are represented spatially in networks or in charts, tell us how these concepts are related to each other; a list of the concepts would not accomplish this. It seems reasonable to suppose that this additional information would make it easier for someone to learn something or to solve a problem.

Another explanation of the effectiveness of visual argument is that it calls on alternative, and usually underused, abilities in students. It has been argued (Olson, 1977) that schooling is biased toward verbal forms of representation and discourse. By presenting information or problems in graphic forms, we encourage students to use mental skills that may be more effective than verbal skills but which they do not usually employ. Often, problems to solve and information to learn are forced into formats, as much by tradition as anything else, which may not be optimal for the student. With alternative graphic forms that use visual argument, the opportunity exists to match format with learning task in a much more productive way.

This line of reasoning is supported empirically in studies demonstrating that attributes of presentation forms (or "symbol systems" as Salomon, 1979, calls them) can model cognitive strategies and get students to use them. In a study by Winn (1986b), a computer screen, displaying letter patterns, was divided into quadrants, modeling a "chunking" strategy. This technique helped students learn the patterns more successfully than students for whom the strategy had not been modeled. Studies by Salomon (1974) and Bovy (1983) demonstrated similar learning advantages for techniques that isolated details in visual displays by zooming and "irising," a technique in which a detail is enclosed in an ever-decreasing circle with the rest of the image turning black. This research suggests that graphic forms, conveying information by means of visual argument, can induce the use of cognitive processes that are themselves "visual" in some way. These might include visual chunking, mental imagery, parallel processing, and so on.

Solving the puzzle of the monk graphically therefore succeeds because it translates the original text into a form that uses a more appropriate visual system of logic and that presents more relevant information. People "see" that the lines must cross. Furthermore, the superimposition of the two plots of time and distance suggests a cognitive strategy by which the events of the two days are processed at the same time. Both the form in which the puzzle is represented for solution and the cognitive processes it induces are alternatives to those forms and processes that might more normally have been used. The result is that the solution is relatively easy to discover.

The monk puzzle and our discussion of visual argument in general have indicated some ways in which graphic forms might make learning easier. There are other factors that might contribute to the advantages of graphics over other forms, and we now turn to some of these.

Physiological Mechanisms

Some writers attribute the advantages of graphic forms and the cognitive skills associated with them to physiological mechanisms. Sless (1981, p. 147) reminds us that the human eye is very well suited for pattern recognition, but very poor at quantitative judgments. For example, the visual system does very well when it encodes and interprets the general pattern of streets and buildings in an aerial photograph, but the system cannot tell you how many houses there are in the photograph without resorting to counting, which is a totally different kind of process. Pinker (1981, 1983), too, points out that the human visual system is very good at recognizing geometric shapes, and he attributes the success of graphic forms largely to this ability.

Another physiological mechanism that has received a lot of attention recently is learning by means of the right cerebral hemisphere. The claim is that, traditionally, education is predominantly "left brained" and that the "right brain" has been neglected (Sylwester, 1981). While it does not seem reasonable that students would be able to switch their hemispheres on and off at will, nor that instruction can be directed to one hemisphere rather than the other, there is certainly evidence that the two hemispheres of the brain process information differently and that the right hemisphere is better suited for processing spatial information (Hellige, 1980; Wittrock, 1980). As far as graphic forms are concerned, Toth (1980) has speculated that the superiority of instruction in sociology that uses diagrams might be accounted for by the fact that this form calls upon right-brain processes that otherwise would not have been used by students. He bases his claim on the argument that the right hemisphere can create images (Wittrock, 1977) that can in turn help the left hemisphere interpret information.

Cognitive Mechanisms

While the advantages of graphic forms might well be accounted for by physiological factors, the majority of research addresses cognitive factors. The psychological literature abounds with dichotomies, whose poles are pairs of abilities, one of which is in some way associated with graphic, or nonverbal, nonlinear systems of representation. For example, Paivio (1971, 1983) has proposed a "dual-coding" theory, according to which we are capable of encoding information both imaginally and verbally. Das, Kirby, and Jarman (1979) have demonstrated the existence of two distinct processes they call "simultaneous" and "successive." A great deal of research on aptitude has made a major division of mental abilities based on differences between spatial and verbal processes (Cattell, 1971; Snow, 1980). In each case, the advantage of using visual argument, presented in graphic forms, lies in the application, by students, of cognitive abilities that are particularly suited to what has to be learned.

IMAGERY

In addition to Paivio, a number of researchers have proposed that certain types of information are stored in memory as image-like structures (Anderson, 1978; Kosslyn, 1980, 1981; Shepard, 1978; Shepard & Cooper, 1982) which retain some, though not all, of the properties of the pictures, the graphic forms, or the direct visual experiences that gave rise to them. It should be added that there has been considerable debate as to whether this is in fact the case, or whether all information in memory is stored as propositions in language-like structures as Pylyshyn (1973, 1981) has suggested.

A number of researchers have used imagery theory as the basis for constructing and testing hypotheses concerning learning from graphic forms. Rigney and Lutz (1976) used computer graphics in a lesson on the battery and found that these helped students learn the material. They accounted for their findings in terms of the images that they suspected the graphics encouraged the students to form. In a subsequent study, Alesandrini (1981) reported that students who had to draw diagrams of the battery and who related specific details to more inclusive concepts performed better than students who did not. In this study, imagery appeared to be related to visual, holistic thinking. Finally, in a study of how spatial processes are applied to the study of maps, Kulhavy, Schwartz, and Shaha (1983) provided evidence that what they called a "quasi-visual image-based process" plays an important role in the retrieval from memory of information that was presented in graphic form. These studies exemplify a body of research that leads to the following conclusion: Graphic forms encourage students to create mental images that, in turn, make it easier for them to learn certain types of material.

SIMULTANEOUS AND SUCCESSIVE PROCESSING

A different dichotomy of processes is suggested by Das, Kirby, and Jarman (1975, 1979). These researchers have developed and tested a theory of simultaneous and successive processing, which they derived from the neurophysiological research of Luria (1970, 1973). Simultaneous processing involves the availability at one time of all the information with which someone has to deal. For example, when you do a jigsaw puzzle, all the pieces can be seen at once. Finding out where the next piece goes requires the simultaneous scanning and processing of the entire puzzle. Successive processing requires only knowledge of preceding and following elements in a series. If one were to thread beads on a string in a sequence determined by the colors of the beads, then successive processing would be involved. Once a bead was placed on the string, you could forget about it and concentrate on the next one.

Das, Kirby, and Jarman have not attempted to relate simultaneous and successive processing specifically to the advantages of graphic forms in instruction. However, as we saw in the monk puzzle, there are sometimes obvious advantages to having all the information needed to solve the problem or to learn something available in one display. Study of the eye movements of students looking at diagrams (Winn, 1983b) has shown that presenting information graphically allows students to scan it rapidly and quickly to discover patterns of elements within the diagram that are meaningful and that lead to the completion of a variety of cognitive tasks. Other studies involving diagrams in the teaching of science, summarized by Winn and Holliday (1982) and discussed in more detail later, have suggested that the ability of students to scan all the information they need simultaneously makes it possible to them to derive meaning from the actual distance between elements in a diagram, to learn sequences by tracing logical paths through diagrams, and to understand the relationships among parts in a process, all of which are visible at once.

GRAPHIC ORGANIZERS

The advantages that accrue to graphic forms from their ability to present information so that it can be processed simultaneously suggest that charts, graphs, and diagrams might also be effective at organizing information for students in the same way that advance organizers do (Ausubel, 1968). There is experimental evidence that this is indeed the case. Jonassen and Hawk (1984) demonstrated that a graphic summarizing information about American industrial growth in the nineteenth century improved the performance of students when compared to students who did not see the graphic organizer. This diagram presented all the main ideas, as well as certain relationships among them, at once. The students were able to access this information in one and the same instant, thus acquiring a concise and accurate overview of the material.

When graphic organizers like these are used to summarize text, Alesandrini (1984) suggests that they can readily be derived from semantic networks (Norman, Rumelhart, & LNR Research Group, 1975) which, like graphic organizers, present concepts and their relationships in diagrammatic form for easy simultaneous processing. Graphics based on network theory have been used effectively to help students organize science material (Stewart, 1984) and all manner of other content (Armbruster & Anderson, 1980, 1982; Holley & Dansereau, 1984; Jones, 1985). We shall return to this technique later.

Summary

It seems, then, that charts, diagrams and graphs are effective in instruction because they allow students to use alternative systems of logic. The advantages of visual argument that arise from these alternative systems seem generally to stem from the fact that in graphic forms the spatial relationships among concepts are made explicit and meaningful. In this way, certain physiological strengths of learners, such as pattern recognition and the ability to recognize geometric shapes, as well as the advantages of "right-brain" processing, can be exploited. Also, a greater range of cognitive abilities can be drawn upon, allowing more effective individualized instruction. These abilities include, but are by no means limited to, mental imagery, simultaneous processing, and "graphic organization" of content.

The Meaningful Use of Space

The previous remarks about the advantages of graphic forms for students have suggested that the key to successful visual argument lies in the way information is represented spatially. Spatial metaphors abound in everyday language. Some people we feel "close to"; others we find "distant." Some people we "look up to," while others are "beneath our contempt." The extension of this characteristic of our language to its deliberate and literal use in instructional graphics is intuitively appealing. Those who have tried to illustrate parts of the animal kingdom by drawing cheetahs and leopards "closer to" lions than to aardvarks or clams do so because they know that representations of ideas placed close together in a layout are thought of as being "close together" conceptually (see Fleming & Levie, 1978, p. 70). The meaning of space in graphs, charts, and diagrams therefore seems to depend on the way in which the relationships among elements in the graphic are displayed.

Elements and Relationships

Any illustration can be thought of in terms of its elements and the relationships among them. In a realistic picture, where one element ends and the next begins is often difficult to determine. However, in graphics the elements are often less ambiguously defined. In charts, the elements might be verbal labels or small drawings arranged in table form. In graphs, they might be labeled points on a line or the blocks of a histogram. And in diagrams they might consist of concepts, described by labels, symbols, line drawings, or small pictures. The relationships among these elements could be expressed in a variety of ways. In charts, relationships might be shown by the relative positions of elements in a table under various column headings; in graphs by the positions of the elements relative to the x and y axes; and in diagrams by where the elements are placed on the page relative to each other, or more explicitly by lines, arrows, inclusion in boxes, or other graphic devices. At all times, the overall meaning is conveyed by both the elements and by how they are connected. Applying a familiar saying to graphic forms, Szlichcinski (1980) reminds us that "the meaning of the whole is greater than the sum of the meaning of the parts" (p. 114).

Knowlton (1966) has analyzed the question of elements in illustrations and their relationships in some detail. He illustrates how the meaning of a visual representation derives from its elements, the pattern that they form, and any "order of connection" that is implied between the elements. What is more, each of these—elements, pattern, and order of connection—may or may not be isomorphic to the reality that the illustration represents. For example, in a map, the "elements," such as topographical features and buildings, might be shown as small pictures or as conventional signs. An example is given in Figure 5.4. The pattern might be realistic if the map were drawn to scale, or the pattern might not be realistic if the map were "schematized" in the way that subway and bus maps often are (see Bartram, 1980). But even in this latter, rather unrealistic, type of illustration, one would expect the sequence of features, such as subway stations and bus stops, to be the same as they would be in the real world.

Clearly, the meaning and the function of a graphic varies as the elements, patterns, and order of connection vary. Realistic elements on a map help you find your way by allowing you to recognize the real features, such as buildings and landmarks, that the elements represent. Realistic patterns help you navigate by measuring distances between points and taking directions from one point to the next. Realistic orders of connection serve to emphasize the sequence of elements, which is all you need to know when riding a bus or subway.

The meaningful use of space in graphics is mainly concerned with the pattern and order of connection, or sequences, of elements. Thus, charts, graphs, and diagrams have to be understood in terms of how they use sequences and patterns

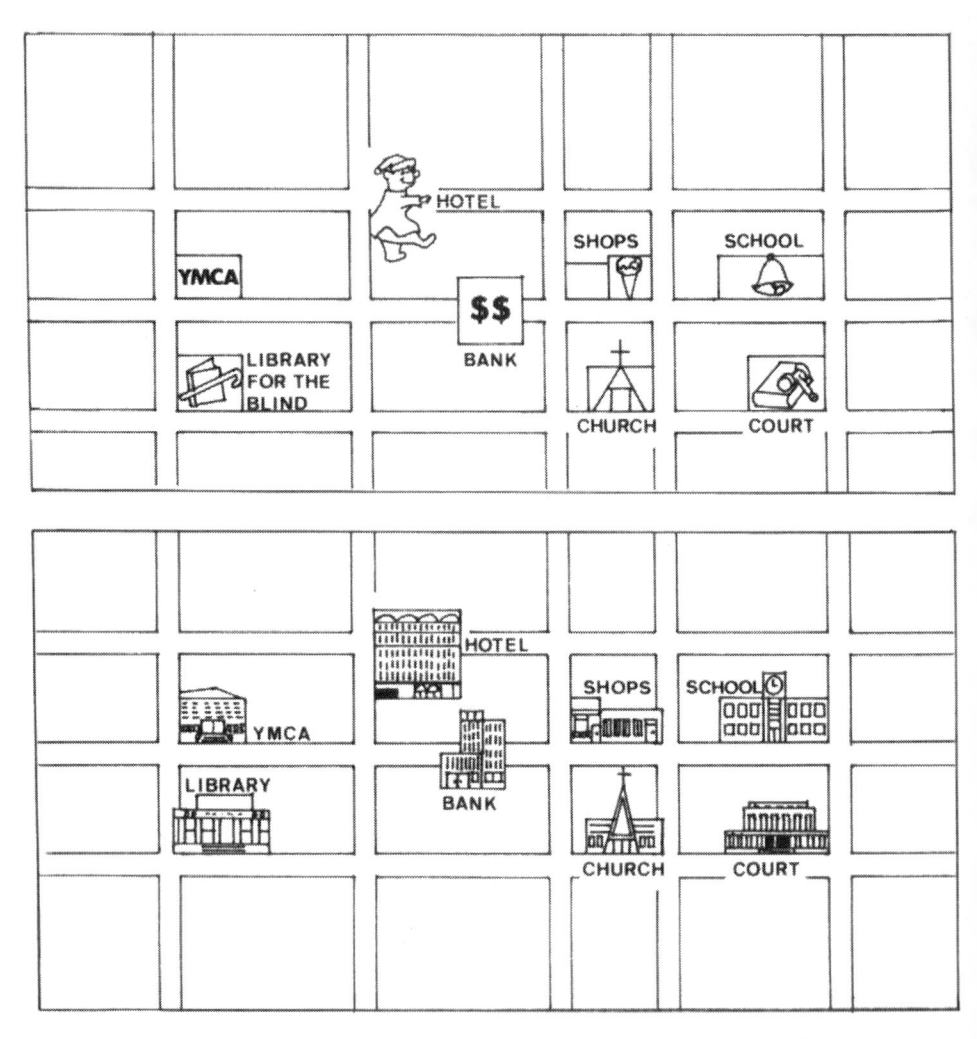

FIGURE 5.4. Two versions of a map of a part of downtown Seattle, using different types of elements.

of elements as visual argument. The following explains how each of the three graphic forms conveys meaning in terms of sequences and patterns.

Charts

SEQUENCE

The elements in a chart are not necessarily always in a particular sequence. For instance, a chart illustrating the main agricultural products of the 50 states might be organized around an alphabetical list of the states or a list that begins from the west and works eastward. The differences in the meaning of each chart would be slight. However, charts often do illustrate sequences. Time charts illustrating events in history are examples. It has been shown that charts organized around events in time can be used effectively in instruction. Winn (1981) demonstrated the effectiveness of a chart (shown in Figure 5.2) that illustrates the stages in insect metamorphosis in teaching middle school students.

The sequence of elements in charts can be arranged along other dimensions. Sternberg and Weil (1980) had students construct simple charts in which the elements of syllogisms were arranged in sequence by size. In problems of the type "If A is smaller than B and B is bigger than C, which is biggest?", Sternberg and Weil found that arranging A, B, and C in a chart by size helped students find the solution.

PATTERN

The patterns of the elements in charts convey meaning in two ways. The first is the relative distance of one element to the next. In any chart-like arrangement of information, some items are physically further away from others on the page. Winn (1980) constructed a chart that showed predator–prey relationships in a simple food chain. Studying the chart helped students develop cognitive structures representing the concepts involved such that an animal immediately next to another in the chain was seen as "closer to" its neighbor than to other animals further along the chain. Also, the chart helped the students classify the animals as different types of consumer, such as first-level and second-level carnivores, again as a result of the way in which these classifications were illustrated by the layout of the chart.

The second way in which charts convey meaning through the patterns of elements involves the relationships among column and row headings and other parts of the chart. In the Holliday and Benson (1981) chart, illustrating the sources and effects of different vitamins (shown in Figure 5.1), the column and row headings named broad categories for classification, like "Source" and "Effect." Each cell of the chart contained a subordinate concept such as "carotene," under "Source," and "premature aging" under "Effect." For those who have developed "chart literacy," the meaning of a column heading is to identify a common category in which all items physically beneath it belong. We can therefore tell at a glance, simply by the general pattern of the chart, which elements are broad and which are specific, and the hierarchies into which they fit.

Graphs

SEQUENCE

In graphs, the sequence of elements is crucial to the information they convey. The continuous variables they describe are, by definition, sequential. The order of the categorical variables likewise has an impact on the meaning of the graph. In a line graph or a histogram, one expects that the categories on either axis will be placed so as to make sense. Thus, a bar graph showing rainfall each month throughout the year would be expected to present the months in sequence, starting with January on the left. This is not only what a "graph literate" person would expect, but it makes the graph easier to read than it would be if the months were placed, say, in alphabetical order.

PATTERN

The overall pattern of a graph conveys meaning primarily in the way its general shape appears at first glance. The student can tell, without reading any labels or looking at any particular elements, what the graph is about and what the general trends are among the relationships that it describes. For instance, one can tell from the shape of the curve of a line graph whether the variables are related in a linear or more complex fashion. Also, it has been pointed out that different types of graph, displaying different types of pattern among elements, serve different functions (Fry, 1983; Wainer & Thissen, 1981). Line graphs illustrate trends and are often interpreted as showing dynamic relationships among variables. Bar and pie graphs always contain at least one categorical variable and therefore display their information as steps or areas (see Figure 5.5). These invite the student to make comparisons among the categories in terms of the values of the continuous variable. A line graph of annual rainfall by month emphasizes how rainfall increases and decreases throughout the year. A bar graph of the same material would invite comparison of one month's rainfall to the next month's. Likewise, a pie graph showing the percentage of sales tax going to various state services would suggest that it was meant to indicate contrasts or discrepancies among the various categories.

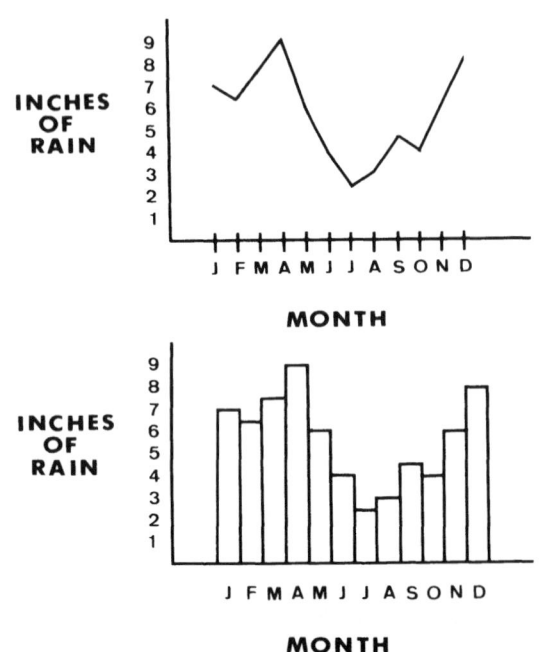

FIGURE 5.5. Line and bar graphs of rainfall by month.

In addition to these general meanings of patterns of elements in different types of graph is the convention that an element placed higher on the page is larger or more valuable than elements placed lower. This convention arises from the tradition that values higher up on the y axis are greater than lower values. (On the x axis, of course, they increase from left to right, in the same direction as we read.) Thus, we interpret the value of points and elements in a graph from their position on the page without necessarily looking at the actual values written along the two axes. Often, values can be omitted from the axes of graphs altogether.

Finally, Macdonald-Ross (1977b) has described a particularly effective way of presenting numeric information in graphs. This involves what he calls the "isotype," a graphic form developed by Neurath in the 1930s (Neurath, 1974). These are forms of graphs in which quantities are represented by small drawings of the elements in question, each of which represents a certain quantity of the concept involved. Thus, the population of Latin America over a period of years might be represented as a series of rows of stick figures, one row for each historical period, in which each figure stands for 100 million people. The isotype graph shown in Figure 5.6 conveys its meaning in three ways. First, the general pattern gives the

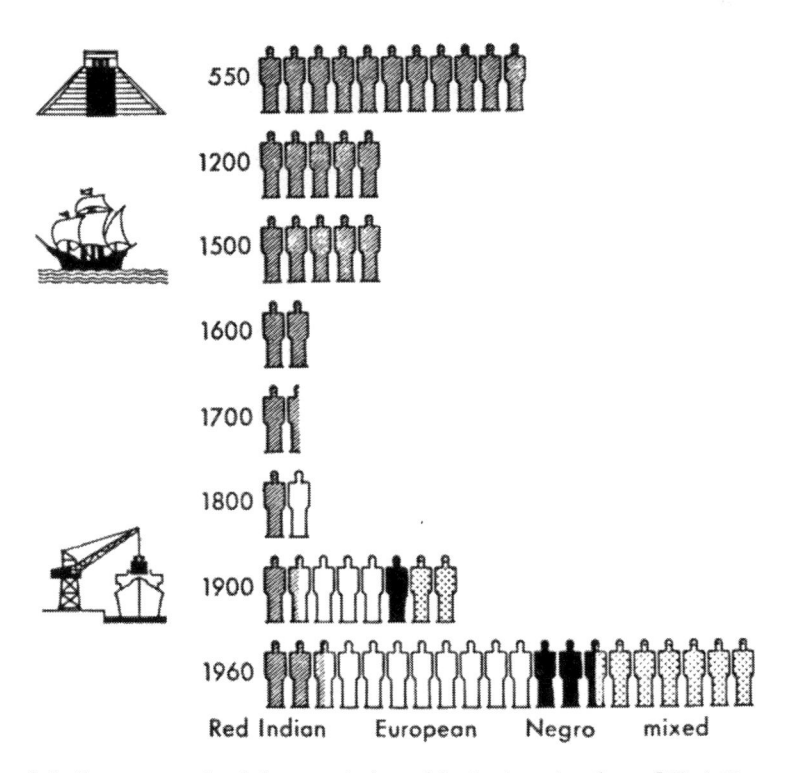

FIGURE 5.6. Isotype graph of the population of Latin America from 550 A.D. to the present. Each figure represents 100 million people. From "Isotype" by M. Neurath, 1974, *Instructional Science*, *3*, p. 13. Copyright 1974 by Nartinus Nijhoff Publishers. Reprinted by permission.

student a picture of the trends that the graph describes. Second, each element is a quasi realistic symbol of what it represents—in this case people. Third, closer scrutiny provides a numerical quantity for each little figure, which allows the student to attach actual values to the graph.

Diagrams

SEQUENCE

Diagrams explain sequences in a number of ways. Like any graphic form, they can follow the conventions of text, meaning that any sequence in the diagram starts with elements in the top left-hand corner and continues across and down the page to the bottom right-hand corner. This has been demonstrated in studies of students' eye movements as they looked at diagrams (Winn, 1983), where the first fixations tended to be in the upper left and scanning tended to be left to right and top to bottom.

However, the sequence of elements in a diagram can be expressed in other ways. Moxley (1983) distinguishes between three types of diagram. A "one-part" diagram has only one component. In our terminology, it consists of just one element and therefore does not exploit space among elements at all. The "two-part" diagram identifies, by means of a line linking two or more elements, the element that is antecedent and the one that follows. Thus, simple lines can indicate sequences of precedence, rules, or chains of reasoning. A "three-part" diagram shows more than linear relationships and is therefore capable of illustrating cycles. These might be shown by arranging elements in circles and linking the elements with arrows.

PATTERN

As in other graphic forms, the patterns formed by placing one element in a diagram closer to another to form clusters have a great deal to convey about how the elements are related. This is because the elements that appear to be physically close are thought of as being conceptually close as well. But as in the case of sequence in diagrams, certain graphic devices can affect how students see and interpret the pattern of elements in a diagram.

Fleming and Levie (1978, pp. 74–77), in what is in effect a rudimentary "syntax" of devices used in graphic forms, note the following techniques. Inclusion of elements within a common category, and, one supposes, their exclusion from others, can be achieved by surrounding the "included" elements with a box or circle. This has the effect of emphasizing the commonness of elements that is achieved by placing them close together. The line of the box or circle creates a boundary that isolates elements within it from others. Superordination can be expressed simply by placement. However, the use of linking lines, commonly found in graphical representations of hierarchies, serves to emphasize which element is superordinate to which other and which is subordinate. Accentuation of important elements can be achieved by pointers, such as arrows or lines, type style, color, and so on. Some of these devices are shown in Figure 5.7.

FIGURE 5.7. Elements of a simple syntax: Boxes and lines help to classify different animals.

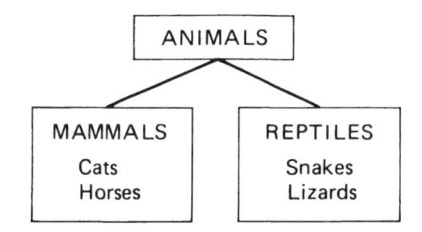

```
          ANIMALS
         /       \
   MAMMALS      REPTILES
   Cats         Snakes
   Horses       Lizards
```

Waller (1981) presents a somewhat different syntax for diagrams. He suggests that the boxes, which Fleming and Levie suggest for indicating which elements go with which, are the graphic equivalents of nouns. This means that, if an element in a diagram is surrounded by a box or circle, it is intended to name something, such as a concept or principle. Arrows correspond to verbs. They suggest actions. Thus, the words "Tyranosaurus" and "Plateosaurus," surrounded by boxes and joined by an arrow, might mean that Tyranosaurus evolved from Plateosaurus. An arrow linking "Lion" to "Gazelle" could suggest that lions eat gazelles. Finally, the graphic equivalents of adjectives and adverbs are, according to Waller, labels, colors, captions, and the like. The word "fierce" added to our lion, or showing it larger than the gazelle, would serve to qualify it just as an adjective would in a text.

Summary

Charts, graphs, and diagrams all convey meaning by exploiting the patterns formed by the elements they contain and by the sequences the elements form. However, each of the graphic forms does this somewhat differently. Charts convey sequences through the order in which elements are encountered as we read them from top to bottom and left to right. They emphasize the patterns of elements, arranged largely so that they convey class memberships, by means of column and row headings. Graphs exploit the convention that higher on the page, or the y axis, means larger or more valuable. They use sequences to convey numerical data, and the general shape of the line or pattern of the bars conveys the general sense of the relationships they describe. Diagrams convey sequence by the placement of elements on the page and through graphic devices like lines and arrows. They emphasize patterns, and thus conceptual organization, by means of boxes, circles, and so on. Some scholars (Fleming & Levie, 1978; Waller, 1981) have even provided simple syntaxes of graphic forms for use in diagrams.

The use of space is therefore central to the ways in which the three graphic forms convey information. We are led to conclude that the relative placement of elements in a chart, graph, or diagram and the devices, like lines, arrows, column headings, and boxes, are the core of visual argument. How successful these attempts have been to make graphic forms meaningful to students in instructional settings is what we turn to next.

Research on Instructional Effectiveness

So far, we have looked at some of the reasons that have been offered for the effectiveness of visual argument in graphic forms and at how these forms convey meaning through the use of space, particularly by means of patterns and sequences of elements. We now turn to research that has studied the effectiveness of graphic forms in instruction.

Characteristics of the Research

As is usually the case, this research does not fit neatly into the schemes and divisions that, theoretically, seem to make sense in terms of what we have said about visual argument and the meaningful use of space. For this reason, it is necessary to make the following points about this body of research.

1. The instructional functions that graphic forms are expected to serve are sometimes confused in studies. (Duchastel & Waller, 1979, have identified a number of these functions, including description, showing structures, showing steps in processes, gaining attention, presenting data, showing algorithms of procedures, and showing logico-mathematical relationships.) It is often not clear whether experimental effects were due to a graphic's explaining effectively how something worked, allowing students to create appropriate mental images, or simply motivating the students. The product of this confounding is results that, at best, tell us *if* charts, graphs, and diagrams are effective, not *why*.
2. It follows that a great deal of the research is concerned simply with whether or not the *presence* of a graphic has a significant effect on what students learn. Many studies compare a treatment that includes a graphic with a textual or some other "traditional" treatment without looking at what the particular features, or "symbol systems" (Salomon, 1979), of the graphic contribute. Again, the emphasis is on the description of effects rather than on explaining them. One is left with the impression of a "shotgun" approach in much of this research in which the theory of visual argument does not feature prominently.
3. On the other hand, there is some research, ostensibly not on graphics, that is extremely useful. This includes research on maps, on visual–spatial ability and learning math and science, on semantic networks (Norman et al., 1975) and how they can be used to help students understand text (see Holley & Dansereau, 1984), and a variety of other areas. This research tends to deal with psychological factors that are fundamental to visual information processing generally and that underlie learning from all forms of visual illustration including, of course, graphics.
4. There is a disproportionate amount of research on what we have defined as "diagrams." There is very little on the instructional effectiveness of graphs, and not much more on charts.
5. The effectiveness of graphics cannot be explained in any simple way. This is because, in a substantial number of studies, the experimental effects have been

found to depend on students' abilities and on the nature of the learning task. A number of studies have confirmed interactions between student ability and experimental treatments (see Cronbach & Snow, 1977, for a comprehensive treatment of Aptitude-Treatment Interactions [ATI]). In many cases, but by no means all the time, the graphics have done more to improve the performance of low-ability students than of those of high ability.

Dependency on task is less easy to generalize about. We shall deal with each instance as it occurs. However, some intuitive suppositions are borne out. For example, recognition is improved when the elements in graphics are shown realistically (Dwyer, 1978; Winn, 1981). Processes are learned more easily when a diagram presents them in sequence (Holliday, 1976; Winn, 1982).

We now look at a representative selection of studies from this body of research, chosen to illustrate a wide variety of functions of graphics and of other important issues.

Realism: The Descriptive Function

In the previous section, we saw that the elements in a chart, graph, or diagram could be represented in a number of ways: by verbal labels, arbitrary symbols, or small realistic pictures. A number of studies have suggested that the use of small pictures to illustrate the single elements in a graphic has certain advantages. These advantages are accounted for by theories concerning alternative coding of information by students where, generally, presenting information in pictures reduces the processing burden, especially among poor readers. For example, Paivio's "dual-coding" theory (1971, 1975) proposes that pictures are encoded both as visual images and as their verbal labels, while words are coded only verbally, thus accounting for the apparent superiority of pictorial presentations when the task is recall. This superiority is affected by both students' ability and the nature of the learning task.

ABILITY

Holliday, Brunner, and Donais (1977) studied the effects of two types of flow diagram, shown in Figure 5.8, used to teach biological cycles to Grade 10 students. The diagrams were complex and illustrated the carbon dioxide, oxygen, nitrogen, and water cycles and how they interact with one another. The diagrams were identical, except that one, the "picture–word" diagram, showed each element, such as plants, animals, clouds, volcanoes, and the like, as line drawings, while the "block–word" diagram showed just their labels. Students' verbal ability was assessed by the V2 vocabulary test from the *Kit of Reference Tests of Cognitive Factors* (French, Ekstrom, & Price, 1963). Students studied the two diagrams (there was no accompanying text) and then completed 30 multiple-choice questions that tested their retention of the material.

Holliday et al. reported a significant interaction between the treatments and the verbal ability of the students such that the picture–word diagram improved the performance of low-ability students more than that of high-ability students when

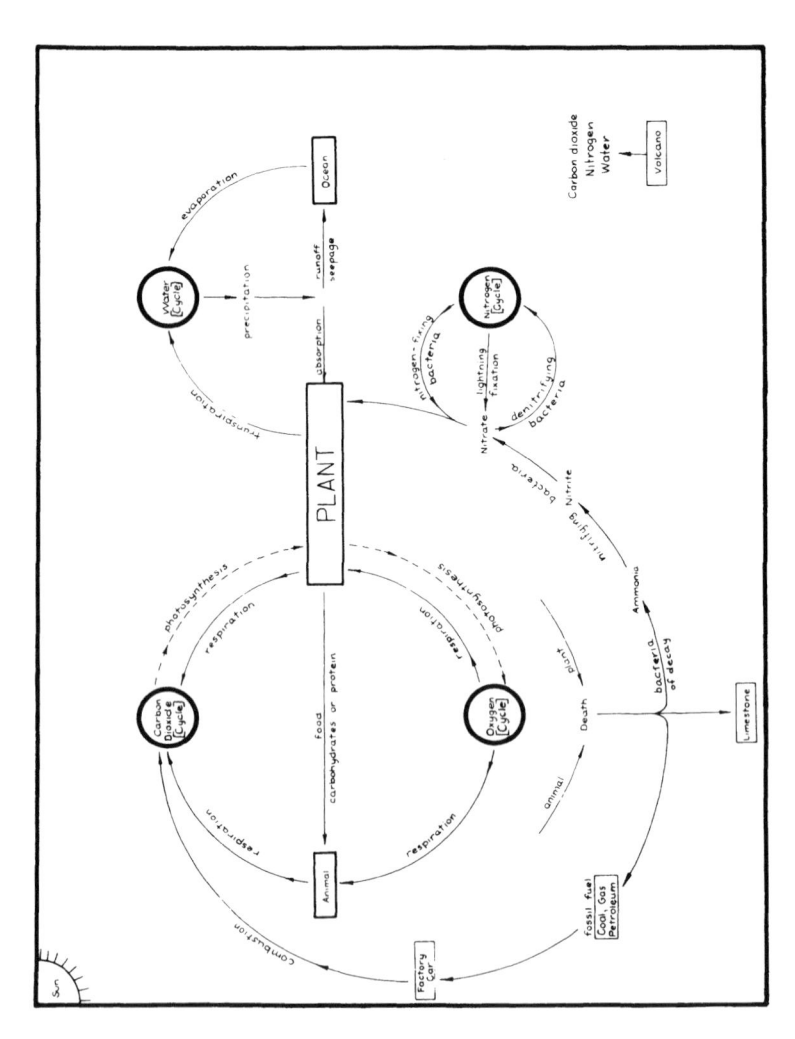

FIGURE 5.8. Two versions of a flow diagram teaching biological cycles and showing elements as pictures or labels. From "Teaching Verbal Chains Using Flow Diagrams and Texts" by W. G. Holliday, 1976, *AV Communication Review*, 24, p. 66–67. Copyright 1976 by Association for Educational Communication and Technology. Reprinted by permission.

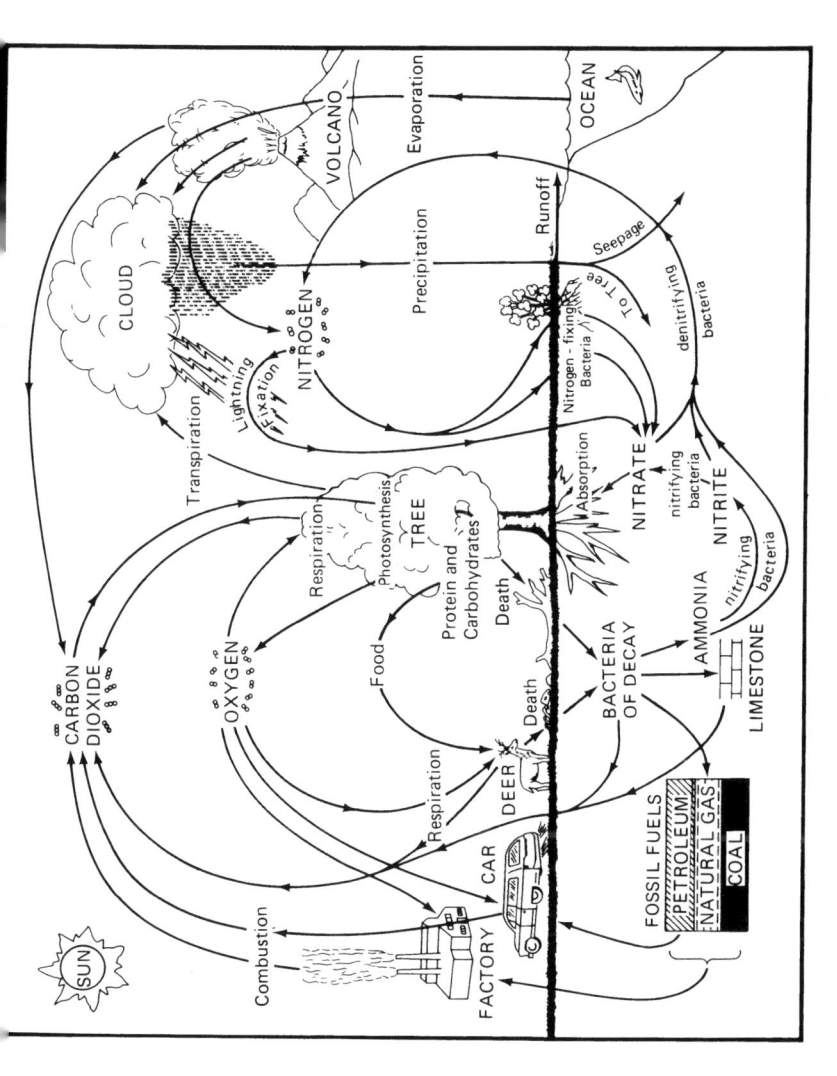

FIGURE 5.8. *Continued.*

compared to the success of the block–word diagram. These results were interpreted in terms of Paivio's theory, mentioned above.

A similar finding was reported in mathematics instruction for a problem-solving task (Moyer, Sowder, Threadgill-Sowder, & Moyer, 1984). Students in Grades 3–11 solved word problems. Three treatments were compared: a regular verbal description of the problem, a verbal description combined with illustrations that showed realistic drawings of the elements in the problem, and a "telegraphic" treatment that described the problems in terse phrases. The format with the drawings led to significantly greater success at solving the problems than either of the two other formats. An interaction with reading ability, where the drawn format was more helpful to low-ability readers than to more able students, was also reported. These results are accounted for by the claim that the drawings reduced the "reading-related working-memory overload" in poor readers.

These two studies suggest that, as one might expect and as theory predicts, the representation of elements in diagrams as pictures rather than as verbal labels helps students who are poor at verbal skills more than it helps verbally competent students. When other measures of ability are used, however, different results sometimes occur.

Parkhurst and Dwyer (1983) had undergraduates study a unit on the human heart presented by programmed instruction. The independent variable of interest was the degree of realism in the illustrations that accompanied the programmed material, and the predictor was IQ. The illustrations ranged from realistic pictures of the heart, to photographs of models of the heart, to line drawings. On a variety of criterion measures (recall, learning spatial information, learning concepts), the study demonstrated that increasing the realism of the elements in the illustrations improved the performance of the high-IQ students, while the performance of the low-IQ students decreased.

This interaction is clearly contrary to the interactions reported by Holliday et al. (1977) and by Moyer et al. (1984), where the predictor was verbal ability. It can be accounted for by the claim (Allen, 1975) that low-ability students have difficulty processing instruction that is informationally rich and redundant. In graphics whose elements are presented as realistic pictures, more information is available to the students. Students of low ability find it difficult to deal with this added information and therefore are less successful than their more able counterparts.

A similar conclusion was reached by Canelos, Taylor, and Gates (1980), using a similar set of materials on the heart, presented this time by slide and tape. Canelos et al. used field dependence (Witkin, Moore, Goodenough, & Cox, 1977) as their predictor. People who are field dependent have more difficulty processing information independent of its context than field-independent people. This means that they are less likely to be able to free themselves from the form in which information is presented in order to manipulate it, restructure it, and solve problems. Canelos et al. reported that field-dependent college students (the "less able" ones) had more difficulty than the field independents extracting information from the illustrations that was necessary for the completion of the more difficult tasks, such as concept learning.

To summarize, these studies exemplify research which suggests, first, that representing the elements of a graphic pictorially will be advantageous to students who are weak in verbal skills. This is because it presents information in a way that is less likely to call on skills in which the student is not particularly adept. However, there are limits to the amount of detail that should be included. There is a point, yet to be defined precisely, at which the addition of detail to elements in graphics begins to interfere with students' more general abilities to extract and process information.

We now turn to an examination of how task interacts with the types of element used in instructional graphics.

Task

Kulhavy et al. (1983) had university students study three types of map showing a grid of streets in a fictitious town for six blocks in all directions. On one map, the features were identified by verbal labels only. On a second map, they were shown by realistic drawings, and on the third by arbitrary geometric symbols. On a "cued recall" test, where students had to fill in the details of blank maps, students who had studied the maps with drawings and labels outperformed those whose maps had symbols. On a "recognition" test, requiring students to state which feature was nearest and which farthest from another, the maps with drawings once again led to better performance than the maps with symbols. Kulhavy et al. account for this by concluding that symbols that are not congruent with what they represent interfere with learning. This study therefore suggests that realistic elements are more effective for recall and recognition tasks.

The conclusion that arbitrary representation of elements in illustrations interferes may not be true for all tasks, however. A study (Winn, 1986a), in which high school students studied electronic circuit diagrams, suggested that symbols might well interfere with recall of elements in a pattern, but not of elements in sequence. The circuit diagrams were presented in two forms, which are shown in Figure 5.9. In one form, each element in the circuit, such as a resistor, capacitor, or diode, was represented by its conventional symbol with a letter beside it, keyed to the component's name at the bottom of the page. In the other form, it was shown as the letter in a small box. Also, each component was numbered in order across the page from the top left corner to the bottom right. It was found that students who had to recall and list the elements in the circuit in their correct order did better if they saw the diagrams with the symbols, while those students who had to draw the circuit diagram, with the elements in the correct position, did best if they saw the diagrams without the symbols.

In this study, the two tasks called on totally different types of cognitive processing. Drawing the diagram, with the elements in the right places, required simultaneous processing (Das et al., 1979), while remembering a sequential list of elements required successive processing. As we saw earlier, simultaneous processing requires that students grasp the "big picture." The greater the detail of the elements, the harder this would be, because the detail of the elements has nothing to do with remembering where they are placed. Successive processing

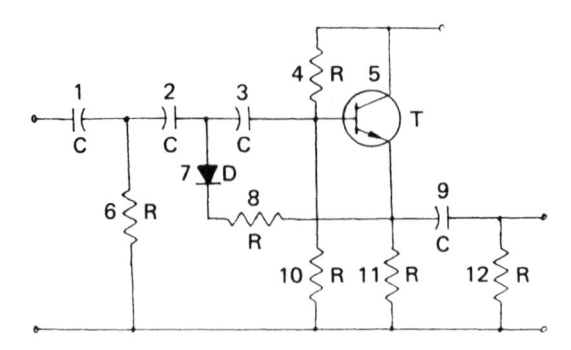

FIGURE 5.9. Detailed and less detailed elements in a circuit diagram. From *Simultaneous and Successive Processing of Circuit Diagrams Having Different Amounts of Detail* by W. D. Winn, 1986, April. Paper presented at the annual meeting of the American Educational Research Association, San Francisco. Reprinted by permission.

C CAPACITOR
D DIODE
G GROUND
R RESISTOR
T TRANSISTOR

requires identifying and remembering each element individually. Here, the more unique each element appears to be, the easier it is to remember.

There are other reasons why representing the elements of a diagram by realistic drawings might help students learn sequences of elements. In a study involving Grade 9 students, Winn (1982) used four flow diagrams to teach the evolutionary sequence of dinosaurs. The diagrams identified the animals either by labeled line drawings or by labels alone. Two of the diagrams showed the evolutionary sequence running in the direction one would normally read, from left to right across the page. The other two diagrams showed the sequence reversed, running from right to left. In each case, the dinosaurs were facing in the direction of the evolutionary sequence.

A number of tests were given. Of interest to this discussion is the finding that, on a posttest of the students' knowledge of the evolutionary sequence, the superior performance of those who saw the normal, left-to-right, diagram was confined to the students whose diagrams showed pictures of the animals. Clearly, they had picked up cues about the sequence of events from the direction in which the dinosaurs were facing. So it seems that, in addition to providing extra details that help students remember the individual elements in a graphic, adding realistic pictures can also provide cues suggesting sequence through details within the drawings themselves.

In this study, it was also found that students who saw elements shown as drawings were better able to identify the animals correctly on a posttest. Presenting the features of elements in the diagram so that the attributes of each species of dinosaur were shown realistically would, in theory, make it much easier to learn concrete concepts and to assign each animal to its correct category (Merrill & Tennyson, 1977), and the results of the study bore this out.

Further support for this comes from another study (Winn, 1981) in which Grade 9 students learned about insect metamorphosis from realistic pictures or from a chart in which only labels and stylized drawings of each insect were presented. It was found that students scoring high on the V2 verbal ability test from the *Kit of Reference Tests for Cognitive Factors* (French et al., 1963) who studied a pictorial treatment, in which the critical attributes of each insect were highlighted by means of arrows and in a spoken narration, performed better on a test of insect identification than high-ability students who studied metamorphosis by means of the chart. (The chart proved to be helpful when the task was to classify insects by type of metamorphosis. We shall return to this later.)

These studies suggest that detail in the elements of graphics may improve student performance on concept identification and on some recall tasks, but not on other tasks. (For further discussion of this point, see Clark & Angert, 1985, and Dwyer, 1978.) Furthermore, for certain tasks, particularly those that are more demanding of students' cognitive resources, the complexity added to elements by increasing detail or by highlighting critical attributes can be handled only by students with a higher capacity for information processing. It therefore seems that three-way interactions among treatment, task, and ability would be more likely to account for the instructional effectiveness of different ways of presenting the elements in graphics than simpler explanations. This would certainly be consistent with the results of the ATI studies, discussed above, which investigated the relationships among abilities and learning from graphics. However, the research in graphics has not yet explored this more complex type of relationship in sufficient detail to permit reliable conclusions to be drawn.

Charts: The Organization of Information

In the earlier section on the function of charts, we noted that these graphic forms convey meaning by organizing categories of concepts on the page in columns and rows. Column and row headings, and the drawing of horizontal and vertical lines to delineate the divisions more clearly, mean that charts are particularly dependent on spatial organization. The meaning of a chart is therefore the result of the actual physical distance of one element to another and of the superordinate column and row categories by means of which they are organized. This section first looks at general research on the effects of spatial organization and headings on learning in laboratory experiments. It then turns to studies that have examined the effectiveness of charts in the instruction of school subjects.

Organization

There is some evidence that simply arranging elements to be learned into groups will improve students' ability to do so. In a study by Decker and Wheatley (1982), university students studied lists of nouns that had either low or high imagery values, according to the Paivio, Yuille, and Madigan (1968) norms. These were presented to the students either in one long list or grouped into three lists placed in the top left portion of the page, in the middle, or in the bottom right portion. Five such sets of lists were prepared. The students studied them for 30 seconds each and then took a 1-minute free-recall test. There were five such trials. A significant interaction was found involving spatial arrangement and trial. By the third trial, students who saw the grouped lists were outperforming students who saw the single list. This effect was independent of imagery.

What this study suggests is that, once students have learned to take advantage of it, the spatial grouping of items that have to be learned improves free recall. This is true regardless of whether the items are likely to facilitate the creation of mental images or not, and regardless of the conceptual coherence of the groupings. (The Paivio et al. norms are not organized around any "families" of concepts named by the nouns.)

When the elements to be learned can be grouped according to some sort of conceptual structure, then their arrangement can help reinforce that structure. Rabinowitz and Mandler (1983) studied the effect of grouping short phrases for two types of category. Each phrase contained a verb and a noun. The phrases, which students were to remember, were grouped either taxonomically (i.e., into a superordinate category) or schematically (according to a story schema). The taxonomic group "Places" included such phrases as "go to mountains," "go to Hawaii," "go to theater." The schematic group "Going skiing" included the phrases "go to mountains," "put on jacket," "buy lift ticket," and so on. In a first experiment, undergraduates were assigned to either the taxonomic, schematic, or a random grouping treatment. They listened to the phrases of tape and then took a recall test. It was found that students in the schematic group outperformed students in the other two groups. They also recalled better formed clusters of phrases and phrases more often in the correct sequence. This superior performance was attributed to the fact that the story schema in the schematic treatment provided a logical sequence of events and made it easier for students to imagine "scenes" in which the events described by the phrases took place. In a second experiment, the schematic grouping was arranged so that such a logical sequence of events was not apparent. The group "Going to the park" included, in order, "play in park," "lick ice cream," "pedal bicycle." It was found that, in most cases, there was now no difference in recall performance between the taxonomic and schematic groups.

This study is interesting for two reasons. First, it confirms that grouping makes elements easier to recall. Second, it shows that when the grouping allows students to form mental images that organize the elements in a meaningful way, as the story schemata did, then recall is improved even further. The sequence in which elements are presented, in time as in this study or in space as we shall see later, is often the means by which such logical structures can be imagined and easily remembered.

However, there is a suggestion in the literature that the structurally meaningful organization of elements is not effective with younger students who fail to make the appropriate associations among the elements. Frankel (1983) presented kindergarten, fourth-grade, and tenth-grade students with a set of 24 pictures, half of which showed items that were highly associated, and half nonassociated items. Not only did the kindergarten and Grade 4 students not group associated material together when they recalled it, but neither recall nor organization improved for these students over three trials with the same materials. This suggests that students have to be at least at the Grade 10 level to be able to notice and take advantage of conceptual coherence in elements in order to form groups that assist memory and recall.

Hartley and Trueman (1985) reported a similar developmental trend after conducting 17 experiments with students of different ages on the effectiveness of headings in text. Students studied a semitechnical text about television and the BBC. Three tasks were involved. Recall required students to write open-ended answers to test questions. Search had them find answers to questions in the passage as they read it and to circle them. The dependent measure was time. Retrieval required them to read the passage for a set length of time and then to find and circle the answers. The results of these experiments provided a lot of information. In summary, it was found that headings improved the performance of 14- and 15-year-old students on all three tasks, but with 11- and 12-year-old students, headings helped only search and retrieval. The failure of headings to improve the recall performance of the younger students suggests that, like the students in Frankel's study, these did not take advantage of headings to form structures organizing the material which would have been helpful for recall. Only the recall task required them to remember information for any substantial period of time.

We can conclude from this research that even the simplest spatial organization of elements into meaningful clusters has the potential for improving learning. However, the last two studies require us to consider the developmental level of students when either assessing the results of research or using charts, with headings, to instruct. It is generally accepted, largely as the result of the work of Piaget (Piaget & Inhelder, 1969), that the stage of a student's development constrains intellectual ability in a number of ways. The developmental nature of students' ability to take advantage of the conceptual coherence of items grouped in clusters on the page conforms to this phenomenon. It is probably premature to attempt to link this ability to a particular developmental stage. However, we have seen evidence that college students, as well as those in Grade 10, have this ability, while younger students do not.

INSTRUCTIONAL CHARTS

When we turn to studies of the use of charts to teach school subjects, we find similar evidence for the advantages of organization on the page, both spatial and conceptual. While charts have obvious applications in a variety of subject areas, most of the research has been concerned with the teaching of science, and it is to this area that our discussion is limited.

The organizational function of charts has been demonstrated in a study of how a chart can teach a simple biological food chain to Grade 9 students (Winn, 1980). This study allows us a particular insight into the question of organization because the principal dependent variable was the degree to which the students' cognitive

178   Bill Winn

structures representing the material corresponded to the actual organization of the concepts presented in the chart. This was achieved, first, by creating a "directed graph" (Harary, Norman & Cartwright, 1965; Shavelson, 1972), which illustrated the structure of the content by the spatial arrangement of the elements in the food chain and the arrows between them, and then by converting this to a matrix of estimated distances among all possible pair combinations of the concepts. (Harary et al., 1965, pp. 134–141, explain how this is done.) Students gave free verbal associations to words naming the elements in the food chain, and from these, matrices representing their cognitive structures were created (see Deese, 1962, and Garskof & Houston, 1963, for the techniques involved). The matrices representing students' cognitive structures were then compared to the matrix derived from the directed graph by calculating the "Euclidean distance" between them (see Shavelson, 1972, for how this is done). The dependent measure was therefore a number representing the proximity of students' cognitive structures to the "ideal" structure of the content.

Grade 9 students either read a text describing a simple food chain or studied a chart, shown in Figure 5.10, that presented the same information along with the text. The students' general ability was estimated from their combined verbal reasoning and numerical ability scores on the Differential Aptitude Test (Bennett, Seashore, & Wesman, 1972). It was found that the cognitive structures of high-ability students were closer to the "target" structure when they studied the chart rather than the text alone, but that there was no difference for the low-ability students. This suggests that the addition of a chart to a text in which conceptual organization is made explicit (e.g., which animal preys on which, and whether they are energy producers or consumers) helps only those students who

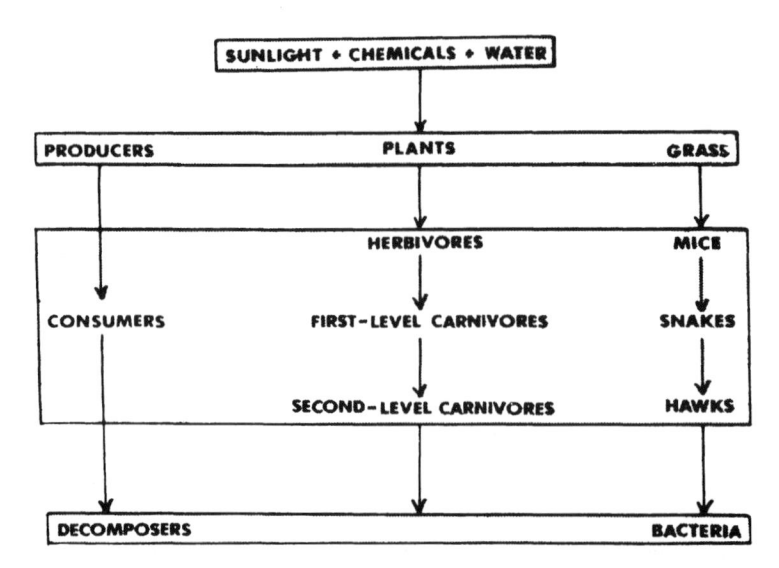

FIGURE 5.10. Chart of a simple food chain showing sequence and category membership.

are able to take advantage of it. But the help it provides comes in the form of a better organization of the elements and the relationships among them, as theory suggests it should.

However, this effect is also constrained by the nature of the task. A study of the use of pictures and charts (Winn, 1981) to teach insect metamorphosis was described in part above. Another aspect of this study was the role of the chart, shown in Figure 5.3, in which insect type and type of metamorphosis were crossed with stage of metamorphosis. Of the Grade 9 students who took part in the study, those who saw the chart rather than pictures of the insects and who were high-verbal made fewer errors when asked to classify the insects by type of metamorphosis than those who saw pictures. There was no difference for low-verbal students. On the other hand, as we saw above, when the task was the identification of insects by type and by stage of metamorphosis, in most instances the high-verbals did best when they saw pictures rather than the chart, while, again, there was no difference for the low-verbals. The interaction between ability and treatment was completely reversed when a different task was required.

In both of these studies, charts improved student performance on tasks requiring a knowledge of structure or relationships provided that the students were capable of taking advantage of the information that the charts gave them about how the content was organized. In the studies we looked at earlier of how subjects used organization in materials to improve recall, search, and retrieval, we saw that the ability to take advantage of this depended on developmental level. We now have evidence that it also depends on ability within a particular developmental level. A developing area of research in education has to do with metacognition, or the ability of students to select and effectively use appropriate learning strategies (Brown, 1981; Brown, Campione, & Day, 1981; Chipman & Segal, 1985). It is generally believed that more able students are better at finding these strategies and using them. Although these studies of the use of spatial organization and charts were not directly concerned with metacognition, it seems that students will benefit from these graphic forms only when they do use their particular abilities as strategies for learning.

One of the simplest and most important of these strategies is finding and attending to the important information in a chart and ignoring the rest. Holliday and Benson (1981) taught high school students about vitamins by means of a chart that crossed vitamins with their sources and with the consequences of their presence and absence in a diet. Study questions were used as a strategy for directing students' attention to different columns. It was found that when the questions directed attention to all the columns in the chart, students' performance was no better than when no study questions were used. When attention was focused on particular columns, students learned more from those columns than students whose questions directed their attention to all the columns, or who had no questions at all.

This study did not consider the influence of student ability or task. It is therefore impossible to say whether the study questions were needed to direct the attention of all the students, or whether they would play a similar role if the task had been other than recall. However, it does appear that strategies that direct attention to relevant parts of a chart, such as study questions, might help students find and attend to important information.

These studies of instructional charts extend the more basic principles of organization by using a number of graphic and other instructional techniques. Generally, the organizational advantages of charts, predicted by theory, receive qualified confirmation. The qualifications arise principally from the need for students to possess the ability to decode and understand the information in the spatial layout—the rows and columns of charts—and to use it appropriately. Also, charts are not appropriate for all types of task. They are particularly useful when students have to recall groups of concepts which may be associated conceptually in a number of ways. They help students classify elements into categories. Their benefits are enhanced if they are used with appropriate learning strategies, which can be guided by such devices as study questions.

Spatial Visualization in Mathematics

We have already seen that one of the general advantages of graphic forms is that they present "pictures" of things that are normally abstract and hard to grasp. Among other things, this encourages students to form mental images of the content that are easier to manipulate and recall than other forms of representation. As the monk puzzle suggested, this has particular advantages in the type of problem solving where the subject matter is abstract and difficult to deal with.

A number of writers on mathematics education have remarked that representing problems in some visual form is particularly advantageous for this potentially abstract and baffling subject area. For Simon and Simon (1978), effective problem solvers develop physical representations of a problem before they select and use mathematical procedures to solve it. That diagrams are useful in this role of giving problems a physical form has been convincingly argued by Schoenfeld (1980). This is because they make apparent the patterns formed by the elements of the problem and their relationships, the recognition and symbolical articulation of which is fundamental to mathematical thinking (Burton, 1984; Mason, Burton, & Stacey, 1982, p. 181). There is a body of research demonstrating the value of the graphic representation of mathematical problems and the use of spatial cognitive processes to solve them. We now look at some representative studies.

Spatial Ability

One line of research has studied the relationship between students' spatial ability and their success in mathematical problem solving. The emphasis in these studies is on student ability rather than the way in which information is presented to them. Their relevance to the present discussion therefore lies in what they reveal about students' internal processes that rely on spatial representation.

Typical of this type of research is a study by Fennema and Tartre (1985). This was a longitudinal study of a group of students while they were in Grades 6, 7, and

8. The students' spatial ability was tested by the Spatial Visualization subtest of the Differential Aptitude Test (Bennett et al., 1973). Periodically during the 3-year period of the study, the students were tested in individual interviews, during which they were given mathematical problems to solve. They were required to make drawings as often as they could during the interviews in order to help them solve the problems. Line drawings, pie graphs, and other "hints" were provided if they were unable to do this. The data were protocols of their performance during the interviews.

The results of this study showed that students high in spatial visualization ability used drawings more often and more successfully to solve the problems than students who were less visually able. The researchers attributed this to the fact that the good visualizers were better able to translate the problem into a physical representation than the poor visualizers. It was also found that the girls were more likely to use pictures to help them than the boys. This conclusion is consistent with apparent gender differences that have been reported for a variety of tasks related to mathematics (see also Fennema & Sherman, 1977).

While the finding that spatial ability makes it easier for students to solve mathematics problems has received wide support, this support is not universal. Battista (1981) conducted a study based on earlier work involving students' "right hemisphere" processing ability (Battista, 1980). University undergraduates studied algebraic structures using either verbal materials or verbal materials with many additional graphic devices. No main effects were found, nor did the treatments interact with the students' spatial ability. While it is possible that the lack of significant differences, particularly for the interaction, could be the result of a small sample (only 36 students in total), it may also be the case that with students this senior, presumably with some background in mathematics, the advantages bestowed by spatial ability and spatial treatments are not necessary for success.

INSTRUCTIONAL GRAPHICS

Another line of research has looked at the use of graphics, particularly diagrams, for representing the problems students have to solve. In this research, the interest is primarily in the facilitative role of the diagrams the students work with, whether produced by them or provided by the instruction, and less on their abilities.

Lindvall, Tamburino, and Robinson (1982) conducted an exploratory study of how diagrams can help younger children learn basic mathematical operations. The students were primary grade children learning to solve story problems. Over a period of twenty-two 40-minute lessons, the students were taught to draw a different diagram for each of eight types of addition and subtraction problem. These were similar to venn diagrams and showed elements in a set as dots, the set boundaries as lines, and the operations, such as combining, separating, increasing, decreasing, comparing, and equalizing, by means of a variety of symbols. Some examples are shown in Figure 5.11. Each diagram was modeled for the

COMBINE

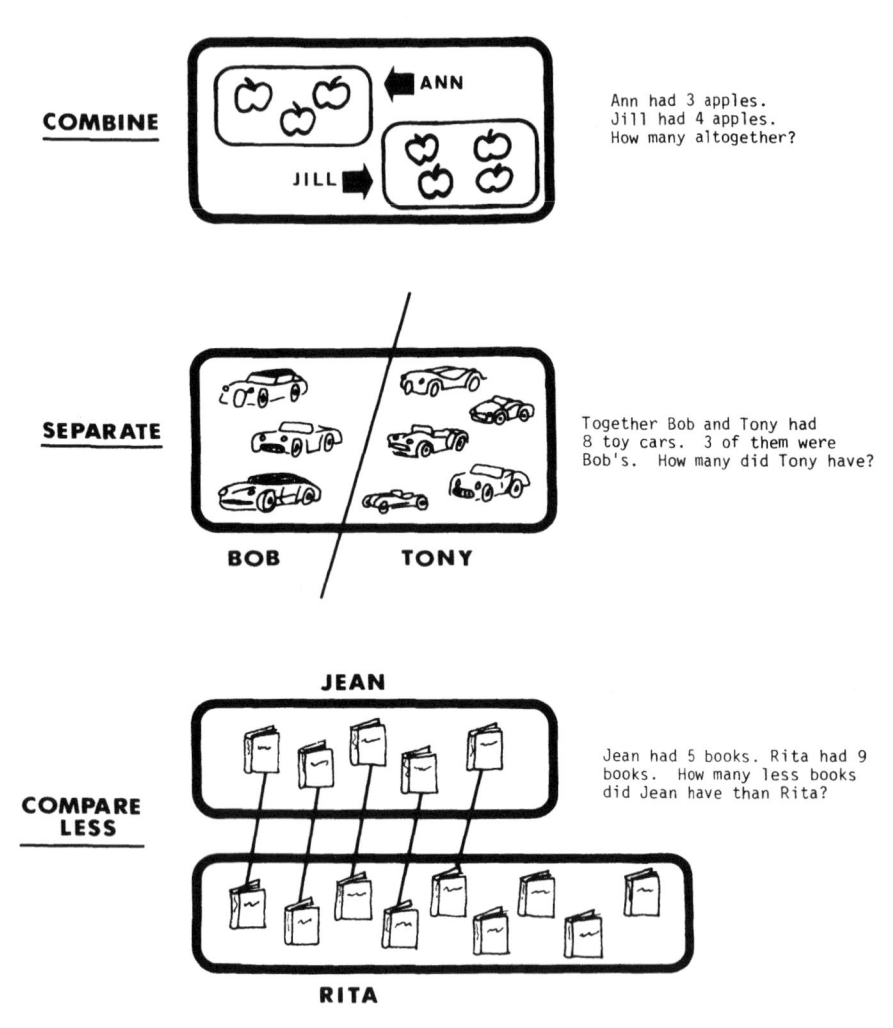

Ann had 3 apples.
Jill had 4 apples.
How many altogether?

SEPARATE

Together Bob and Tony had 8 toy cars. 3 of them were Bob's. How many did Tony have?

COMPARE LESS

Jean had 5 books. Rita had 9 books. How many less books did Jean have than Rita?

FIGURE 5.11. Examples of diagrams used to help children learn arithmetic. Based on *An Exploratory Investigation of the Effect of Teaching Primary Grade Children to Use Specific Problem-Solving Strategies in Solving Simple Story Problems* by C. M. Lindvall, J. L. Tamburino, and L. Robinson, 1982, March. Paper presented at the conference of the American Educational Research Association, New York. Reprinted by permission.

students individually using chips and yarn. Once the students had learned how to use the diagram, how to translate it into a number sentence, and how to find the answer to the sentence, they went and worked individually on story problems.

The design was a pretest–posttest design, and all students received the same treatment. Comparisons were made between pretest and posttest scores on the students' ability to draw the appropriate diagram, on their construction of the correct number sentence, and on their getting the right answer. Significant gains were reported on all three measures. In addition, a transfer test was given with story problems involving more than one operation, two-digit numbers, and topics, such as length, that were new to the students. Significant gains were also found for this test.

One of the problems with this kind of study is that it is difficult to attribute performance gains to the use of diagrams or simply to more general familiarity and practice with solving story problems. However, the study does demonstrate that a learning strategy that requires students to draw diagrams to represent story problems is effective in teaching young children how to solve this type of problem.

A more traditional use of graphics in mathematics is to present information to students, rather than have them draw their own. And, not surprisingly, there is a growing interest in the use of graphics to teach mathematics by computer, as the following two studies illustrate.

Carrier, Post, and Heck (1985) used computer graphics to teach Grade 4 students basic arithmetic skills. Graphics were used to fulfill a variety of functions. To enhance motivation, for example, a drawing of a racing car moved around a track. To highlight the structural properties of such problems as "$7 \times 3 = \underline{}?$," a chart showing a 7×3 array of drawings of objects was displayed. A computer version of the worksheet used by one of the experimental groups was also shown. On a posttest and a retention test of multiplication facts, instruction by computer proved to be more successful than instruction by paper-and-pencil worksheets. For division facts, the superiority of computerized instruction was confined to the posttest alone.

For the researcher, it is unfortunate that the report of this study does not attribute the superiority of the computer treatments to particular aspects of the graphics. It is not possible to determine whether the effects were due to enhanced motivation as a result of moving the racing car, or to the chart that visualized in an array the structural features of multiplication problems. Confounding like this has been problematic in many studies of computer-assisted learning (Clark, 1985). However, for practical purposes, where identifying causes is of less importance, this study demonstrates the superiority of graphic forms in instruction over more traditional ways of teaching. The graphic treatment, irrespective of why, turned out to be more effective.

Computer graphics are extremely effective in simulations. Reed (1985) used animated diagrams to simulate such things as tanks filling through one or two pipes, fluids mixing, and so on. The objective was to improve undergraduates' estimates of correct answers when they solved word problems in algebra. It was found that the diagrams were useful only on some tasks. For example, on a problem involving the mixing of acids, verbal information was sufficient to enable the students to solve the problem. On other tasks, the graphics only helped if the parts of the problem were displayed simultaneously, not one after another, and if students were given feedback after each problem. Again, we find it necessary to qualify the general conclusion that graphic forms are superior by taking the task and the nature of other aspects of the interaction between students and instruction into account.

All these studies of the use of graphics in mathematics instruction were based on the premise that representing abstract problems in a concrete, visual form makes them easier to solve. We have seen evidence that the cognitive processes these visual representations activate (spatial ability, imagery) do indeed serve mathematical thinking, with some qualifications on account of gender and intellectual maturity. We have also seen some evidence, from primary grade children and college students, that the representations themselves are helpful. This, again, depends on the type of task and on other instructional strategies that may be used concurrently with the graphics. For instance, their advantages might be canceled out if good instructional practices, like giving feedback on performance, are ignored. Basically, then, the study of spatial ability in learning mathematics and of how diagrams can capitalize on that ability is in line with the study of realism in elements and of spatial organization. Graphic representations can make abstract relationships concrete and explicit and therefore easier to learn. And if students have sufficient spatial ability to deal easily with graphic forms, then their performance will be noticeably superior.

Diagrams and Science Instruction

In earlier sections on the elements in graphics and on charts, we looked at a number of studies that examined the effectiveness of graphic representations in teaching science. We now return to this topic, but from a slightly different direction. As we saw in our study of graphics in mathematics instruction, there is a great advantage to be derived from representing abstract concepts and relationships concretely in ways that encourage students to create visual internal representations. This idea has been applied in science instruction to the study of the "mental models" students construct in order to understand the principles and problems of science (Gentner & Stevens, 1983; Larkin, 1985). Earlier studies in science instruction were more concerned simply with the effectiveness of diagrams, representing through their elements and patterns the structure of conceptual domains, and less with the mental models that students derive from instruction. We begin with these simpler studies and then look at how diagrams can improve understanding by helping students to develop accurate mental models of science content.

Diagrams of Processes

A great deal of science instruction has to do with processes. In science textbooks, these are often taught by means of flow diagrams that accompany the text (Holliday, 1975). It is easy to see why this approach should be effective. In teaching the common biological cycles, like the nitrogen cycle, a diagram could show not only which elements are present in the cycle but also the way in which they interact, by means of arrows, labels, and placement on the page. The ability of diagrams to teach processes has been the subject of a number of studies.

Holliday (1976) used a flow diagram to teach the nitrogen, water, oxygen, and carbon dioxide cycles to high school students. One diagram represented the elements in the cycles as small pictures; another showed them as verbal labels. Students studied either one of the diagrams, or one of the diagrams alongside a text that presented the same material, or the text alone. On a multiple-choice verbal test of comprehension, students who studied the diagrams on their own outperformed those who saw the diagrams alongside the text or who just read the text. Students who saw text and diagrams performed no better than those who saw just text.

These results suggest that the superiority of instructional diagrams over text for teaching science processes is attenuated when they are used, as they usually are in textbooks, alongside text. The reason for this, offered by Holliday, is based on earlier work by Anderson (1970) and Samuels (1970), which suggests that students tend not to look at illustrations in texts because they believe they can get all the information they need from what they read. In Holliday's experiment, this meant that those students who saw text and diagram did not take advantage of the simultaneous and logically organized presentation of information in the diagrams and thus did no better than if they had only read the text.

The facilitative effect of diagrams in teaching science processes also appears to depend on student ability and intellectual maturity. Koran and Koran (1980) used a flow diagram similar to Holliday's to teach Grade 7 and 8 students the water cycle. The diagram made explicit the relationships among the concepts involved. Three treatments were prepared. In the first, the diagram was placed before a 4-page text. In the second, it was placed after. The third treatment used just the text. Student ability was assessed through the Letter Series subtest from the *Kit of Reference Tests for Cognitive Factors* (French et al., 1963) which measures inductive reasoning and general intelligence.

It was found that, irrespective of placement, the diagrams helped the Grade 7 students but not those in Grade 8, suggesting a developmental factor. A significant interaction also occurred between ability and treatment, such that both diagram treatments helped low-ability students but did not help those of higher ability.

At first glance, it appears that these results contradict those reported by Holliday (1976), who found that adding a diagram to text did not improve performance. However, Koran and Koran reported significant improvements only for Grade 7 students and for those of low ability. Holliday's students were in high school, and if the developmental factor is an important one in learning from flow diagrams, then the presence of a diagram in the materials these students studied could be expected to have no effect. Why this is so is open to question. Maybe younger and less able students pay attention to diagrams in text while older and more able students do not. Or maybe, as we have seen earlier, more mature students, like more able ones, do not need the information about structure and interelement relationships that the others do because they are better at deriving it from text alone. The resolution of this issue will require further research. But in any event, the advantages bestowed by diagrams making intangible and often invisible processes concrete and visual are again generally found in research on teaching science, with the now familiar qualification on account of intellectual ability.

MENTAL MODELS

Mental models are students' representations to themselves of the world around them whose purpose is to help them understand that world. They are usually thought of as networks (Norman et al., 1975) in which concepts are identified and the relationships among them are made specific (De Kleer & Brown, 1981; Gentner & Stevens, 1983). In a sense they can be thought of as internalized diagrams. We have seen how representing information in a diagram can assist students in developing cognitive structures (Winn, 1980), and that having students draw their own graphics, thus forcing them to think spatially, can improve performance on a number of tasks (Lindvall et al., 1982). The following studies are concerned primarily with teaching students to develop these internal spatial models.

While creating a mental model is necessary for understanding, simply being able to do so does not mean that satisfactory understanding will be forthcoming. The networks of concepts begin as simple structures (Fisher & Lipson, 1985), which often represent a naive and erroneous view of science (Larkin, 1985). As knowledge is acquired and refined, the basic model is elaborated and the model grows in complexity, evolving from a naive representation to a more abstract "scientific" one, and finally to an even more abstract "mathematical" form (Larkin, 1985, pp. 147-150).

All this takes time. Lehman, Carter, and Kahle (1985) compared the effectiveness, for black high school students, of outlining and of preparing concept maps of science content. The concept mapping technique (Novak, 1981) has students draw network diagrams of the content in question, thus making them seek out the relationships among the concepts to be learned. No significant differences between outlining and mapping were found, leading the authors to conclude that the technique takes a relatively long time to learn before it can be used effectively.

However, in an earlier study, Sherris and Kahle (1984) found that drawing concept maps (Novak, 1979) was advantageous for some students. High school biology students learned about humans and the environment from one of two treatments. The first involved reading, activities, and study guides. In the second treatment, the study guides stressed interconcept relationships, based on a concept map. Students in this group were also taught a mapping strategy. On a delayed posttest of the content, a significant interaction was found between the treatments and the students' locus of control. The mapping treatment helped students with an external locus of control, but not internals. Since externals typically require more instructional support while internals do not, it seems that the mapping strategy provided this support where it was needed. The authors also mentioned that the students tended to have difficulty drawing the concept maps, which suggests, as the other study did, that this is not a skill that is learned easily and quickly.

Mayer, Dyck, and Cook (1984) used a variety of techniques in three experiments to help high school students develop good mental models of causal systems, such as the nitrogen cycle. These techniques included training them in definitions of the key concepts, or "nodes," in the systems, and "signaling" the relationships among these by means of headings and diagrams. It was found that students who received such training, and worked with the materials having headings and diagrams, outperformed students in a control group. Evidence that their superior performance was the result of better formed mental models comes from the observation that they scored higher on tests of the relationships among the concepts, and on problem solving tests whose answers could not be derived from the material presented during instruction, and that they did not do better on verbatim tests that required no additional manipulation of the information other than remembering it.

Pallrand and Seeber (1984) took the time to train their students in the visualization skills that are necessary if students are to construct spatial mental models. College students took an introductory physics course in one of three modes: a normal college class; the same class plus training in spatial skills; a normal class taught by the same person who taught the spatial skills. A group of liberal arts students served as a control. The spatial training involved 11 hours of instruction in such things as drawing, geometry, locating objects, and work with lines and angles. Students took tests of their perceptual ability, spatial orientation and spatial visualization, and a final exam for the course.

Improvements from pre- to posttests on all measures of spatial ability were noted for the group who received the training. In addition, these students outperformed all others on those items on the final exam requiring spatial abilities, and they also performed better in laboratory activities and on the final grade.

The general conclusions we can draw from this set of studies are: (a) mental models of the content, defined as having similar spatial properties to diagrams, are necessary if people are to understand the concepts of science and the way in which they are related; and (b) the abilities required to develop these models, a large component of which is spatial in nature, can be taught if enough time is taken. The difference in effectiveness between teaching students these skills and presenting them with materials that have already been reduced to concept maps and networks in the form of diagrams probably comes down to cost effectiveness. While it is an advantage to train students to derive their own mental models, it may sometimes be more efficient to present them with the models, ready made, as instructional graphics.

Graphics and Text Comprehension

We have seen that, in mathematics and science, training students to translate information from text into some type of graphic form is often beneficial. This form of visualization allows students to scan all the relevant information in a conceptual domain simultaneously, which makes it easier to understand just how each idea is related to the others.

Research in language comprehension has contributed much to developing techniques for reducing text to graphic form. Armbruster and Anderson (1982, 1984) have developed a technique they call "idea mapping," which is based on the

188   Bill Winn

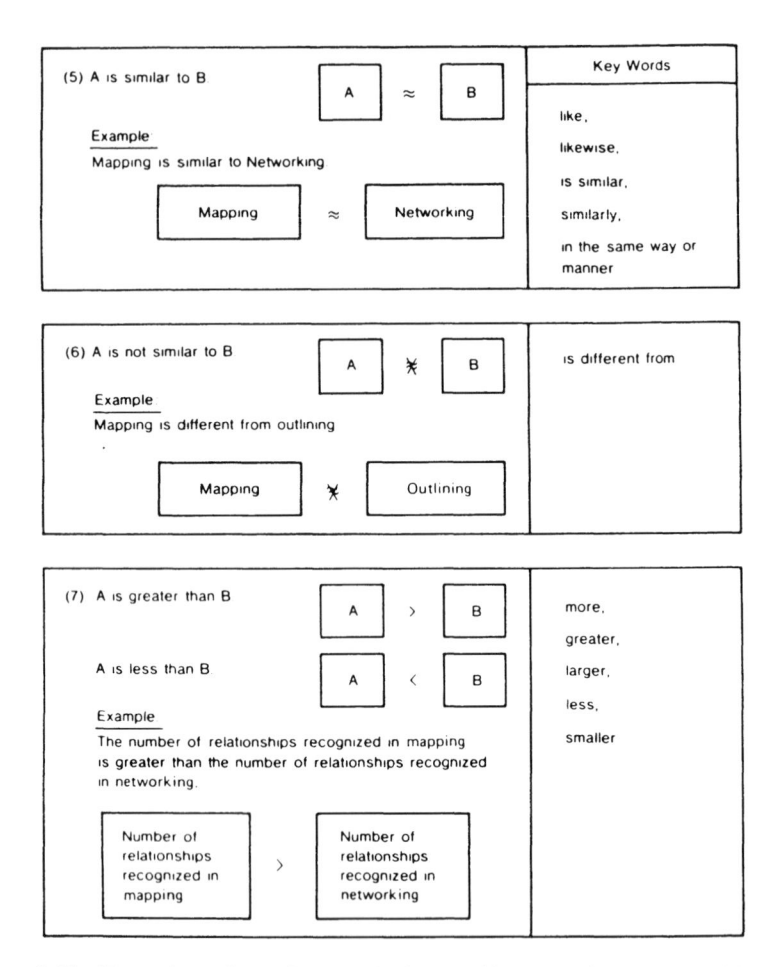

FIGURE 5.12. Examples of Armbruster–Anderson idea mapping. From "Mapping: Representing Informative Text Graphically" by B. B. Armbruster and T. H. Anderson, 1984. In C. D. Holley and D. F. Dansereau (Eds.), *Spatial Learning Strategies* (pp. 190, 192), New York: Academic Press. Copyright 1984 by Academic Press. Adapted by permission.

notion that ideas in text can be connected by a few fundamental relationships. The technique relies on a set of symbols, shown in Figure 5.12, that express these relationships as different types of lines, arrows, and other graphic symbols. This enables a person to draw "maps" of domains of concepts in which A might be an instance of B, might cause B, might precede B, or might enable B. The technique has been used successfully to analyze the structure of information presented in history texts (Armbruster & Anderson, 1980).

Empirical support for the effectiveness of this kind of technique is presented in a study by Geva (1983). In two experiments, community college students

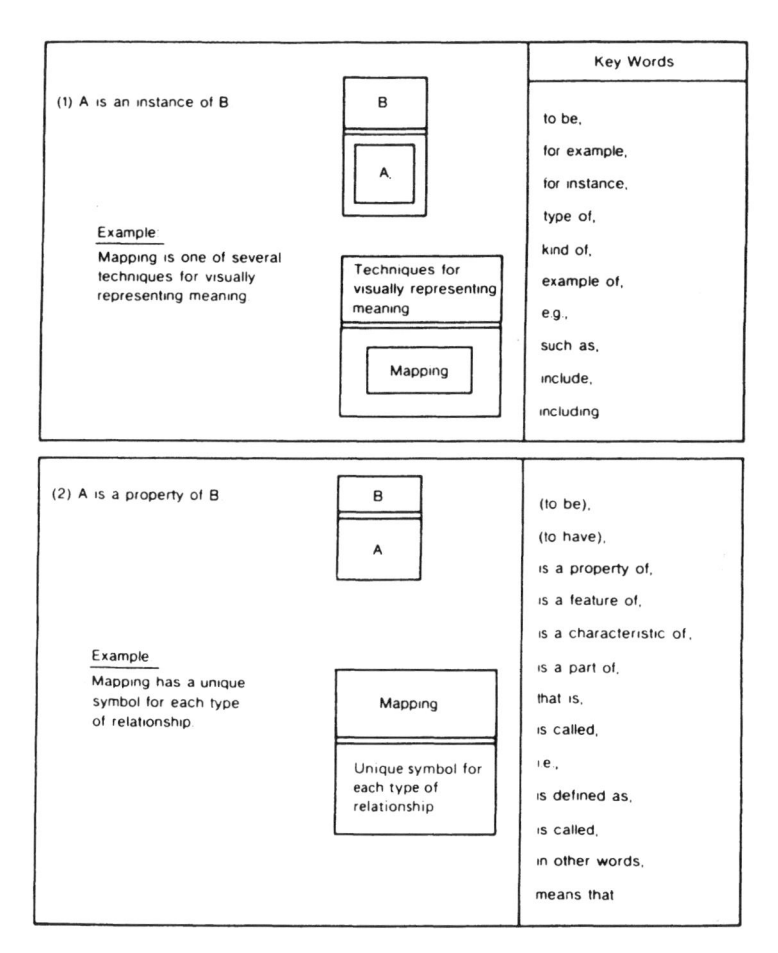

		Key Words
(1) A is an instance of B Example Mapping is one of several techniques for visually representing meaning	B [A] Techniques for visually representing meaning [Mapping]	to be, for example, for instance, type of, kind of, example of, e.g., such as, include, including
(2) A is a property of B Example Mapping has a unique symbol for each type of relationship	B A Mapping [Unique symbol for each type of relationship]	(to be), (to have), is a property of, is a feature of, is a characteristic of, is a part of, that is, is called, i.e., is defined as, is called, in other words, means that

FIGURE 5.12. *Continued.*

learned to draw flow diagrams which represented graphically the "nodes" and the "relations" in text. The symbols used for the relations—for example, elaboration, cause and effect, process, detail—were different from those proposed by Armbruster and Anderson. But the technique was essentially the same.

In the first experiment, students in the experimental group worked on developing flow diagram skills for 7 weeks. Over this period, their diagrams improved, but their comprehension ability was no better than that of a control group. In a second experiment, however, the students in the experimental group outperformed those in the control group on tests that measured whether or not they noticed connections between related phrases or sentences. Since the diagramming technique was based on skill at identifying and drawing relationships among nodes, it seems that the diagrams did what they were intended to do. An interaction between treatment and students' scores on the Nelson–Denny Reading

Comprehension Test (Nelson & Denny, 1973) was also reported. Low-ability students benefited more from the diagramming technique than high-ability students. This was presumably because the highs could understand the material sufficiently well without the extra support provided by drawing the diagrams.

A different approach to improving comprehension through the use of graphics was taken in a study by Dean and Kulhavy (1981). In two experiments, students learned information about the features of a fictitious country. In the first experiment, the information was presented in a text. One group of students was told to draw a map of the country as they read the text. The other group was not. On a comprehension test, the students who drew the map performed better than those who did not on the number of idea units they got correct, on a multiple-choice test of the content, and on constructed responses.

In the second experiment, students either studied a labeled map or copied in the details on a blank map from the complete map projected on an overhead transparency. Students in a control group studied an unrelated map. The students who copied the details, who were in effect forced to process the information spatially, outperformed the students in the other two groups on a free-recall test. Taken with the results of the first experiment, this suggests that the act of constructing a graphic is what is important for improving comprehension, not simply the presence of a graphic. This conclusion is reinforced by the finding of an interaction between vocabulary ability and the treatments in the second experiment. Forced processing benefited the students whose vocabulary was weak more than it helped the more able students. This is further evidence that students of high ability may derive benefits from the information about elements and their relationships in graphics without prompting, while weaker students may not. As with some of the research in mental models and in learning mathematics, it appears that having students actually draw graphics that explain the structure and meaning of text is advantageous.

Summary

In this section we have looked at studies of many different types that have demonstrated various aspects of the instructional effectiveness of graphic forms. Most have also demonstrated that the instructional advantages of graphics depend on many things. In all subject matters and for most tasks, student ability is a factor that determines their usefulness. The studies we have looked at have examined the impact of general ability, IQ, spatial reasoning, locus of control, field dependence, verbal ability, vocabulary, age, and gender on performance. On most of these measures, the better students have had less need of the explicit descriptions of elements and patterns that graphics provide than the less able ones. We have seen a number of cases where the presence of a diagram, or the drawing by the students of a chart or diagram, helped the low-ability students but not the high-ability students. But there are also limits to the amount of information about elements and their relationships that low-ability students can take in. In some instances, we saw that the additional processing load imposed by graphics impeded the performance of low-ability students.

As far as task is concerned, it seems that graphics are most useful where it is necessary for students to pay attention to the elements and their relations. This would certainly include recognition and recall of concepts in a domain and solving problems in mathematics and science where pattern and structure are themselves important properties of the content area.

There also appears to have been a shift in the research away from the study of the facilitative effects of graphics, that themselves capture and express the structure of content, to an interest in the way students represent such structures internally as mental models of the content. These models are based on theoretical constructs, such as networks and concept maps, that have many of the characteristics of diagrams. And it appears that getting students to draw diagrams and make maps of content is one useful way of developing good mental models. But this process takes time to learn, and even then may not be of use to brighter students, who can make the translation from information presented in text to a satisfactory structural image without going through the intermediate step of drawing a diagram or chart.

Finally, let us not lose sight of the fact that a lot of the research that we have found useful in explaining the success of graphic forms in instruction was, ostensibly, not primarily concerned with graphics at all. As Clark (1983) has pointed out, what really has an effect on learning is the instructional method that is used, not the form in which information is presented. Sometimes, of course, simply presenting information in graphic forms will activate the appropriate cognitive processes that facilitate learning. As such, the graphic may then be thought of as embodying a particular method. However, we have seen that it is more frequently the case that students need instructional support in addition to the graphic in order to learn effectively. Developing visual and spatial skills, directing attention by means of study questions, forcing students to copy material, and giving them prompts, hints, and feedback, are all examples of this support. It is therefore inappropriate to consider the effectiveness of graphic forms separate from these other instructional strategies which amplify their advantages to the point where they are optimally useful.

Conclusions

In this chapter we have looked at how graphic forms convey information by means of the elements within them and through the patterns that these elements form in space. We have noted how these two factors are related to students' abilities and to the tasks they have to perform. We have looked at a selection of studies that have reported on various aspects of their effectiveness in instruction. From this, we can conclude that charts, graphs, and diagrams do communicate with people in a unique way and can therefore be used where other forms of communication, such as written text, are not successful. This would include communication with students whose ability to decode, understand, and remember text is not satisfactory, and communication concerning learning tasks where organization, structure, and spatial sequences are important.

The research that has studied the effectiveness of graphics in communication and instruction is uneven in its emphasis. Only a very few of the studies we looked at had anything to say about graphs. This may be because these graphic forms, while very efficient at presenting data, are not particularly good at teaching. Their function is mainly descriptive and not really instructional. Charts, and diagrams, on the other hand, have great variety and can express easily and explicitly the structure of content domains that students have to learn. They are very good at teaching things, not just describing them.

In many studies, further unevenness comes from the lack of a sound grounding in theory. These are the studies that are concerned with the mere presence of graphics in instructional materials and not with the mechanisms that lead to their effectiveness (or lack of it). It is encouraging, however, to see a body of research developing around the theory of mental models, in which the effectiveness of a variety of graphic strategies, whether they involve presenting information to students in spatial form or whether they require students to draw their own charts and diagrams, is tied directly to mental processes. This is the kind of research that needs to be conducted if we are to learn anything substantial about how graphic forms can be used effectively in instruction. It is also research, as we have seen, that has as much, if not more, to do with internal processes than with the external forms that are used to convey information to students.

It is also important to develop lines of inquiry into the learning strategies students use when working with graphic forms. How do they extract information? Are they conscious of using particular cognitive strategies when they do so? Do some students need training in these strategies, and are some already sufficiently "graphic literate" to be able to learn from these forms without instruction or prompting? The research in learning strategies that is currently being conducted is relevant here. Again, this is not work that has to do specifically with charts, graphs, and diagrams. However, the general principles that it is generating will apply here as they do in other areas.

Finally, more effort needs to be put into developing ways to teach students to use charts, graphs, and diagrams, and the appropriate learning strategies that must accompany them. A number of the studies we have looked at have demonstrated that this type of training is both feasible and effective. However, we know very little about why this is so and we need to find out more.

These are just some of the ways in which the unevenness of the research in graphic forms can be corrected. While the translation of the findings of research studies of the type we have examined into prescriptive principles for the design of instruction is not straightforward (Landa, 1983), it is still important for us to find out as much as we can about how students learn from charts, graphs, and diagrams. The theory that this research allows us to construct will, eventually, be sufficiently complete to allow more efficient and effective instruction to be developed.

References

Alesandrini, K. L. (1981). Pictorial-verbal and analytic-holistic learning strategies in science learning. *Journal of Educational Psychology, 73*, 358–368.

Alesandrini, K. L. (1984). Pictures and adult learning. *Instructional Science, 13*, 63–77.

Allen, W. H. (1975). Intellectual abilities and instructional media design. *AV Communication Review, 23*, 139–170.

Anderson, J. R. (1978). Arguments concerning representations for mental imagery. *Psychological Review, 85*, 249–277.

Anderson, R. C. (1970). Control of student mediating processes during verbal learning and instruction. *Review of Educational Research, 40*, 349–369.

Armbruster, B. B., & Anderson, T. H. (1980, July). *Structures for explanations in history textbooks: Or so what if Governor Sanford missed the spike and hit the rail?* (Technical Report No. 252). Urbana, IL: University of Illinois at Urbana–Champaign, Center for the Study of Reading. (ERIC Document Reproduction Service No. 218 595)

Armbruster, B. B., & Anderson, T. H. (1982, October). *Idea mapping: The technique and its use in the classroom or simulating the "ups" and "downs" of reading comprehension* (Reading Education Report No. 36). Urbana, IL: University of Illinois at Urbana–Champaign, Center for the Study of Reading. (ERIC Document Reproduction Service No. ED 221 842)

Armbruster, B. B., & Anderson, T. H. (1984). Mapping: Representing informative text graphically. In C. D. Holley & D. F. Dansereau (Eds.), *Spatial learning strategies* (pp. 189–209). New York: Academic Press.

Ausubel, D. P. (1968). *The psychology of meaningful verbal learning*. New York: Grune & Stratton.

Bartram, D. J. (1980). Comprehending spatial information: The relative efficiency of different methods of presenting information about bus routes. *Journal of Applied Psychology, 65*, 103–110.

Battista, M. (1980). Interrelationships between problem-solving ability, right hemisphere processing facility and mathematics learning. *Focus on Learning Problems in Mathematics, 2*, 53–60.

Battista, M. (1981). The interaction between two instructional treatments of algebraic structures and spatial-visualization ability. *Journal of Educational Research, 74*, 337–341.

Bennett, G. K., Seashore, H. G., & Wesman, A. G. (1972). *Differential aptitude tests*. New York: The Psychological Corporation.

Bovy, R. (1983, April). *Defining the psychologically active features of instructional treatments designed to facilitate cue attendance*. Paper presented at the meeting of the American Educational Research Association, Montreal.

Brown, A. L. (1981). Metacognition: The development of selective attention strategies for learning from texts. In M. L. Kamil (Ed.), *Directions in reading research and instruction* (Thirtieth Yearbook of The National Reading Conference) (pp. 21–43). Washington, DC: National Reading Conference.

Brown, A. L., Campione, J. C., & Day, J. D. (1981). Learning to learn: On training students to learn from texts. *Educational Researcher, 10*(2), 14–21.

Burton, L. (1984). Mathematical thinking: A struggle for meaning. *Journal for Research in Mathematics Education, 15,* 35-49.

Canelos, J. J., Taylor, W. D., & Gates, G. B. (1980). The effects of three levels of visual complexity on the information processing of field-dependents and field-independents when acquiring information for performance of three types of instructional objective. *Journal of Instructional Psychology, 7,* 65-70.

Carrier, C., Post, T. R., & Heck, W. (1985). Using microcomputers with fourth-grade students to reinforce arithmetic skills. *Journal for Research in Mathematics Education, 16,* 45-51.

Cattell, R. B. (1971). *Abilities: Their structure, growth and action.* Boston: Houghton Mifflin.

Chipman, S. F., & Segal, J. W. (1985). Higher cognitive goals for education: An introduction. In S. F. Chipman & J. W. Segal (Eds.), *Thinking and learning skills* (Vol. I, pp. 1-19). Hillsdale, NJ: Erlbaum.

Clark, F., & Angert, J. (1985). *Synthesizing the research findings of Dwyer and his associates: A quantitative assessment.* Unpublished manuscript.

Clark, R. E. (1983). Reconsidering research on learning from media. *Review of Educational Research, 53,* 445-460.

Clark, R. E. (1985). Confounding in educational computing research. *Journal of Educational Computing Research, 1,* 137-148.

Cronbach, L. J., & Snow, R. E. (1977). *Aptitudes and instructional methods.* New York: Irvington.

Dale, E. (1946). *Audio-visual methods in teaching.* New York: Dryden Press.

Das, J. P., Kirby, R. F., & Jarman, R. F. (1975). Simultaneous and successive syntheses: An alternative model for cognitive abilities. *Psychological Bulletin, 82,* 87-103.

Das, J. P., Kirby, J. R., & Jarman, R. F. (1979). *Simultaneous and successive cognitive processes.* New York: Academic Press.

Dean, R. S., & Kulhavy, R. W. (1981). Influence of spatial organization on prose learning. *Journal of Educational Psychology, 73,* 57-64.

Decker, W. H., & Wheatley, P. C. (1982). Spatial grouping, imagery, and free recall. *Perceptual and Motor Skills, 55,* 45-46.

Deese, J. (1962). On the structure of associative meaning. *Psychological Review, 69,* 161-175.

De Kleer, J., & Brown, J. S. (1981). Mental models of physical mechanisms and their acquisition. In J. R. Anderson (Ed.), *Cognitive skills and their acquisition* (pp. 285-310). Hillsdale, NJ: Erlbaum.

Doblin, J. (1980). A structure for non-textual communications. In P. A. Kolers, M. E. Wrolstad, & N. Bouma (Eds.), *Processing visible language* (Vol. II, pp. 89-111). New York: Plenum Press.

Duchastel, P. C., & Waller, R. (1979). Pictorial illustration in instructional text. *Educational Technology, 19*(11), 20-25.

Dwyer, F. M. (1972). *A guide for improving visualized instruction.* University Park, PA: State College, Pennsylvania State University, Learning Services Division.

Dwyer, F. M. (1978). *Strategies for improving visual learning.* State College, PA: Learning Services.

Fennema, E., & Sherman, J. (1977). Sex-related differences in mathematics achievement, spatial visualization, and affective factors. *American Educational Research Journal, 14,* 51-71.

Fennema, E., & Tartre, L. A. (1985). The use of spatial visualization in mathematics by girls and boys. *Journal for Research in Mathematics Education, 16*, 184-206.

Fisher, K. M., & Lipson, J. I. (1985). Information processing interpretation of errors in college science learning. *Instructional Science, 14*, 49-74.

Fleming, M. L., & Levie, W. H. (1978). *Instructional message design: Principles from the behavioral sciences.* Englewood Cliffs, NJ: Educational Technology Publications.

Frankel, M. C. (1983). Children's recall and organization of noncategorical associated pictures. *Psychological Reports, 52*, 787-790.

French, J., Ekstrom, R., & Price, L. (1963). *Kit of reference tests for cognitive factors.* Princeton, NJ: Educational Testing Service.

Fry, E. (1983). *A theory of graphs for reading comprehension and writing communication.* New Brunswick, NJ: Rutgers University, Reading Center. (ERIC Document Reproduction Service No. 240 528).

Garskof, B. E., & Houston, J. P. (1963). Measurement of verbal relatedness: An ideographic approach. *Psychological Review, 70*, 277-288.

Gentner, D., & Stevens, A. L. (Eds.). (1983). *Mental models.* Hillsdale, NJ: Erlbaum.

Geva, E. (1983). Facilitating reading comprehension through flowcharting. *Reading Research Quarterly, 18*, 384-405.

Harary, F., Norman, R. Z., & Cartwright, D. (1965). *Structural models: An introduction to the theory of directed graphs.* New York: Wiley.

Hartley, J., & Trueman, M. (1985). A research strategy for text designers: The role of headings. *Instructional Science, 14*, 99-155.

Hellige, J. (1980). Cerebral hemispheric asymmetry: Methods, issues and implications. *Educational Communication and Technology Journal, 28*, 83-98.

Holley, C. D., & Dansereau, D. F. (Eds.). (1984). *Spatial learning strategies: Techniques, applications and related issues.* New York: Academic Press.

Holliday, W. G. (1975). What's in a picture? *The Science Teacher, 42*, 21-22.

Holliday, W. G. (1976). Teaching verbal chains using flow diagrams and texts. *AV Communication Review, 24*, 63-78.

Holliday, W. G., & Benson, G. (1981, April). *Using questions to focus students' attention on non-prose science materials.* Paper presented at the conference of the National Association for Research in Science Teaching, New York.

Holliday, W. G., Brunner, L. L., & Donais, E. L. (1977). Differential cognitive and affective responses to flow diagrams in science. *Journal of Research in Science Teaching, 14*, 129-138.

Jonassen, D., & Hawk, P. (1984). Using graphic organizers in instruction. *Information Design Journal, 4*, 58-68.

Jones, B. F. (1985, April). *Graphic text structures should reflect prose structures.* Paper presented at the meeting of the American Educational Research Association, Chicago.

Knowlton, J. Q. (1966). On the definition of "picture." *AV Communication Review, 14*, 157-183.

Koran, M. L., & Koran, J. (1980). Interaction of learner characteristics with pictorial adjuncts in learning from science text. *Journal of Research in Science Teaching, 17*, 477-483.

Kosslyn, S. M. (1980). *Image and Mind.* Cambridge, MA: Harvard University Press.

Kosslyn, S. M. (1981). The medium is the message of mental imagery. *Psychological Review, 88*, 46-66.

Kulhavy, R. W., Schwartz, N. H., & Shaha, S. H. (1983). Spatial representation of maps. *American Journal of Psychology, 96*, 337-351.

Landa, L. N. (1983). Descriptive and prescriptive theories of learning and instruction: An analysis of their relationships and interaction. In C. M. Reigeluth (Ed.), *Instructional design theories and models: An overview of their current status* (pp. 55-73). Hillsdale, NJ: Erlbaum.

Larkin, J. (1985). Understanding, problem representations, and skill in physics. In J. W. Segal & S. F. Chipman (Eds.), *Thinking and learning skills* (Vol. 2, pp. 141-159). Hillsdale, NJ: Erlbaum.

Lehman, J. D., Carter, C., & Kahle, J. B. (1985). Concept mapping, vee mapping and achievement: Results of a field study with black high school students. *Journal of Research in Science Teaching, 22,* 663-673.

Levie, W. H., & Dickie, K. E. (1973). The analysis and application of media. In R. M. W. Travers (Ed.), *Second handbook of research on teaching* (pp. 858-882). Chicago, Rand McNally.

Lindvall, C. M., Tamburino, J. L., & Robinson, L. (1982, March). *An exploratory investigation of the effect of teaching primary grade children to use specific problem-solving strategies in solving simple story problems.* Paper presented at the conference of the American Educational Research Association, New York. (ERIC Document Reproduction Service No. 216 904).

Luria, A. L. (1970). The functional organization of the brain. *Scientific American, 222*(3), 66-78.

Luria, A. L. (1973). *The working brain.* London: Penguin.

Macdonald-Ross, M. (1977). Graphics in text. In L. S. Shulman (Ed.), *Review of research in education* (pp. 49-85). Itasca, IL: Peacock. (a)

Macdonald-Ross, M. (1977). How numbers are shown: A review of research on the presentation of quantitative data in texts. *AV Communication Review, 25,* 359-410. (b)

Macdonald-Ross, M. (1979). Scientific diagrams and the generation of plausible hypotheses: An essay in the history of ideas. *Instructional Science, 8,* 223-234.

Mason, J., Burton, L., & Stacey, K. (1982). *Thinking mathematically.* London: Addison-Wesley.

Mayer, R. E., Dyck, J. L., & Cook, L. K. (1984). Techniques that help readers build mental models from scientific text: Definitions, pretraining and signaling. *Journal of Educational Psychology, 76,* 1089-1105.

Merrill, M. D., & Tennyson, R. D. (1977). *Teaching concepts: An instructional design guide.* Englewood Cliffs, NJ: Educational Technology Publications.

Moxley, R. (1983). Educational diagrams. *Instructional Science, 12,* 147-160.

Moyer, J. C., Sowder, L., Threadgill-Sowder, J., & Moyer, M. B. (1984). Story problem formats: Drawn versus verbal versus telegraphic. *Journal for Research in Mathematics Education, 15,* 342-351.

Nelson, N. J., & Denny, E. C. (1973). *Nelson-Denny reading test.* Boston: Houghton Mifflin.

Neurath, M. (1974). Isotype. *Instructional Science, 3,* 127-150.

Norman, D. A., Rumelhart, D. E., & LNR Research Group. (1975). *Explorations in cognition.* San Francisco: Freeman.

Novak, J. D. (1979). Applying psychology and philosophy to the improvement of laboratory teaching. *American Biology Teacher, 41,* 466-470.

Novak, J. D. (1981). *The use of concept mapping and Gowan's "vee" mapping instructional strategies in junior high science.* Ithaca, NY: Cornell University Press.

Olson, D. (1977). The languages of instruction: On the literate bias of schooling. In R. C. Anderson, R. C. Spiro, & M. C. Montague (Eds.), *Schooling and the acquisition of knowledge* (pp. 65-69). Hillsdale, NJ: Erlbaum.

Paivio, A. (1971). *Imagery and verbal processes*. New York: Holt, Rinehart & Winston.
Paivio, A. (1975). Imagery and long-term memory. In A. Kennedy & A. Wilkes (Eds.), *Studies in long-term memory* (pp. 57–85). New York: Wiley.
Paivio, A. (1983). The empirical case for dual coding. In J. C. Yuille (Ed.), *Imagery, memory and cognition* (pp. 310–332). Hillsdale, NJ: Erlbaum.
Paivio, A., Yuille, J. C., & Madigan, S. (1968). Concreteness, imagery and meaningfulness values for 925 nouns. *Journal of Experimental Psychology, 76*, Monograph Supplement, 1–25.
Pallrand, G. J., & Seeber, F. (1984). Spatial ability and achievement in introductory physics. *Journal of Research in Science Teaching, 21*, 507–516.
Parkhurst, P. E., & Dwyer, F. M. (1983). An experimental assessment of students' IQ level and their ability to profit from visualized instruction. *Journal of Instructional Psychology, 10*, 9–20.
Piaget, J., & Inhelder, B. (1969). *The Psychology of the Child*. New York: Basic Books.
Pinker, S. (1981). *A theory of graph comprehension* (Occasional Paper No. 10). Cambridge, MA: Center for Cognitive Science, Massachusetts Institute of Technology.
Pinker, S. (1983). *Pattern perception and comprehension of graphs*. Cambridge, MA: Department of Psychology, Massachusetts Institute of Technology.
Pylyshyn, Z. (1973). What the mind's eye tells the mind's brain. *Psychological Bulletin, 80*, 1–24.
Pylyshyn, Z. (1981). The imagery debate: Analogue media versus tacit knowledge. *Psychological Review, 88*, 16–45.
Rabinowitz, M., & Mandler, J. M. (1983). Organization and information retrieval. *Journal of Experimental Psychology: Learning, Memory, and Cognition, 9*, 430–439.
Reed, S. K. (1985). Effect of computer graphics on improving estimates to algebra word problems. *Journal of Educational Psychology, 77*, 285–298.
Rigney, J. W., & Lutz, K. (1976). Effect of graphic analogies of concepts in chemistry on learning and attitude. *Journal of Educational Psychology, 68*, 305–311.
Salomon, G. (1974). Internalization of filmic schematic operations in interaction with learners' aptitudes. *Journal of Educational Psychology, 66*, 499–511.
Salomon, G. (1979). *Interaction of media, cognition and learning*. San Francisco: Jossey Bass.
Samuels, S. J. (1970). Effects of pictures on learning to read, comprehension and attitude. *Review of Educational Research, 40*, 398–407.
Schoenfeld, A. H. (1980). Heuristics in the classroom. In S. Krulik & R. E. Reys (Eds.), *Problem solving in school mathematics* (pp. 9–22). Reston, VA: Council of Teachers of Mathematics.
Shavelson, R. J. (1972). Some aspects of the correspondence between content structure and cognitive structure in physics instruction. *Journal of Educational Psychology, 63*, 225–234.
Shepard, R. (1978). The mental image. *American Psychologist, 33*, 125–137.
Shepard, R., & Cooper, L. A. (1982). *Mental images and their transformations*. Cambridge, MA: MIT Press.
Sherris, J. D., & Kahle, J. B. (1984). The effects of instructional organization and locus of control orientation on meaningful learning in high school biology students. *Journal of Research in Science Teaching, 21*, 83–94.
Simon, H. (1981). *The sciences of the artificial*. Cambridge, MA: MIT Press.
Simon, D. P., & Simon, H. A. (1978). Individual differences in solving physics problems. In R. Sieger (Ed.), *Children's thinking: What develops?* (pp. 325–348). Hillsdale, NJ: Erlbaum.

Sless, D. (1981). *Learning and visual communication*. New York: Wiley.

Snow, R. E. (1980). Aptitude processes. In R. E. Snow, P. A. Federico, & W. E. Montague (Eds.), *Aptitude, learning and instruction* (Vol. I, pp. 27–64). Hillsdale, NJ: Erlbaum.

Sternberg, R. J., & Weil, E. M. (1980). An aptitude × strategy interaction in linear syllogistic reasoning. *Journal of Educational Psychology, 72*, 226–239.

Stewart, J. H. (1984). The representation of knowledge: Curricular and instructional implications for science teaching. In C. D. Holley & D. F. Dansereau (Eds.), *Spatial learning strategies: Techniques, applications and related issues* (pp. 235–254). New York: Academic Press.

Stewart, J. H., Van Kirk, J., & Rowell, R. (1979). Concept maps: A tool for use in biology teaching. *The American Biology Teacher, 41*, 171–175.

Sylwester, R. (1981). Educational implications of recent brain research. *Science Digest*, November, p. 64.

Szlichcinski, K. P. (1980). The syntax of pictorial instruction. In P. A. Kolers, M. E. Wrolstad, & H. Bouma (Eds.), *Processing visible language* (Vol. II, pp. 113–124). New York: Plenum Press.

Toth, M. A. (1980). Figures of thought. The use of diagrams in teaching sociology. *Teaching Sociology, 7*, 409–424.

Wainer, H., & Thissen, D. (1981). Graphical data analysis. *Annual Review of Psychology, 32*, 191–241.

Waller, R. (1981, April). *Understanding network diagrams*. Paper presented at the annual meeting of the American Educational Research Association, Los Angeles. (ERIC Document Reproduction Service No. 226 695).

Winn, W. D. (1980). The effect of block–word diagrams on the structuring of science concepts as a function of general ability. *Journal of Research in Science Teaching, 17*, 201–211.

Winn, W. D. (1981). The effect of attribute highlighting and spatial organization on identification and classification. *Journal of Research in Science Teaching, 18*, 23–32.

Winn, W. D. (1982). The role of diagrammatic representation in learning sequences, identification and classification as a function of verbal and spatial ability. *Journal of Research in Science Teaching, 19*, 79–89.

Winn, W. D. (1983). Perceptual strategies used with flow diagrams having normal and unanticipated formats. *Perceptual and Motor Skills, 57*, 751–762.

Winn, W. D. (1986, April). *Simultaneous and successive processing of circuit diagrams having different amounts of detail*. Paper presented at the annual meeting of the American Educational Research Association, San Francisco. (a)

Winn, W. D. (1986). Knowledge of task, ability and strategy in the processing of letter patterns. *Perceptual and Motor Skills, 63*, p. 726. (b)

Winn, W. D., & Holliday, W. G. (1982). Design principles for diagrams and charts. In D. Jonassen (Ed.), *The technology of text* (Vol. 1, pp. 277–299). Englewood Cliffs, NJ: Educational Technology Publications.

Witkin, H. A., Moore, C. A., Goodenough, D. R., & Cox, P. W. (1977). Field-dependent and field-independent cognitive styles and their educational implications. *Review of Educational Research, 47*, 1–64.

Wittrock, M. C. (Ed.). (1977). *The human brain*. Englewood Cliffs, NJ: Prentice-Hall.

Wittrock, M. C. (Ed.). (1980). *The brain and psychology*. New York: Academic Press.

Author Index

Ackerman, B. P., 12, 14, 35, 36
Adams, M. J., 21, 37, 45
Alcorn, M. D., 117, 145
Alderton, D. L., 20, 44
Alesandrini, K. L., 13, 37, 60, 78, 80, 81, 115, 141, 144, 145, 158, 160, 193
Allen, W. H., 172, 193
Alley, G. R., 74, 80, 85
Ally, M., 81, 118, 145
Alvarado, V., 41, 119, 130, 150
Anderson, D. R., 5, 22, 28, 44, 45, 46
Anderson, J. R., 10, 33, 158, 193
Anderson, R. C., 81, 111, 118, 124, 185, 193
Anderson, R. E., 14, 37
Anderson, T. H., 160, 187, 188, 193
Andreassen, C., 38, 89, 114
Andreoli, V., 25, 48
Angert, J., 175, 194
Anglin, G. J., 55, 78, 81, 96
Antes, J. R., 5, 9, 28, 32
Armbruster, B. B., 160, 187, 188, 193
Arnheim, R., 4, 19, 27, 42, 49
Arnold, D. J., 58, 64, 78, 81
Ashwin, C., 17, 39
Ashworth, C., 20, 44
Atkins, C. L., 22, 44
Ausubel, D. P., 58, 78, 118, 136, 145, 159, 193

Babich, J. M., 13, 36
Bacharach, V. R., 135, 145, 146

Baggaley, J., 25, 48
Baggett, P., 22, 44, 106, 111
Bailis, K., 35
Baker, E. L., 24, 47
Baker-Ward, L., 108, 111
Baratz, D., 17, 41
Barnard, P., 17, 40
Barsam, H. F., 20, 43
Barnsley, R. H., 126, 149
Bartlett, J. C., 34
Bartram, D. L., 161, 193
Battista, M., 181, 193
Baumeister, A. A., 36
Beagles-Roos, J., 22, 44, 106, 111
Beck, C. R., 4, 28
Beck, J., 7, 30
Becklen, R., 9, 32
Beilen, H., 20, 24, 44, 49
Biesbrock, E., 23, 48
Bell, G., 24, 47
Bell, R., 24, 47
Bell, S. M., 8, 24, 32
Belleza, F. S., 61, 78
Bender, B. G., 55, 78, 81, 83, 94, 95, 99, 111, 112, 129, 142, 148
Bengston, J. K., 30
Bennet, G. K., 178, 181, 193
Benson, G., 153, 154, 163, 179, 195
Berbaum, K., 7, 30
Berg, W. K., 17, 40, 41
Berlyne, D. E., 5, 23, 25, 28, 46, 49, 122, 145
Bernard, R. M., 81, 118, 145
Berry, C., 16, 22, 45

Berry, J. K., 40, 61, 73, 76, 77, 79, 83, 93, 94, 112
Beveridge, M., 83, 120, 149
Biaggio, M. K., 25, 49
Bialystok, E., 20, 44
Biddle, W. B., 118, 124, 145
Biederman, I., 5, 7, 9, 28, 30, 32
Bieger, G. R., 17, 39
Biesbrock, E., 24
Binet, A., 133, 134, 145
Binnie-Dawson, J. L. M., 5, 28
Birnbaum, D., 25, 50
Biron, J., 14, 37
Blake, T., 21, 44
Blanchard, F. A., 24, 49
Bland, D., 90, 111
Blank, P., 50
Blinder, D., 27
Bock, M., 124, 142, 143, 145
Borg, W. R., 17, 39
Borges, M. A., 12, 34, 81, 120, 145
Borkowski, J. G., 108, 113
Bornstein, M. H., 94, 99, 113
Borwick, D., 122, 144, 151
Boselie, F., 24, 47
Bourne, L. E. Jr., 12, 35
Boutwell, R. C., 60, 80, 81, 83, 130, 141, 149
Bovair, S., 16, 40
Bovy, R., 157, 193
Bower, G. H., 7, 30
Bowers, D., 46
Bowling, A., 15, 38
Boyer, B. A., 25, 49
Braine, L. G., 20, 43
Brainerd, C. J., 14, 38, 87, 111
Bransford, J. D., 64, 78, 81, 120, 121, 136, 145
Bray, N. W., 14, 36
Brems, D. J., 13, 36
Bridger, W. H., 31
Briggs, N., 83, 120, 149
Brimer, R. W., 37
Brinkerink-Carlier, M., 125, 150
Brison, S. J., 10, 34
Brody, P. J., 137, 143, 144, 145–146
Bromage, B. K., 64, 79
Brooks, P. H., 7, 30, 58, 64, 78, 81
Brooks, V., 7, 31

Brotsky, S. J., 14, 37
Brown, A. L., 108, 111, 179, 193
Brown, D., 117, 122, 140, 146
Brown, J. S., 186, 194
Brown, J. W., 116, 146
Brown, N. L., 14, 38
Brown, R. M., 14, 38
Brown, S. J., 83
Bruner, J., S., 5, 29, 134, 148
Brunn, J., 20, 29, 43
Brunner, L. L., 136, 147, 169, 172, 195
Bryant, J., 22, 44, 117, 122, 140, 146
Bryant, S. L., 99, 100, 106, 107, 108, 113
Buchanan, J. A., 48
Buescher, K., 12, 35
Bullock, M., 7, 30
Burch, G., 24, 49
Burton, L., 180, 194, 196
Buswell, G. T., 28
Butcher, J., 23, 46
Butler, D. L., 30
Butler, L., 6, 28
Byram, M., 8, 28, 30

Cabe, P. A., 7, 30
Cable, G. W., 17, 43, 60, 64, 80, 84, 125, 128, 142, 149
Caelli, T., 7, 30
Caldwell, C., 102, 103, 105, 112
Calvert, S. L., 46
Campeau, P. L., 21, 45
Camperell, K., 65, 79
Campione, J. C., 179, 193
Canelos, J. J., 39, 172, 194
Cantor, D. S., 38, 47
Cantor, J., 23
Caplan, P. J., 43
Carney, R. N., 94
Carnine, D., 16, 39
Carothers, T., 49
Carr, T. H., 10, 33, 135, 145, 146
Carrier, C., 136, 146, 183, 194
Carrier, D., 27
Carroll, J. M., 22, 45
Carroll, R. W., 37
Carroll, W. R., 37
Carter, C., 186, 196
Carter, J. M., 24, 48

Author Index

Cartwright, D., 178, 195
Cassidy, D. J., 108, 111
Cassidy, M. R., 20, 43
Castano, D., 34
Caterino, L. C., 22, 45
Cattell, R. B., 158, 194
Cave, K. R., 20, 43
Cervone, D., 9, 32
Chaiklin, S., 38
Chance, J. E., 12, 20, 35, 43
Chase, P., 31
Chatterjea, R. G., 13, 34
Chen, H., 12, 36
Chevrier, J., 47
Cheyne, W. M., 82, 126, 147
Chipman, S. F., 179, 194
Choi, P. P., 5, 28
Christ, R. E., 17, 39
Chu, G. C., 22, 45
Chute, A. G., 138, 146
Ciancolo, P. J., 91, 111
Cimino, M., 90, 111
Clark, F., 175, 194
Clark, R. E., 21, 22, 45, 183, 191, 194
Clifford, B., 22, 45
Cocklin, T., 12, 35
Coffman, W. E., 39
Cohen, J., 67, 69, 78
Cohen, P. A., 21, 45
Cohen, S. R., 30
Coldevin, G. O., 46
Collingbourne, R., 82, 126, 147
Collins, A., 21, 45
Collins, W. E., 5, 29
Coltheart, M., 15, 38, 56, 80, 84, 136, 150
Coltheart, V., 84, 136, 150
Conezie, J., 126, 150
Cook, L. K., 186, 196
Cooper, L. A., 158, 197
Coscarelli, W. C., 42
Coulter, M. L., 14, 37
Coulter, R. G., 13, 37
Courtois, M. R., 12, 34
Cox, M. V., 20, 43
Cox, P. W., 172, 198
Crandall, T. L., 120, 150
Cronbach, L. J., 169, 194
Cross, H. A., 12, 35

Csapo, K., 37, 128
Culbertson, H. M., 23, 46
Culhane, J. W., 119, 149
Cundick, B. P., 84
Cunningham, D. J., 71, 80, 81, 84, 141, 150
Cupchik, G. C., 23, 46, 49
Cutting, V., 12, 35
Cykowski, F., 83

Danilovics, P., 83
Danset-Léger, J., 134, 146
Davidoff, J. B., 7, 31
Davidson, G. R., 13, 35
Davidson, R. E., 64, 78
Dale, E., 116, 117, 137, 138, 146, 152, 194
Dansereau, D. F., 160, 168, 195
Das, J. P., 158, 159, 173, 194
Davies, G., 14, 34
Dawson, J., 49
Day, J. D., 179, 193
Day, M. C., 108, 111
Dean, R. S., 56, 78, 81, 121, 131, 132, 133, 136, 141, 142, 146, 190, 194
Decker, W. H., 175, 194
Deese, J., 178, 194
Deffenbacher, K. A., 10, 33
DeGood, H., 82
DeKleer, J., 186, 194
DeKosky, S. T., 46
Delaney, H. D., 61, 79
Delhaye, P., 12, 34
DeLoache, J. S., 108, 111
DeLorme, A., 24, 47
DeMelo, H., 144, 146
Denny, E. C., 190, 196
Denny, M. R., 23, 47
Deregowski, J. B., 8, 30, 31, 82, 126, 147
DeRose, T. M., 13, 35, 81
DeSoto, C. B., 18, 42
DeSousa, M. A., 25, 49
Desrochers, A., 14, 38
D'Hondt, W., 24, 47
Dick, M. B., 14, 37
Dickie, K. E., 21, 45, 152, 196
Diesch, E., 33

Author Index

Digdon, N., 81, 92, 100, 108, 111
DiGeorge, W., 14, 37
Dillingofski, M. S., 81
Divine-Hawkins, P., 83
Dixon, D., 16, 40
Doan, R. L., 83
Doblin, J., 152, 156, 194
Donais, E. E., 136, 147, 169, 172, 195
Donald, D. R., 81, 120, 128, 146
D'Onofrio, A., 26, 49
Dos Santos Veiga, J., 20, 44
Dowling, S. B., 84
Dretzke, B. J., 16, 40
Duchastel, P. C., 53, 78, 81, 96, 111, 116, 117, 118, 119, 142, 144, 146, 168, 194
Duck, S. W., 25, 48
Duncan, J., 6, 28
Dunham, T. C., 81, 92, 111
Durso, F. T., 10, 33
Dwyer, F. M., 4, 15, 16, 17, 29, 39, 40, 67, 78, 81, 135, 137, 138, 139, 140, 142, 144, 146, 147, 153, 169, 172, 175, 194, 197
Dyck, J. L., 186, 196
d'Ydewalle, G., 12, 34

Ebeling, B. J., 21, 45
Edmondson, D., 48, 50
Efran, J. S., 23, 46
Egan, D. E., 18, 42
Ehrenfeucht, A., 22, 44, 106, 111
Eijkman, E. G. J., 7, 30
Eisner, E., 25, 50
Ekstrom, R., 169, 175, 185, 195
Elkind, D., 9, 32
Elliott, S. C., 117, 122, 140, 146
Ellis, A. W., 47
Ellis, H., 14, 34
Emmerich, H. J., 12, 35
Enemoh, P. A., 121, 132, 133, 142, 146
Engblom, P., 23, 47
Engle, R. W., 14, 37
Epstein, W., 9, 32
Erdelyi, M. H., 15, 38
Ernest, C. H., 13, 35
Espe, H., 48
Evans, R. A., 75, 78, 82
Evans, T., 23, 47

Everett, R. J., 23, 47
Eysenck, H. J., 50

Farah, M. J., 33
Farley, F. H., 47
Faulconer, B. A., 10, 34
Feaver, W., 90, 111
Feinstein, H., 19, 42
Fennema, E., 180, 181, 194, 195
Fenton, T., 136, 143, 147
Fernie, D. E., 20, 44
Field, D. E., 45
Fields, W. C., III, 34
Findlay, J. M., 5, 28
Fink, S. I., 28
Finke, R. A., 33
Fischer, C., 22, 46
Fisher, C. B., 20, 43
Fisher, D. F., 27, 28, 29
Fisher, K. M., 186, 195
Flagg, B. N., 136, 143, 147
Flavell, J. H., 31, 108, 114
Fleming, M. L., 17, 40, 135, 138, 147, 152, 160, 166, 167, 195
Forbes, N. E., 20, 44
Forrest-Pressley, D. L., 75, 78
Foss, S. K., 50
Frank, A. R., 16, 40
Frankel, M. C., 176, 195
Franken, R. E., 12, 35
Freedman, J., 32
Freeman, N. H., 20, 43
Freiheit, R., 33
French, J., 169, 175, 185, 195
Freyd, J. J., 7, 30
Friedman, A., 9, 32, 126, 147
Friedman, S. L., 7, 30
Frost, A. G., 24, 47
Fry, E., 164, 195
Fry, M. A., 17, 40, 52, 78, 82, 124, 130, 141, 147
Fulton, J. L., 40
Fulton, O., 40
Fussell, D., 7, 30

Gaffney, J. S., 16, 41
Gage, N. L., 39
Gambrell, L. B., 82

Author Index

Gardner, H., 20, 26, 43, 50
Garforth, C., 8, 28, 30
Garskof, B. E., 178, 195
Gat, I., 22, 44, 106, 111
Gates, G. B., 172, 194
Gelade, G., 5, 29
Gelatt, R., 136, 143, 147
Gelman, R., 7, 30
Gentner, D., 18, 42, 184, 195
George, S. G., 25, 48
Geva, E., 188, 195
Ghatala, E. S., 13, 14, 35, 37, 89, 111
Gibson, J. J., 2, 27
Gick, M. L., 18, 42
Gillespie, G. L., 15, 39
Gillund, G., 14, 37
Ginn, M., 13, 32, 35
Glaser, R., 87, 111
Glass, A. L., 7, 30
Glass, G. V., 67, 78
Glock, M. D., 17, 39, 41, 56, 80, 84, 120, 150
Glover, J. A., 14, 37
Gluck, M. A., 16, 40
Go, E., 9, 32
Goessens, L., 12, 34
Goldberg, F., 82, 136, 147
Goldsmith, E., 39, 109, 111
Goldsmith, L. T., 7, 32
Goldstein, A. G., 12, 20, 35, 43
Goldstein, E. B., 22, 28, 45
Goldstein, R., 135, 147
Goldston, D. B., 82, 99, 101, 112
Golinkoff, R. M., 82
Gombrich, E. H., 2, 27, 50
Goodenough, D. R., 172, 198
Goodman, G. S., 13, 14, 37
Goodman, N., 4, 27
Gottfried, A. W., 31
Goud, A., 118, 125, 149
Gould, J. D., 5, 28
Graefe, T. M., 13, 35, 36
Grant, A. P., 47
Green, D., 12, 35
Greene, R., 30
Greer, D., 25, 48
Gregory, R. L., 2, 27
Griffiths, B., 83
Griffitt, W., 24, 49
Grimes-Farrow, D. D., 18, 42

Grossberg, S., 7, 31
Grotzbach, H., 33
Gunter, B., 22, 45
Guri, S., 75, 78
Guttman, D., 6, 29
Guttmann, J., 71, 78, 82, 83, 89, 96, 97, 98, 99, 101, 112

Haake, R. J., 14, 39
Haaland, A., 7, 30
Haber, R. H., 7, 31
Haber, R. N., 12, 13, 15, 17, 32, 35, 38, 40, 126, 150
Hackling, M., 102, 103, 105, 112
Hadamard, J., 19, 42
Haertel, E. H., 20, 44
Haertel, G. D., 20, 44
Hagen, M. A., 4, 7, 8, 17, 27, 31, 40
Haith, M. M., 13, 36
Hallstrom, J. L., 7, 32
Hampson, P. J., 12, 35
Handel, S., 18, 42
Hanes, M. L., 130, 147
Hannafin, M. J., 17, 40, 94, 112
Harary, F., 178, 195
Harber, J. R., 74, 78
Harcleroad, F. F., 116, 146
Hardiman, G. W., 24, 26, 47, 50
Haring, M. J., 17, 40, 52, 78, 82, 124, 130, 141, 147
Harris, R. J., 92, 94, 112, 113
Harris, W. J., 64, 80, 84
Hartley, J., 16, 40, 177, 195
Harvey, D. A., 82
Hasenfus, N., 25, 50
Hatfield, G., 19, 32
Hawk, P., 160, 195
Hayes, D. A., 82, 124, 128, 142, 147
Hayes, D. S., 22, 45
Hayvren, M., 122, 144, 151
Hayward, C., 12, 36
Hayward, L., 104, 112
Heck, W., 183, 194
Heckler, J. H., 82
Heibeck, T. H., 37
Heidt, E. U., 45
Heilman, K. M., 46
Heinrichs, R. W., 24, 48
Hellige, J., 158, 195

Hempstead, J. O., 82
Hengen, N., 47
Henley, S. H. A., 25, 48
Hersh, R. E., 14, 36
Hicks, C., 14, 38
Higbee, K. L., 84
Higgins, L. C., 20, 31, 43, 75, 78, 103, 109, 112, 135, 147
Hintzman, D. L., 14, 38
Hochberg, J., 4, 7, 9, 27, 31, 33
Hock, H. S., 32
Hodapp, T. V., 43
Hoege, H., 25, 50
Hoffman, D. D., 7, 31
Hohle, B., 33
Hoisington, M., 12, 35
Holden, D. J., 108, 111
Hollenberg, C. K., 16, 40
Holley, C. D., 160, 168, 195
Holliday, W. G., 82, 135, 136, 140, 147, 153, 154, 159, 163, 169, 170-171, 172, 179, 184, 185, 195, 198
Holmes, C. B., 24, 48
Holt, L. H., 12, 34
Homa, D., 16, 40
Honeck, R. P., 18, 42
Hope, D. J., 64, 80, 107, 108, 113, 127, 149
Hörmann, H., 12, 35, 135, 142, 145, 147
Houston, J. P., 178, 195
Hovespian, W., 25, 48
Howe, M. J. A., 45
Howe, M. L., 14, 38
Hughes, J., 81
Hughes, L., 101, 114
Hunt, E. B., 19, 42
Hunter, M. A., 37
Huston, A. C., 25, 46, 48

Inhelder, B., 177, 197
Intraub, H., 5, 6, 13, 14, 29, 35, 37
Ives, S. W., 50

Jagodzinska, M., 116, 147
Jahoda, G., 82, 126, 147
Jamison, D., 21, 45

Jankovic, I. N., 42
Jarman, R. F., 158, 159, 173, 194
Jennings, L. B., 25, 29
Jennings, T., 4, 48
Jester, R. E., 30
Johnson, C. A., 14, 38
Johnson, D., 122, 148
Johnson, H. E., 82
Johnson, M. K., 10, 33, 64, 78, 81, 120, 121, 126, 145, 148
Johnson, N. S., 9, 32
Jolicoeur, P., 16, 40
Jonassen, D., 160, 195
Jones, B. F., 160, 195
Jones, B. J., 26, 50
Jones, R. K., 7, 8, 31
Jörg, S., 12, 35, 134, 147
Joseph, J. H., 137, 140, 147
Joseph, M. R., 136, 146
Justice, E. M., 12, 35

Kagan, J., 13, 36
Kahle, J. B., 186, 196, 197
Kallman, H. J., 8, 12, 32, 35
Kari, J., 48
Katz, A. N., 42
Katz, S., 27
Kaufmann, G., 19, 42
Kee, D. W., 14, 38
Kellogg, R. T., 12, 35
Kelly, J. S., 25, 48
Kelly, S. B., 22, 45
Kelter, S., 33
Kennedy, J. M., 4, 7, 19, 27, 42
Kerst, S. M., 75, 78, 82, 83
Kiefer, B., 20, 43
Kieras, D. E., 10, 16, 33, 40
Kinder, J. S., 116, 117, 122, 137, 145, 147
King, D. L., 16, 40
Kintsch, E., 14, 39
Kintsch, W., 14, 39
Kiphart, M. J., 12, 35
Kirasic, K. C., 13, 36
Kirby, J. R., 158, 159, 173, 194
Kirkpatrick, E. A., 37
Kjorup, S., 22, 45
Kleinbard, J., 15, 38

Author Index

Klich, L. Z., 13, 35
Knowlton, J. Q., 20, 28, 43, 115, 147, 152, 161, 195
Kobayashi, S., 33
Kobasigawa, A., 89, 112
Koegler, R. R., 9, 32
Koenderink, J. J., 7, 31
Koenke, K., 120, 148
Kok, I., 125, 150
Kolbe, R., 25, 48
Kolbet, L., 6, 29
Kolers, P. A., 4, 7, 10, 28, 31, 34
Koran, J. J., 136, 142, 143, 148, 185, 195
Koran, M. L., 136, 142, 143, 148, 185, 195
Koroscik, J. S., 20, 43
Kose, G., 22, 24, 45, 49
Koskinen, P. S., 82
Kosslyn, S. M., 10, 16, 20, 34, 40, 43, 158, 195
Krebs, E. W., 84
Kreszock, C. M., 22, 45
Krey, C. L., 136, 146
Kroll, J. F., 34
Kubovy, M., 9, 32
Kulhavy, R. W., 22, 45, 56, 78, 81, 82, 84, 131, 132, 136, 141, 146, 159, 173, 190, 194, 195
Kulik, J. A., 21, 45
Kundel, H. L., 5, 29
Kunen, S., 12, 35
Kuskowski, M., 20, 44
Kyllonen, P. C., 43

LaChapelle, J. R., 42
LaCroix, P., 136, 146
Lagerspetz, K. M. J., 23, 47
Lamberski, R. J., 17, 40
Landa, L. N., 192, 196
Lansing, K. M., 20, 43
Larkin, J., 184, 186, 196
LaVole, J., 25, 48
Lawrence, V., 15, 38
Leach, M. L., 20, 43
Lean, D. S., 15, 39
LeComte, M., 64, 80, 107, 108, 113, 127, 149

Ledger, G. W., 14, 20, 38, 43
Lee, J. B., 45
Lee, P. L., 22, 24, 48
Leeuwenberg, E., 24, 47
Legenza, A., 143, 146
Lehman, J. D., 186, 196
Lehmkuhle, S. W., 33, 126, 130, 150
Lehrer, A., 22, 46
Leicht, K. L., 141, 150
Leifer, A. D., 22, 45
Lentz, R., 52, 53, 67, 68, 79, 91, 92, 93, 112, 115, 116, 117, 119, 124, 125, 129, 136, 141, 142, 144, 148
Leondar, B., 27
Lesgold, A. M., 51, 52, 65, 71, 75, 78, 79, 82, 88, 92, 93, 95, 99, 112, 129, 130, 144, 148
Leu, J. R., 10, 33
LeVesconte, S., 20, 44
Levie, W. H., 8, 21, 31, 45, 52, 53, 67, 68, 78, 91, 93, 112, 115, 116, 117, 119, 124, 125, 129, 136, 141, 142, 144, 148, 152, 160, 166, 167, 195, 196
Levin, J. R., 13, 14, 16, 17, 35, 37, 40, 41, 51, 52, 53, 55, 58, 61, 62, 63, 64, 65, 67, 69, 70, 75, 76, 77, 78, 79, 80, 81, 82, 83-84, 87, 88, 89, 92, 93, 94, 95, 96, 97, 98, 99, 100, 101, 103, 107, 108, 111, 112, 113, 116, 127, 128, 129, 130, 142, 144, 148, 149, 150
Levin, S. R., 5, 28
Levine, M., 42
Levy, E. I., 128, 147
Lewis, M., 5, 29
Lewis, R. B., 116, 146
Lindauer, M. S., 24, 49, 103, 113
Lindvall, C. M., 181, 182, 186, 196
Lippman, M. Z., 14, 38
Lipson, J. I., 186, 195
Litcher, J., 122, 148
Liu, I., 42
LNR Research Group, 160, 168, 186, 196
Lockheart, L., 84
Loftus, E. F., 14, 35
Loftus, G. R., 5, 8, 13, 15, 29, 32, 35, 38, 130, 148
Lohman, D. F., 43

Author Index

London, M., 18, 42
Long, G. M., 15, 38
Lonner, W. J., 20, 44
Loomis, R. J., 12, 35
Lootsteen, P. J., 36
Lorraine, W., 109, 112
Lovano-Kerr, J., 26, 50
Lovegrove, W., 15, 38
Lovett, S. B., 84
Low, W. C., 81
Luke, C., 9, 32
Luria, A. L., 159, 196
Lutz, K. A., 17, 43, 84, 158, 197
Lynes, J. A., 2, 28

McCauley, C., 33
McCormick, C. B., 16, 40, 70, 80, 82, 83, 84
Macdonald-Ross, M., 156, 165, 196
McEvoy, C. L., 11
MacFadyen, J., 89, 113
McFee, J. K., 26, 50
McGee, M. G., 44
McGinnis, J. J., 29
McGivern, J. E., 41, 70, 76, 79, 83
Machotka, P., 9, 32
McIsaac, M. S., 22, 46
McKay, M. E., 23, 47
McKay, T. D., 23, 47
McKelvie, S. J., 6, 13, 14, 28, 36, 37
MacKinnon, G. E., 75, 78
Mackworth, N. H., 5, 29, 134, 148
MacLennan, D. W., 22, 46
MacLeod, C. M., 19, 36, 42
McLoone, B., 76, 80
McMahon, C. M., 17, 40
McManus, I. C., 24, 48, 50
MacPherson, G. M., 43
Madigan, S., 15, 38, 175, 197
Magee, L. E., 10, 34
Magne, O., 144, 148
Maher, J. H., 83
Makoid, L. A., 13, 35
Main, R. E., 83
Mandler, J. M., 9, 32, 126, 148, 176, 197
Manelis, L., 141, 150
Mann, S. W., 9, 32

Marcel, T., 17, 40
Marchant, H., 22, 45
Margolin, V., 25, 49
Marks, D. F., 136, 148
Marr, D., 4, 28
Marschark, M., 42
Martindale, C., 25, 50
Mason, J., 180, 196
Massey, C., 50
Mastropieri, M. A., 16, 41, 76, 80, 83
Mathews, N. N., 19, 42
Matz, R. D., 84
Mayer, R. E., 17, 42, 64, 79, 186, 196
Meck, E., 7, 30
Medhurst, M. J., 25, 49
Medin, D. L., 16, 40
Mehner, D. S., 135, 145, 146
Meringoff, L. K., 22, 46, 106, 112
Merril, M. D., 174, 196
Metzger, R. L., 5, 9, 28, 32
Metzler, J., 36
Mewborn, C. R., 23, 47
Meyer, B. J. F., 141, 148
Meyer, S. E., 90, 112
Mezzanotte, R. J., 5, 9, 28, 32
Miccinati, J. L., 83
Miller, D., 47
Miller, R. B., 81
Miller, G. E., 16, 40, 65, 71, 73, 102, 103, 105, 112
Miller, R. J., 48
Milz, B., 124, 142, 143, 145
Mingolla, E., 7, 31
Mitchell, W. J. T., 28
Monty, R. A., 28, 29
Moore, C. A., 172, 198
Moore, D. M., 22
Moore, D. W., 52, 80
Moore, P. J., 120, 128, 130, 136, 142, 148
Moore, R. L., 24, 48, 84, 117, 140, 150
Morrison, C. R., 76, 79, 80, 83
Morrison, F. J., 13, 36
Morton, J., 88, 112
Mosley, M. L., 22, 46
Moss, V., 24, 48
Moxley, R., 166, 196
Moyer, J. C., 18, 42, 43, 172, 196

Moyer, M. B., 18, 42, 43, 172, 196
Mroczek, K., 7, 30
Mueller, J. H., 12, 34, 37
Muir, P., 90, 112
Murphy, C. M., 16, 41
Murphy, G. L., 16, 41
Murray, F. S., 18, 41
Myatt, B., 24, 48
Myers, B. L., 12, 13, 35

Nadaner, D., 22, 46
Nakayama, S. Y., 14, 38
Nall, L., 101, 114
Navon, D., 8, 32
Neisser, U., 9, 12, 32, 36, 134, 148
Nelson, D. G. K., 16, 41
Nelson, D. L., 10, 11, 34, 128, 148
Nelson, N. J., 190, 196
Nelson, T. O., 36, 38
Nelson, W. W., 5, 8, 29, 32
Neurath, M., 165, 196
Newman, L. A., 16, 40
Newton, D. P., 17, 41
Nicholson, J. R., 20, 44
Nickerson, R. S., 37, 126, 148
Nicki, R. M., 24, 48
Nicklos, S., 14, 37
Nodine, C. F., 5, 26, 27, 29, 49, 50
Norman, D. A., 104, 112, 160, 168, 186, 196
Norman, R. Z., 178, 195
Norton, D. E., 90, 91, 112
Novak, J. D., 156, 196
Nugent, G. C., 83

O'Brien, E. J., 14, 38
O'Connor, J., 24, 49
O'Donnell, H., 119, 148
O'Hare, D., 25, 50
Oliver, E., 24, 49
Olson, D. R., 20, 39, 44, 125, 148, 156, 196
Ornstein, P. A., 108, 111
Osaka, N., 5, 29
Osgood, C. E., 49
Ostergaard, A. L., 7, 31
Ostry, D. J., 27

Otto, W., 65, 79, 120, 146
O'Sullivan, C. S., 10, 33
Owen, L. A., 6, 29
Owens, R. D., 46

Paivio, A., 10, 14, 33, 34, 37, 38, 42, 88, 89, 113, 124, 128, 148, 158, 169, 175, 197
Palij, M., 42
Pallrand, G. J., 187, 197
Palmer, S. E., 8, 9, 31, 32
Paradowski, W., 23, 47, 118, 149
Paris, S. G., 39, 103, 113
Park, D. C., 13, 36
Parker, R. E., 5, 29
Parkhurst, P. E., 172, 197
Parkin, A. J., 12, 36
Parknäs, L., 144, 148
Parmelee, C. M., 33
Paul, B., 13, 34
Payne, D. G., 15, 39
Peacock, J., 50
Peeck, J., 14, 36, 64, 74, 83, 116, 117, 118, 122, 123, 124, 125, 126, 127, 128, 129, 132, 136, 141, 142, 149
Pellegrino, J. W., 20, 44
Peng, C-Y., 83, 94, 113
Peppin, B., 90, 113
Perkin, G. W., 17, 41
Perkins, D. N., 17, 27, 40, 41, 42
Perlmutter, M., 32
Perry, F. L., 81
Peters, E. E., 41, 62, 70, 79, 83
Petersen, C. H., 81, 118, 145
Peterson, M. A., 9, 33
Petros, T., 83
Pew, R. W., 21, 45
Peynircioglu, Z. F., 13, 36
Pezdek, K., 12, 22, 36, 46, 106, 113, 129, 149
Philipchalk, R., 14, 38
Phillips, P. E., 5, 29
Piaget, J., 177, 197
Pigott, S., 64, 80, 99, 100, 106, 107, 108, 113, 127, 149
Pillow, B. H., 31
Pinker, S., 34, 157, 197
Pitz, H. C., 90, 113

Author Index

Plouffe, L., 14, 36
Plug, C., 24, 48
Pollatsek, A., 5, 29
Pollock, I., 110, 113
Pomerantz, J. R., 9, 32
Popham, W. J., 24, 47
Porter, M. C., 138, 150
Post, T. R., 183, 194
Potash, L. M., 22, 46
Potter, M. C., 10, 34, 130, 149
Potts, R., 46
Poulsen, D., 14, 39
Pratt, F., 31
Pray, R., 136, 143, 147
Prazdny, S., 7, 30
Premack, D., 14, 39
Pressley, G. M., 83
Pressley, M., 13, 16, 40, 41, 58, 61, 64, 65, 70, 71, 73, 75, 78, 79, 80, 81, 82, 83, 84, 88, 89, 94, 96, 97, 98, 99, 100, 101, 102, 103, 104, 105, 106, 107, 108, 111, 112, 113, 114, 127, 142, 148, 149
Presson, C. C., 42
Price, L., 169, 175, 185, 195
Puff, C. R., 37
Puglisi, J. T., 13, 36
Purkel, W., 94, 99, 113
Pylyshyn, Z. W., 10, 34, 158, 197

Quatman, G., 25, 48

Rabinowitz, J. C., 9, 32
Rabinowitz, M., 176, 197
Radich, A. J., 50
Raeissi, P., 46
Ramsey, I. L., 24, 48
Randhawa, B. S., 39
Rankin, E. F., 119, 149
Rasco, R. W., 60, 80, 83, 130, 141, 149
Rauch, T., 101, 113
Rayner, K., 5, 29
Read, J. D., 25, 49, 149
Readence, J. E., 52, 80, 82, 124, 128, 130, 142, 147
Reed, D. A., 36
Reed, E. S., 7, 31

Reed, S. K., 18, 42, 183, 197
Reed, V. S., 10, 11, 34, 128, 148
Reid, D. J., 83, 120, 149
Reid, J. C., 22, 46
Reynolds, R. I., 33
Rice, D. R., 83
Richards, W. A., 7, 31
Rickards, J. R., 143, 149
Richman, C. L., 82, 99, 101, 112, 114
Riding, R. J., 84, 136, 149
Rigney, J. W., 17, 43, 60, 78, 81, 84, 158, 197
Ritchey, G. H., 14, 37
Ritter, K., 108, 114
Robins, S. L., 81, 120, 145
Robinson, C. A., 9, 32
Robinson, E. H., 74, 80
Robinson, L., 181, 182, 186, 196
Rock, I., 6, 29
Rodger, J., 48, 50
Roediger, H. L., 15, 39
Rogers, C. A., 37
Rogers, R. W., 23, 47
Rohwer, W. D. Jr., 64, 80, 84, 89, 94, 113
Rolandelli, D., 46
Rosch, E., 31
Rose, M. C., 84
Rose, S. A., 31
Rose, T. L., 74, 80
Ross, R. P., 25, 46, 48
Rowe, E. J., 14, 38
Rowell, R., 156
Royer, J. M., 17, 43, 60, 64, 80, 84, 125, 128, 142, 149
Ruch, M. D., 84, 99, 101, 103, 113, 129, 150
Rudnick, M. F., 138, 150
Rumelhart, D. E., 160, 168, 186, 196
Rush, J. C., 25, 26, 50
Russell, A., 5, 29
Rusted, J., 56, 80, 84, 136, 150
Ryan, E. B., 14, 20, 38, 43
Ryan, M., 24, 49
Ryan, T. A., 17, 18, 41

Sabbah, D., 7, 31
Sabers, D. L., 25, 50

Salomon, G., 20, 21, 22, 28, 39, 44, 45, 46, 157, 168, 197
Saltz, E., 16, 40
Samuels, S. J., 24, 48, 53, 80, 124, 143, 150, 185, 197
Savarese, J. M., 48
Schallert, D. L., 52, 80, 92, 93, 114, 124, 142, 144, 150
Schmelzkoph, K. F., 32
Schmidt, C. R., 39
Schneider, W., 108, 113
Schoenfeld, A. H., 180, 197
Schramm, W., 22, 45
Schuller, C. F., 17, 39, 116, 137, 151
Schunert, J. R., 117, 145
Schwartz, C. B., 17, 18, 41
Schwartz, N. H., 84, 159, 173, 195
Schwen, T. M., 42
Scott, K. P., 25, 49
Scruggs, T. E., 16, 41, 76, 79, 80, 83
Seashore, H. G., 178, 181, 193
Seddon, G. M., 20, 44
Seeber, F., 187, 197
Seefeldt, C., 20, 44
Segal, J. W., 179, 194
Seidman, S., 20, 44
Seiler, W., 49
Senders, J. W., 28, 29
Serpell, R., 8, 31
Sewell, E. H. Jr., 24, 48, 84, 117, 140, 150
Shaha, S. H., 159, 173, 195
Shanahan, M. W., 14, 38
Shannon, P., 20, 44
Shavelson, R. J., 178, 197
Sheikhian, M., 138, 147
Shepard, R. N., 10, 12, 34, 36, 126, 129, 150, 158, 197
Shepherd, J., 14, 34
Sheppard, A., 23, 47
Sherman, J. L., 84, 181, 194
Sherman, T., 14, 37
Sherris, J. D., 186, 197
Shiffrin, R. M., 14, 37
Shimamura, A. P., 15, 38
Shimron, J., 71, 78, 82, 84, 96, 114
Shore, J. M., 84
Shriberg, L. D., 92, 96, 114

Shriberg, L. K., 61, 62, 70, 76, 79, 80, 83, 84, 92, 96, 114
Shute, V. J., 20, 44
Siegel, A. W., 13, 36
Sigel, I. E., 8, 31
Silberberg, A. R., 117, 122, 140, 146
Silver, R. A., 44
Silvern, S. B., 84, 92, 114
Simon, D. P., 180, 197
Simon, H., 155, 197
Simon, H. A., 180, 197
Simon, S., 22, 46
Simon, Th., 133, 134, 145
Simonson, M. R., 24, 49
Simpson, W., 19, 42
Simutis, Z. M., 20, 43
Singer, D. G., 25, 49
Singer, J. L., 25, 49
Singaas, P. A., 5, 28
Sinha, D., 82, 126, 147
Sjogren, D. D., 12, 35
Skinner, M. J., 120, 128, 130, 136, 142, 148
Sless, D., 39, 157, 198
Slythe, R. M., 90, 114
Small, M. Y., 84
Smillie, R. J., 17, 41
Smith, E. E., 16, 40, 41
Smith, J. D., 9, 33
Smith, K. U., 116, 117, 118, 150
Smith, M. C., 10, 34
Smith, M. F., 116, 117, 118, 150
Smith, R., 22, 46
Smith, S., 36
Smith, S. L., 17, 41
Smythe, W. E., 28
Snodgrass, J. G., 10, 33, 34
Snow, R. E., 43, 158, 169, 194, 198
Snowman, J., 71, 80, 81, 84, 141, 150
Somerville, S. C., 14, 39
Sorce, J. F., 31
Sowder, L., 18, 42, 43, 172, 196
Sowry, B. M., 18, 42
Spangenberg, R., 21, 46
Spangler, T. J., 23, 46
Spaulding, S., 130, 135, 140, 150
Sperber, R. D., 33
Spiegel, J. P., 9, 32
Spoehr, K. T., 33, 126, 130, 150

Author Index

Stacey, K., 180, 196
Standing, L., 12, 36, 126, 150
Stanny, C. J., 13, 36
Stein, J. B., 15, 38
Steingart, S. K., 84
Stelmack, R. M., 13, 36
Stepanowsky, M. A., 12, 34
Stergios, J. C., 30
Stericker, A., 20, 44
Stern, L. D., 14, 38
Stern, W., 133, 150
Sternberg, R. J., 18, 43, 163, 198
Sternfels, S., 20, 44
Stevens, A. L., 184, 195
Stevens, E., 22, 46, 106, 113
Stevenson, M. B., 7, 30
Stewart, G., 101, 114
Stewart, J. H., 156, 160, 198
Stewig, J. W., 24, 48
Stober, S., 39
Stone, D. E., 17, 41, 56, 80, 120, 150
Story, N., 22, 46
Sullivan, H., 83
Suppes, P., 21, 45
Supplee, K. A., 25, 49
Suydam, E. L., 138, 150
Swenson, I., 82
Sylwester, R., 158, 198
Szlichcinski, K. P., 17, 41, 161, 198
Szymczyk, J. M., 17, 18, 41

Tabachnick, B., 14, 37
Tamburino, J. L., 181, 182, 186, 196
Tariq, R. J., 20, 44
Tartre, L. A., 180, 195
Taunton, M., 26, 50
Taylor, S. E., 24, 49
Taylor, W. D., 39, 172, 194
Teitelbaum, R. C., 5, 28
te Linde, J., 11, 34
Tennyson, R. D., 16, 41, 60, 80, 83, 130, 141, 149, 174, 196
Terry, P. R., 24, 48
Tharp, D., 7, 30
Thies, P., 24, 49
Thissen, D., 164, 198
Thomas, J. L., 85
Thompson, S. C., 24, 49

Thorndike, R. M., 20, 44
Threadgill-Sowder, J., 18, 42, 43, 172, 196
Thursby, P. M., 140, 147
Tidhar, C. E., 20, 44
Till, R. E., 34
Tirre, W. C., 141, 150
Tobin, P., 43
Todd, J. T., 7, 31
Toppino, T. C., 14, 37
Toth, M. A., 158, 198
Travers, R. M., 41, 116, 117, 118, 130, 138, 150
Treisman, A., 5, 29
Triplett, D., 85
Trueman, M., 177, 195
Tsal, Y., 6, 29
Tulving, E., 36, 89, 114
Turner, L. A., 14, 36
Turnure, J. E., 104, 105, 114
Tversky, B., 14, 17, 37, 41
Twyman, M., 17, 41, 109, 114
Tyrrell, D. J., 37

Underwood, G., 135, 147

Valenstein, E., 46
Van Dam, G., 125, 150
Van den Bosch, A. B., 135, 151
Vanderwart, M., 33
Vanderwiele, M., 24, 47
Van Kirk, J., 156, 198
van Lieshout, C. F. M., 23, 47
Van Parreren, C. F., 134, 151
Van Slyke, D. A., 37
Veltrusky, J., 28
Verhaegen, L. J. J., 132, 151
Vernon, M. D., 122, 151
Voegtle, K., 18, 42
Vokey, J. R., 25, 49
Von, 110, 114
Vygotsky, L., 106, 114

Wacker, D. P., 16, 17, 40, 41
Wainer, H., 164, 198
Walberg, H. J., 20, 44

Author Index

Wall, M. U., 13, 36
Wallach, R. W., 20, 43
Waller, R., 53, 78, 156, 167, 168, 194, 198
Waller, T. G., 75, 78
Walling, J. R., 10, 34, 128, 148
Walton, R., 104, 105, 114
Ward, J. L., 30
Wardle, K. F., 136, 151
Warner, M. M., 74, 80, 85
Waterman, D., 12, 35
Waters, H. S., 38, 89, 114
Watkins, M. J., 13, 35, 36
Weaver, G. E., 13, 36
Weaver, P. A., 136, 143, 147
Weeks, L. A., 46
Weil, E. M., 163, 198
Weisberg, J. S., 118, 125, 151
Weisstein, N., 7, 31
Welch, R., 25, 48
Wellman, H. M., 14, 39, 108, 114
Wells, S., 21, 45
Wesman, A. G., 178, 181, 193
Westwood, H., 26, 50
Whalen, D. H., 24, 49
Whalley, J. I., 91, 114
Wheatley, P. C., 175, 194
Whissell, C., 23, 46
White, S., 65, 79
Whiteside, C., 22, 46
Wicks, B. J., 136, 149
Wieland, L. D., 13, 36
Wiggers, M., 23, 47
Williams, L. J., 5, 29
Williams, P. A., 20, 44

Willows, D. M., 51, 64, 80, 85, 118, 122, 126, 127, 135, 137, 138, 142, 144, 151
Wilson, B. J., 23, 47
Winn, W. D., 17, 23, 41, 47, 75, 135, 151, 153, 157, 159, 163, 166, 169, 173, 174, 177, 179, 186, 198
Winner, E., 26, 50
Wiseman, S., 12, 36
Wittich, W. A., 116, 137, 151
Witkin, H. A., 172, 198
Wittrock, M. C., 158, 198
Wohlwill, J. F., 5, 26, 30, 50
Wolford, C. R., 14, 38
Wong, E., 7, 31
Wood, D. J., 16, 41
Wood, E., 104, 105, 114
Wooldridge, P., 101, 114
Worchel, S., 25, 48
Worsnop, J. G., 20, 44
Wright, J. C., 22, 25, 46, 48
Wutzig, S., 33

Yarbus, A. L., 30
Yonas, A., 7, 20, 32, 44
Yuille, J. C., 33, 175, 197
Yussen, S. R., 114

Zarate, O., 110, 114
Zernich, T., 24, 26, 47, 50
Zimmerman, M. L., 17, 41
Zuckerman, D. M., 25, 49
Zwarts, J., 14, 36

Subject Index

Adjunct aids, 118, 125, 144; *see also* Graphic forms
Adults, 7–8, 20, 23, 52, 66, 110, 126, 130, 135
Advance organizers, 58, 64, 118, 159–160
Affective responses
 aesthetic reactions, 1, 25–26
 arousal and emotional reactions, 1, 23, 117, 122, 140
 attitudes, 24–25, 117, 122
Ambiguous figures, 6
Aptitude-treatment interactions (ATI), 169, 175
Arrows and labels, 4, 17, 161, 188
Audio-visual communication, 20–22, 116, 117

Brain
 hemispheric processing, 157–158, 181

Cartoons and caricatures, 17–18, 110
Charts
 conveyance of meaning, 162–163, 175–180
 definition, 152–153
 elements, *see* Graphic forms, relationship of elements
 examples of, 154–155
Children
 economically disadvantaged, 94
 general, 12, 20, 22, 24, 52, 65, 66, 72, 75, 87–110, 119, 130, 136, 141; *see also* Students, middle school
 retarded, 16–17, 94
 young, 5, 7–8, 9, 16, 20, 24, 26, 65, 75, 87–110, 130, 133, 172, 176, 181
Children's books, 51, 53–56, 87, 90–91, 117
Computers, 4, 7, 16, 157, 158, 183

Decoding, 7, 87, 180
Diagrams
 conveyance of meaning, 166–167
 definition, 152–153
 effects of, 169–175, 181–187, 190
 elements, *see* Graphic forms, relationship of elements
 examples of, 170–171, 188–189
 types, 169, 174, 181, 183, 184
Drawings
 incomplete, 17, 18, 89, 92, 96–110
 line, 16, 17, 18, 75, 90, 135, 138, 140, 174
 outline, 6, 13
Differential Aptitude Test, 178, 181

Film, 15, 20–22, 24, 106, 157

Graphic forms
 advantages of, 153–160, 190
 instructional functions of, 168

Subject Index

relationship of elements, 159, 160-167, 175-180

Graphs
conveyance of meaning, 163-166
definition, 152-153
elements, *see* Graphic forms, relationship of elements
types, 164-165

Illustrations
in books, 90-91, 116-117, 142-143
theories of, 109-110

Kit of Reference Tests for Cognitive Factors, 169, 175, 185

Learning and cognition
cognitive skills, 19-20, 119-121, 129, 142, 153-157, 172, 181
developmental aspects, 9, 12, 26, 87, 89, 101-103, 106, 133-134, 176-177, 179, 185
factual knowledge, 15-17
instruction and training, 12-13, 15-17, 20, 21, 22, 73-77, 88, 89, 96-108, 110, 135, 175, 186-191; *see also* Advance organizers; Mnemonic learning techniques
problem solving, 15, 17-19, 153-157, 172-173, 180-184
reasoning and critical thinking, 17, 136, 153-157
text illustration, 15-17, 51-77, 87-110, 114-145
Listening studies, 52, 87-110, 115-145

Maps
concept, 156, 186-191
other research, 22-23, 132
types, 131-132, 161-162, 173
Media research, 21-22, 106
Memory
encoding, 12, 14, 89, 102-106, 127, 135, 158-159, 169; *see also* Symbol systems
models, 8-11, 14, 26, 88-89, 109, 128, 158-159, 169
other research, 14-15
recall and retrieval, 8, 12, 14, 93-108, 118, 125-127, 136, 140, 141-142, 159, 172, 173, 175, 176, 177, 190
recognition, 9, 12-13, 93-108, 126, 135, 173
retention, 1, 8, 12, 14, 61-62, 119, 122-129, 135, 136, 140, 142, 144
Mental imagery, 10, 16, 18, 19, 20, 52, 61, 66, 69, 70, 71-74, 88-89, 92, 94, 96-102, 157-158, 168, 175-176
Meta-analysis, 55, 63, 77
Mismatched pictures, 64, 73, 92, 106-108, 126-129, 143
Mnemonic learning techniques, 16, 61-62

Nelson-Denny Reading Comprehension Test, 190
Neurological research, 159

Orienting response, 5, 117, 130, 138

Photographs, 6, 7, 17, 20, 23, 24, 75, 137-140
Paintings, 26
Picture perception
attention and scanning, *see* Orienting response; Selective attention
interpreting figures and cues, 1, 6-8, 121, 174
perceiving global meaning, 1, 8-9, 12, 121, 173-174
theoretical approaches to, 1, 2-4
Pictures
drawn by learners, 141; *see also* Illustrations
Poor readers, 62, 65, 74, 75, 135-136, 169
Processing mode, 70, 129, 158-159, 173-174

Prose
  picture effects on learning of, 93–110, 115–145
  picture functions in, 53–63, 66–77, 96, 115–137

Radio, 21
Representational pictures, 1, 7, 13, 55–56, 67–77, 87–110, 115–145, 174–175; *see also* Learning and cognition, text illustration
Research
  broad topics, *see* Affective responses; Learning and cognition; Memory; Picture perception
  illustrations, *see* Prose, picture functions in
  listening comprehension, *see* Listening studies
  methodological issues, 63–66, 91–92, 141
  stimuli, types of, *see* Cartoons and caricatures; Charts; Diagrams; Drawings; Film; Graphic forms, Graphs; Maps; Paintings; Photographs; Radio; Representational pictures; Slides; Symbols, TV and video
  stimuli variables, 5, 6–8, 12, 13, 14, 24, 65–66, 75, 116, 120, 129, 137–143, 172
  subject variables, 13, 66, 87, 94, 122, 129, 130–137, 144, 169, 172–173, 178, 180–181, 185, 186, 190; *see also* Aptitude-treatment interactions (ATI)
  subjects, *see* Adult; Children; Poor readers; Students
  time variables, 16, 120, 130, 144, 177
Selective attention, 5–6, 9, 106–108, 131–132, 134–136, 138, 144, 157, 166, 179
Slides, 5, 12, 16, 21, 138
Spatial-structural relationships, 142–143, 160–167, 175–180
Students
  college and university, 12, 118, 119–120, 122, 125, 132, 172, 173, 175, 181, 187
  high school, 66, 122, 125, 137, 169, 172–175, 178–179
  middle school, 62, 76, 117, 120, 122, 124, 126, 132, 135, 142, 172, 176, 180–181, 183, 185
Symbols, 1, 6, 13, 20, 21–22, 155, 162, 165, 169, 173, 181, 188
Symbol systems, 21–22, 88, 157, 168

TV and radio, 9, 15, 20–22, 23, 24, 25, 106, 157

Visual argument, 156–157, 167–168

Printed in Great Britain
by Amazon